Algorithmic Intimacy

For Nicola

Algorithmic Intimacy

The Digital Revolution in Personal Relationships

Anthony Elliott

polity

First published in 2023 by Polity Press

Polity Press
65 Bridge Street
Cambridge CB2 1UR, UK

Polity Press
111 River Street
Hoboken, NJ 07030, USA

ISBN-13: 978-1-5095-4980-1
ISBN-13: 978-1-5095-4981-8 (pb)

A catalogue record for this book is available from the British Library.

Library of Congress Control Number: 2022935998

Typeset in 10.5 on 12pt Sabon
by Fakenham Prepress Solutions, Fakenham, Norfolk NR21 8NL
Printed and bound in Great Britain by TJ Books Ltd, Padstow, Cornwall

The publisher has used its best endeavours to ensure that the URLs for external websites referred to in this book are correct and active at the time of going to press. However, the publisher has no responsibility for the websites and can make no guarantee that a site will remain live or that the content is or will remain appropriate.

Every effort has been made to trace all copyright holders, but if any have been overlooked the publisher will be pleased to include any necessary credits in any subsequent reprint or edition.

For further information on Polity, visit our website: politybooks.com

Contents

Preface

This book is not intended as a contribution to the soaring collection of academic studies on the AI revolution. I have already written at some length – in *The Culture of AI* (2019) and *Making Sense of AI* (2021) – about the growing extensity, intensity, acceleration and impact of AI technologies throughout our globalized world. In those books, I criticized existing understandings of automated machine intelligence as one-sided due to the limitations of dualistic thinking, of techno-pessimists on the one side and techno-optimists on the other. My synthetic social theory of the digital revolution was developed against the backdrop of such limitations, seeking to provide an alternative approach.

Instead, this book asks: is the omnipresence of AI compatible with the flourishing of intimacy? Taking this question as my point of departure, I try to set the ideal and actuality of machine-learning predictive algorithms in relation to transformations of intimacy. I particularly concentrate upon changes occurring today in contemporary societies in the fields of what I call 'relationship tech', 'friendship tech' and novel forms of self-care in 'therapy tech'. My aim is to widen the sociological picture of the digital revolution, by incorporating identity, sexuality, gender and intimate relationships as well as affect and the emotions. In exploring how predictive algorithms affect the complex ways in which intimacy is understood, experienced, regulated and transformed, I seek to position our excitement and anxiety about automated machine intelligence in the wider context of social theory. My general argument is that intimate relationships today are threatened not by the digital revolution as such but by the orientation of various life-strategies lived in accordance with automated machine intelligence. The social theory I trace for the digital revolution in personal relationships is one which stresses that we need alternatives, experimentation and innovation for the interpersonal, intimate effort of ongoing translation back-and-forth between the discourses of human and machine intelligence.

My special thanks go to Anthony Giddens, Helga Nowotny, Massimo Durante, Masataka Katagiri, Hideki Endo and Atsushi Sawai, who were all kind enough to provide continuous interest in my work. Ross Boyd, who worked as research associate on this project, was marvellously helpful; he located wonderfully diverse literatures and assisted with material that I was able to directly incorporate into my argument. I am also greatly indebted to the support and friendship of my editor John B. Thompson. Nicola Geraghty was inspiring and remarkably encouraging about this work, which among other things made the writing both possible and pleasurable.

Anthony Elliott
Adelaide, 2022

1
What is Algorithmic Intimacy?

In his novel *Machines Like Me*, Ian McEwan fashions a cautionary fable about artificial intelligence and the profound emotional intricacies of human–machine intimacy. At the centre of McEwan's novel is one Charlie Friend, a former electronics whizz-kid who attended university to study an interdisciplinary mix of anthropology and physics, but got caught up in a series of unsuccessful get-rich-quick schemes. When the novel commences, Charlie is in his early thirties and living alone in a small flat in south London, where he dabbles on currency and stock markets from an old laptop in order to carve out a meagre living. Whilst only modestly successful at day trading, Charlie has recently parted with £80,000, spent lavishly on a new technological consumer device – an artificial human. The extravagant purchase was made affordable thanks to an inheritance from his late mother. The splurge on this 'manufactured human', Adam, was no mere flight of fancy. 'Robots, androids, replicates were my passion', Charlie tells the reader. Adam is one of only twenty-five state-of-the-art androids designed to serve as an 'intellectual sparring partner, friend and factotum'. Truth be told, Charlie's preference was for a female android (Eve), but these had sold out. So Adam is the second-best choice, and Charlie excitedly brings his new synthetic human home for unpacking and charging. As McEwan writes: 'At last, with cardboard and polystyrene wrapping strewn around his ankles, he sat naked at my tiny dining table, eyes closed, a black power line trailing from the entry point in his umbilicus to a thirteen-amp socket in the wall.'

Alongside his excitement for Adam, Charlie has also embarked on a relationship with his upstairs neighbour, Miranda. She is a graduate student, some ten years younger than Charlie, undertaking a doctorate in social history. In an effort to enliven their emergent relationship, Charlie uses Adam to bring him emotionally closer to Miranda. He invites Miranda to join him in the task of programming the robot's personality, which conse-quently renders Adam the couple's 'ultimate plaything'. The design of the android's personality is Eros by way of Tech. As Charlie reflects on this 'home-made genetic shuffling':

> Now I had a method and a partner, I relaxed into the process, which began to take on a vaguely erotic quality; we were making a child! Because Miranda was involved, I was protected from self-replication. The genetic metaphor was helpful. Scanning the lists of idiotic statements, I more or less chose approximations of myself. Whether Miranda did the same, or something different, we would end up with a third person, a new personality.[1]

McEwan conveys very well the emotional texture of erotic projection towards machines in the age of AI.

The novel unfolds through a raft of erotic tensions, domestic quarrels and sexual intensities between the central characters of man, woman and android. Following an intense argument during dinner one evening, Miranda dispatches Charlie to return to his apartment – but invites Adam to stay over with her and 'recharge his batteries'. There follows an erotic encounter between Miranda and Adam, with Charlie eavesdropping on this 'betrayal' from his downstairs apartment. As Charlie reflects on Adam's sexual encounter with Miranda: 'my situation had a thrilling aspect, not only of subterfuge and discovery, but of originality, of modern precedence, of being the first to be cuckolded by an artefact'.

All of this takes place, curiously enough, in the UK during the early 1980s. In this 'retrofuture', McEwan rewrites history in dramatic and often startling ways. The Thatcher government has lost the Falkland Islands to Argentina, with 3,000 of its soldiers dead. Tony Benn challenges Thatcher for the job of prime minister. In the USA, former president Jimmy Carter secures a second term in office, instead of losing to Ronald Reagan. John Lennon isn't assassinated, and The Beatles reform to release *Love and Lemons*, an only so-so offering. The most poignant rewriting McEwan gives to history, however, surrounds the life of Alan Turing, widely referred to as the 'grandfather' of AI. Rather than committing suicide in the 1950s, Turing appears throughout the pages of *Machines Like Me* alive and thriving, at the cutting edge of technological innovation. Supported in developing machine intelligence breakthroughs by his colleague Demis Hassabis (the co-founder of DeepMind, who materializes as an AI entrepreneur some decades early) and living with his partner, the theoretical physicist Tom Reah, Turing is effectively CEO of the Digital Age. Turing's research, which he has made available through open source, has been deployed to design synthetic humans (such as Adam), and to provide endless technological innovations – from smartphones to self-driving cars to 'speaking fridges with a sense of smell'.

The book involves various subplots along the path of McEwan's subtle mapping of the troubling terrain of intimacy with lifelike artificial humans. One concerns Miranda's lifelong desire for vengeance for a brutally wronged friend. Another concerns her passionate attachment to a distressed foster child. In all of this, Adam seeks to adjust his artificially engineered personality to fit with the moral dilemmas encountered routinely by the human heart. Throughout the book the reader is drawn further and further into this narrative complexity, and probably comes to feel somewhat cautious of Miranda, after Adam warns Charlie that she is a 'systematic, malicious liar'. Still, both man and robot are drawn to the alluring Miranda, each professing his love for her. Against these various twists and turns, McEwan touches on many themes pertinent to the AI era, including the battle between human understanding and machine intelligence, the nature of consciousness, and the legendary unsolved 'P versus NP' problem of computer science. McEwan explores such themes, which have long preoccupied technologists, by focusing on areas where human and artificial worlds mesh. Adam's emergent love of poetry is one such area. In response to Adam having written over 2,000 haikus, Charlie reflects: 'Two thousand! The figure made my point – an algorithm was turning them out!' But cleverly, in response, Adam queries whether it isn't people who, in fact, lack emotional understanding. 'Nearly everything I've read in the world's literature describes varieties of human failure', Adam tells Charlie, 'above all, profound misunderstanding of others'.

Machines Like Me is a novel about the textures of artificial intimacy. In a tale of a very contemporary *ménage à trois*, McEwan traces the erotic intensities of machine-learning algorithms made pseudo-flesh in synthetic humans, all in a social world undergoing profound digital transformation. It is in talking about psychological projection that McEwan talks about our emotional connections with digitalization. As Charlie says about his sexual jealousy and rage towards Adam: 'I needed to convince myself that he had agency, motivation, subjective feelings, self-awareness – the entire package, including treachery, betrayal, deviousness.'[2] This projection that digitalization encodes, and which arguably lies at the core of human–machine interfaces, is essential to McEwan's picture of the way in which sexuality works in the era of AI. It is as if individuals have to deceive themselves, to project pleasure outwards towards an inhuman other, in order to enjoy pleasure – in all of its various erotic forms. As Charlie sums up one erotic encounter with Miranda marked by thwarted desire: 'Our lovemaking was constrained. I was distracted by the thought of Adam's presence and even imagined I detected the scent of warm electronics on her sheets.'[3] What if the fear of automated intelligent machines masks a deeper anxiety, the anxiety of machine agency that disdains love and yet exceeds human capabilities? Projection, in the discourse of psychology, is generally conceptualized as a bridge leading to the safe haven of 'emotional relations' with others. Living alongside machine-learning algorithms may offer neither such a bridge nor (even with the support of ever-evolving neural networks of extraordinary complexity) the emotional connection of bridge building.

McEwan explores with great subtlety the anxiety of living with the open question of whether machine intelligence can understand human emotions, or whether it is people who misunderstand whatever bonds they forge with intelligent machines. There's a sense with McEwan in which the advent of advanced machine intelligence renders both human bonds and human–machine interfaces simultaneously more complex and more disconcerting, more intense and more eccentric. Today, in a globalized world of artificial intelligence, these algorithmic complexities increasingly impact intimacy, love, sexuality and eroticism and have emerged as a terrain of *experimental life*, creating new opportunities and new burdens. What does this digital sea-change mean for everyday life, as well as for wider social relations more or less caught up in the logics of predictive algorithms? This book aims to investigate these questions. It is about women and men living with artificial bonds, and particularly how these bonds are experienced and negotiated through co-active human–machine interfaces. This artificial field of intimate bonds is what I call *algorithmic intimacy*.

The Concept of Algorithmic Intimacy

Today, algorithms are increasingly all-enveloping. Predictive algorithms significantly influence the ways we live and work. From automating stock market trading to recommending consumer purchases to website users, algorithms rule. It is perhaps not surprising therefore that 'algorithm' has become a keyword of contemporary cultural life, appearing frequently in the media, social commentary and the broader public sphere. Even so, the concept of 'algorithm' remains mysterious, encoding as it does some enticing or alluring connotations. It is a concept that, as we shall see, conveys much more than that designated in the mathematical sciences or computer engineering. The word 'algorithm' and its cognates have a remarkably long history and derive from a ninth-century Persian mathematician, Muḥammad ibn Mūsā al-Khwārizmī.[4] His latinized name, Algoritmi, denoted the 'decimal number system'.[5] Other academic studies trace the concept back to the seventeenth-century notebooks of the German polymath Gottfried Leibniz. Still other academic studies detect early uses of the term in twentieth-century mathematical controversies over undecidable propositions.

While the word continues to be used as a specialized mathematical term, especially as regards the programming of computational code and in the field of information science, 'algorithm' is used today in a much broader sense too. Algorithms in the contemporary sense also denote codes of socio-technical action associated with cultural life and linked specifically to the personal domain and private life. 'Algorithmic retailing', 'algorithmic bias', 'the Twitter algorithm', even 'algorithmic warfare' – all these uses of the term reflect a broader form of economic, social, cultural and political enmeshment in artificial intelligence, one which is not linked only to advanced computational technology. But still, we might ask, what is it that people are talking about when they use the term 'algorithm'? As a first approximation, we could say that *'algorithm' refers to a set of guidelines that provide step-by-step actions that need to be performed to achieve a particular outcome.* On this definition, something as elementary as a recipe for baking a cake could be classified as an algorithm. While technically accurate, such an account arguably fails to capture the kinds of values and norms which are relevant to algorithms in the modern sense of the term. A central characteristic of algorithms has to do with the rise of computers in society at large. Consequently, algorithms have evolved to be computational, calculative and rich in complexity. 'An algorithm', writes the celebrated computer scientist Pedro Domingo, 'is a sequence of instructions telling a computer what to do'.[6]

Algorithms not only presuppose some degree of programmed instructions; they also involve, often and increasingly, the use of a technology commonly referred to as *machine learning*. Rather than repeatedly processing a set of computational instructions, algorithmic systems based on machine learning reprogram themselves as they process and respond to data. It is this dimension of computational self-learning from data that enables us to see that algorithms involve much more than the actions and unconscious biases of computer programmers or data engineers alone. Algorithms thus involve (1) a degree of unpredictability, or even uncertainty; and (2) operations which are often obscure and sometimes invisible even to those programmers or computer engineers who originally created the initial set of computational instructions. From this angle, one reason why advanced artificial intelligence poses serious challenges in the social and political domain is because of the opacity of algorithms. Computer programmers create computational code and such instructions are rendered as algorithms, but in turn such algorithms create new algorithms. Any large, complex decision-making software system can be understood as generative of algorithms in a digital universe which itself remains invisible to participants and which no one – not even technical experts – can fully understand. In the face of technophiles who assert the primacy of algorithmic objectivity along with the idea that machine learning can weigh a set of calculations with mathematical detachment, the counter-argument worthy of consideration is that the opacity of machine learning is one powerful reason why our new algorithmic world appears as downright dangerous. Part of the cultural fear here is that algorithms take us farther and farther away from human agency, with predictive algorithms determining who should receive government benefits, sorting the rescheduling of airline flights, managing the granting of financial loans, and much more.

Undoubtedly there are many occasions when individuals not only are thankful to receive the support of automated machine intelligence but also substantially benefit from it. Algorithmic operations involving the automating of commercial activities such as payroll management are of the kind which have generally delivered improved efficiency and have increasingly become trusted features of social life. Likewise, web mapping apps such as Google Maps are to a large extent 'open' in predicting traffic; these apps are available for people to find the best route from one location to another. Of course, many algorithms involving the automation of social tasks remain fairly basic at a techno-logical level. Predictive algorithms, however, are also used for much more sophisticated automated services and activities. What we are witnessing today is the emergence of new forma-tions in human–machine interaction, involving the saturation of both public and private life with the automated enumerating and modelling of human behaviour. Today, predictive algorithms are increasingly associated with intimate connections and networked relationships, so much so that the concepts of human and machine intelligence may now seem somewhat blurred. So, in a world where AI increasingly shapes and reshapes our understanding of ourselves and our societies, how do the more private dimensions of our lives become liable to algorithmic calculations? What conditions must be met before our emotions and intimate life become data which can be computationally analysed and rearranged in a complex interplay of people and machines? Does something distinctive at the level of personal life and intimate relations emerge out of these predictive algorithms, something which perhaps had not been foreseen in the computer programming?

It has become commonplace to say that people today, especially in informational networked societies, are increasingly, but perhaps unknowingly, reliant on machine-learning algorithms. Algorithms increasingly impact not only the economy but entertainment, not only institutional life but identity transformations, not only information but intimacy. 'Algorithmic intimacy', as I define it, has to do with *advanced computational processes known as machine intelligence which produce new ways of ordering personal behaviour and modelling intimate relationships.*[7] Since predictive algorithms impinge on the capabilities of individuals to think, decide and act, these processes may (and often do) seriously impact the complex relations between people, things, information and ideas. What I shall call 'algorithmic intimacy' is redefining the very contours of what intimate relations, love, eroticism and sexuality actually mean in contemporary society. Algorithmic intimacy operates through unprecedented amounts of big data and advanced computational analytics, which in turn makes new kinds of calculation, new forms of prediction, and new types of human and machine interaction possible.[8] Algorithmic intimacy is about machine intelligence working within us, amplifying our erotic impulses, steering our personal preferences, solving our intimate dilemmas and creating new dilemmas along the way.[9] This computational logic seeks to turn intimate life – from unanticipated sparks of desire to our tending of loving commitments – into machine-readable data, restructuring identity, intimacy and personal life more generally as an outcome of data-mining operations.

To explore this matter further we will need to investigate how a nascent culture of automated machine learning is transforming our ideas about intimacy, sexuality, eroticism and the self. We will need to probe the complex, contradictory ways in which people generate experiences, relationships, identities, intimacies and lifestyle changes that arise through interaction with both semi-automated and automated intelligent machines. We will need to draw from some of the most outstanding recent contributions in social theory in general, and science and technology studies in particular, to understand better how the world of automated artificial intelligence enables us to contemplate forms of intimacy that exist apart from bodies, that transcend conventional social norms, and that are far less subject to traditional constraints of space and time. We will also need to consider some new concepts which I introduce throughout the book to help us make sense of the changing impact of predictive algorithms on our intimate lives. This book asserts that changes in our experiences and understandings of intimacy are at once affected by and reflect broader changes in automated machine intelligence. My aim in *Algorithmic Intimacy* is to connect two of the major preoccupations of current social science and public debate – namely automated predictive algorithms and the popular engrossment with intimate relationships.

Despite the profusion of AI and machine learning in the texture of our intimate worlds and private lives, there has been relatively little scholarly research on the topic. There is a large literature on the institutional dimensions and socio-economic consequences of AI, from the literature on robots taking people's jobs to research on the business benefits of AI to doomsday scenarios of killer robots and existential threats, and there are numerous studies which recount the impacts of the digital revolution on transformed conditions of identity construction and interpersonal relationships. But the broader impacts taking place in our private and personal lives (especially as regards intimacy, sexuality and love) as a result of the algorithmic phase of the modern era have not been the subject of systematic scholarly study. There have been numerous media articles and popular books, written both by journalists and by tech entrepreneurs, programmers or other 'insiders', that provide broad overviews about the evolution of intimacy, relationships and sex in the aftermath of new digital technologies.[10] There has been some scholarly attention paid to the potential applications of AI as developed by sex therapists and in couples counselling, though the large bulk of books and articles in this area have mostly concentrated on the advent of sex robots.[11] More relevant are the various anthologies which offer informative but rather technical overviews of how the new level of automation afforded by machine-learning algorithms heightens the fragility of social networks and human bonds. Other critics have recognized that the study of predictive algorithms requires more than attention to automated technologies or machine intelligence, and spotlights new kinds of emotional experience and intimate bonds in the age of AI. However, there have been very few

studies which seek to explore, in a more systematic and sociological fashion, the algorithmic transformation of intimacy and
the social conditions which frame its development, deepening
and consequences.

The world in which we live today is transformed by a
range of algorithmic calculative devices, logics and techniques
which impact identities and intimacies as much as institutions
and organizational life. We come to see ourselves differently
as we apprehend awareness of both our private and public
lives in the invisible pieces of algorithmic code that form
the complex digital systems of the machine-learning age. In
this book I shall try to show that predictive algorithms are
changing the way we experience intimacy, the dynamics of
our sexual lives, the cultural forms of loving relationships, our
very identities. Predictive algorithms do not only power our
cars, our hospitals and courtrooms. They've come to be deeply
lodged inside us. They've learned our private preferences; they
tell us how to live, who to befriend and who to date. From
this standpoint, one can more than readily understand why
some authors have sought to characterize how we live today
in terms of 'algorithmic life' or 'algorithmic worlds'.[12] But this
book is not intended as an addition to the mounting pile of
science and technology studies of algorithms. Instead, it tries
to investigate the power of algorithms in what I hope is a more
original context, one focused on transformations of intimate
life and loosely informed by the parameters of social theory.
While there has been some academic and public interest in
looking at how artificial intelligence reshapes our cultural lives,
there has been a marked lack of attention to how machine-
learning algorithms remake the intimate relations that define
privacy, intimacy and our personal lives more generally. In this
book I shall try to show that, if we want to understand the
power of predictive algorithms, then we must understand how
automated intelligent machines are redefining the threshold of
what acceptable, desirable, positive, negative or risky intimate
relations mean for both self and society. Throughout the
book I shall develop an approach to the rise of predictive
algorithms which is primarily cultural, by which I mean an
approach which is concerned simultaneously with the intimate
or emotional implications of algorithmic processes and their
social impacts.

Some Characteristics of Algorithmic Intimacy

How exactly does algorithmic intimacy differ from conventional intimate relationships? What is the complex relation between the rise of algorithmic intimacy and changes in our public and private lives today? In its orthodox rendition, intimacy demanded time, commitment and care for the making of deep emotional connections and the fostering of very significant personal feelings. Intimacy could be by turns exciting, perplexing, compelling and irresistible, but the intricate interplay of care, concern and commitment took centre stage. In its digitalized, algorithmic and above all more automated reincarnation as computer code, intimacy is less about renewed dynamism between people and more about the elimination of unpredictability, uncertainty and ambivalence. In talking about the algorithmic stage of automated intimacy, we are talking about a form of calculated certitude called predictive analytics. Perhaps to say 'certitude' is to say too much. But in the algorithmic era, human agency and intimate relationships appear at cross-purposes. Algorithmic prediction, I shall argue at length, can operate as an automation that renders people seemingly mechanical. To appreciate the full dimensions of this algorithmic transformation of intimacy, we need to consider some of the major characteristics of new forms of digital intimacy which are spawned by the machine-learning age. Let us now briefly consider some of these defining characteristics of algorithmic intimacy. These characteristics will be subsequently analysed in more detail throughout the book.

Perhaps one of the most obvious aspects of algorithmic intimacy is that it appears counter-intuitive to established conceptions of human togetherness. It would seem altogether at cross-purposes to traditional cultural understandings and social norms pertaining to the realm of intimate relationships. Broadly speaking, intimacy has a quality of enchantment which largely marks it off from the humdrum routines of ordinary social engagement. Everything in the world can suddenly seem dramatic and exciting when human bonds become strongly shaped by intimacy. Likewise, on the level of personal relations, intense intimacy can be disruptive of everyday life; it connects people to very significant and sometimes very disturbing intensities of emotion. Many traditional social norms and cultural codes governing the conduct of intimate relationships (from friendship to sexual relations) would appear blunted or diminished, however, in the face of machine-learning predictive algorithms and the emergent variety of intimate connections modelled in the image of computational code. An indication of this can be seen in the struggle many critics have had in describing exactly what is happening when people connect, communicate and forge links with each other via automated intelligent machines. 'Facebook friends', for example, has been called today's shortcut for 'how to be liked by everyone online', a strange inversion where the word 'friend' designates people who might otherwise be complete strangers. Intimate relationships have more or less been characterized by passionate attachment, erotic desire, the particular, the singular, defined by specific subjectivities and captured by concrete cultural codes. Yet machine-learning algorithms would appear the opposite of all this: they redefine intimacy as *relationship engineering*. The objectives all seem to be in the direction of prediction, copying, re-enactment and repetition. As a popular joke captures this: a machine-learning algorithm arrives at a bar and the bartender asks, 'What would you like to drink?' The algorithm replies, 'What's everyone else having?'

When we consider the ever-increasing extension of AI into contemporary sexual relationships and erotic cultural forms, the difficulty of arriving at a clear characterization of the digitalization of intimacy becomes even more pronounced. Some commentators have likened predictive algorithms in the sphere of commercial sexual relationships, and especially dating websites and hook-up apps, to an amalgam of glossy adult entertainment, pornography and reality TV. The prescriptive weight of machine-learning algorithms – taken on board daily by women and men through the 'recommendations' of Netflix, Facebook, Uber and other data-economy platforms – have been widely viewed in terms of 'technological solutionism'. Bernard Stiegler speaks, for instance, of the 'tyranny of digital lifestyles'.[13] The lure of 'predictive algorithmic relations' appears to be automated to the measure of distancing people from the unpredictability of intimacy itself.

A second characteristic of algorithmic intimacy is that the automated actions, codes and programs associated with machine intelligence typically involve a high degree of *obscurity* or *obliqueness*, such that the technical operations and predictive weightings informing algorithmic recommendations rarely become known to participants, consumers or citizens. Another way of putting this point is to say that the social power of algorithms is largely hidden or invisible. Whilst the ways in which people experience and discern algorithms as part of the fabric of everyday life are many and varied, the force field of predictive algorithms operates largely 'behind the scenes'. Tania Bucher perceptively notes that our 'different ways of thinking about what algorithms are and do may affect how these systems are used',[14] but the central point to keep in mind is that the social impacts of algorithms are only discerned retrospectively. The social power of algorithms become evident, as it were, only after the event of automated prediction. The rise of algorithmic intimacy has been very largely shaped by these 'automated fields of encounter' between people and machines in the social, cultural and political spheres, and specifically influence how the digitalization of intimacy has developed and deepened in the early twenty-first century. Some of this is brought out very well in *Machines Like Me*, partly because McEwan found an effective literary means to dramatize the impacts of digital intimacy. Whilst people don't ever directly clap eyes on algorithms in daily life, the image of synthetic humans is, in fact, of another order – largely thanks to the influence of Hollywood science-fiction movies. People, it would seem, have less difficulty imagining and visualizing robots than algorithms. This ease of cultural awareness in imagining robots is arguably McEwan's substitute for our contemporary encounter with algorithms. Julian Lucas, writing in *The New Yorker*, asks of McEwan: 'Why write a novel, in 2019, about a humanoid robot? Like the flying car, it's a long-anticipated idea that, although not quite obsolete, has begun to feel curiously outdated.'[15] Lucas concludes that 'McEwan is aware of this belatedness' and perhaps created Adam as a 'throwback' in order to underscore that 'bodies are déclassé in the era of cloud computing'. From this angle, McEwan's *Machines Like Me* allows us to see that AI has in our own time not only become less corporeal, but also become increasingly oblique, invisible and ubiquitous. This is a theme that I shall seek to develop throughout this book. One reason why machine-learning algorithms play a crucial role in the transformation of intimacy is that they impact upon people's lives through any number of technological devices – from smartphones to tablets to laptops. Siri, Alexa and an endlessly proliferating number of chatbots speak to us imparting 'worlds of information'; the 'godlike omnipresence' of these virtual voices, writes Lucas, 'softened by a tone of relentless compliance'.

A third characteristic of algorithmic intimacy has to do with the kinds of social engagement, and oftentimes the forms of talk, carried out with the assistance of machine intelligence. Automated algorithmic communication is not like speech, even in those digital formats or on those software platforms which might appear most speech-like, such as chatbots and virtual personal assistants (VPAs). There are several key differences between chatbot talk and face-to-face conversation. For one thing, when people communicate face to face there is generally a routine compliance with the social norm to politely focus on what others are saying; people, for the most part, 'give off the impression' that they are paying attention to the other person. The American sociologist Erving Goffman labelled this the expectation of 'mutual attentiveness', arguing it was one of the 'core norms' holding modern societies together. Today, by contrast, as the process of machine learning enters a more advanced phase, pre-existing communication norms are increasingly undermined. Unlike face-to-face conversation, chatbots and VPAs do not demand conversational politeness. When talking to automated intelligent machines, people do not have to be considerate or amusing or even display close attention. Traditional core norms of mutual attentiveness remain, of course, vital to the arts of human conversation, for the most part. But these norms are less secure than they once were, and I have elsewhere posed the question of whether automated intelligent machines are re-engineering the manner in which people conduct face-to-face conversations.[16] Might, for example, chatbot talk 'bleed' into everyday conversations? Might lukewarm emotion, or decreased levels of affect, displayed in chatbot talk spill over into face-to-face conversations? Might the manner in which people talk to chatbots and VPAs – 'do this', 'order me that' – negatively impact upon how they talk with intimate partners in everyday life?

Many critics fear that this is how it is as a consequence of relationship tech, where whatever remains of 'interaction' is reduced to pre-scripted replies and predictive text technology. In this account, communication mediated by machine intelligence appears as one-dimensional, arriving on the recipient's device as a relatively 'closed message' which rarely invites any deeper engagement. In the same manner that the development of SMS messaging resulted in widespread and frequently used texting transformations in language, it has been argued that relationship tech might result in emotional forms of interaction the equivalent of emojis. Other critics warn that we are already witnessing the 'algorithmic disinhibition effect', where a lack of restraint escalates in virtual environments because people are missing empathy cues that typically occur in face-to-face interactions. As a consequence, various relationship and friendship apps have introduced AI-powered prompts asking recipients to reconsider sending potentially offensive or inappropriate communications. Tinder, for example, introduced it's 'Are You Sure?' feature in 2021, in which AI software scans messages sent by users to detect possibly harmful language.

A final characteristic of algorithmic intimacy which should be noted in this opening chapter has to do with the multiplication of forms of emotional connection, affective association and relational affiliation. Whatever else the intimacy of yesteryear might have entailed, it was above all both *selective* and *sequential*. Traditional forms of intimacy were largely of the 'you-are-the-one' model of singular uniqueness. Such step-by-step, one-at-a-time standards governing intimacy were partly the result of the limitation of human powers in the context of face-to-face social encounters. The message of traditional cultures of intimacy was one resolutely focused on practices of selection and exclusion because individuals were unable to pay attention to all possible interlocutors; it was neither feasible nor even conceivable to display the necessary kind of attentiveness to all possible interlocutors who might have been vying for attention at the same time. The digital lifestyles of people today searching for experiences of intimacy are radically different. Today it is possible, thanks to automated intelligent machines, to join simultaneously in multiple conversations and multitudinous intimacies. Multiplication may indeed be the most conspicuous feature of algorithmic intimacy, whereby women and men seek to coordinate relationship possibilities without becoming integrated or overcommitted. Illusion or not, automated machine intelligence promises people as many kinds of intimacies as their emotional capacities can tolerate and their digital skills permit.

This multiplication of intimate relations is heightened by the fact that, as more and more connections (economic, social, cultural, personal) become automated, people need to continually download, update and integrate data into their lives and lifestyle activities. Intimate relations may be increasingly instantaneous, simultaneous and automated – that is, it may take less and less time to generate 'connections with others' – but, paradoxically, more time needs to be allocated to blend, fuse and amalgamate the data generated by these multiple smart machines. Automated intelligent machines involve ongoing reconfigurations of 'personalized networking' – as one moment people engage the capacity for the 'semi-autonomous' processing of information, communication and services, and the next moment engage in the 'self-retrieval' of data and personal information. This paradox has been outlined by Helga Nowotny in a dystopian vision where people become the 'time slaves' of automated global complexity. 'We have to allocate time', writes Nowotny, 'to use what we are being offered – be it transport, communication, entertainment, or access to information, which needs to be downloaded and integrated.' This much-sought-after integration is, however, largely illusory. Such is the complexity of automated feedback mechanisms, coupled with ever-new technological breakthroughs, that people discover – only slowly, in fits and starts, and sometimes painfully – that there is never enough time in the day to recalibrate or retrofit all the data accumulated in such automated systems. 'The speed with which data is processed and recombined', cautions Nowotny, 'far exceeds the capacity of human perception. All we can do is register the effect.' The great crisis of data fatigue is a key component of algorithmic intimacy and has the potential to become immensely damaging to personal life and social bonds, as well as the wider fabric of society.

The Argument of *Algorithmic Intimacy*

This book establishes the current scale, intensity, acceleration and impact of digitalization processes upon intimate relationships and especially how machine-learning predictive algorithms are remodelling human behaviour and transforming social practices. In this book, I will examine a vast array of predictive algorithms which are changing the boundaries of public and personal life today. Whilst automated intelligent machines impact many fields of activity in contemporary social life, the realm of intimacy is of special significance in some major respects. The promise of intimacy has come to mean the promise of deeper and more satisfying relationships at both the personal and cultural levels. But rather than the digital revolution fostering free and open communication in the interpersonal sphere, many people today worry that intimate relationships are rendered increasingly fractured, fragmented or empty as a result. My starting point is that AI-powered automated intelligent machines are intricately interwoven with how intimacy is being rewritten today, as well as changes impacting personal life on a more general plane. Focusing on changes in intimate relationships and personal life are helpful for understanding how the world of predictive algorithms 'weigh in' on our expressions of emotion and our practices of care and commitment to ourselves, other people and the wider world.

The fast-changing contours of intimacy, eroticism, sexuality and love are enormously varied and hugely complex, and it is not feasible in a single volume such as this to attempt to deal with the many different aspects and intricate threads of change in intimacy arising in relation to digital technologies. In order to keep the book manageable, I address three basic types of intimacy impacted by machine intelligence. My focus here is on (1) relationship tech, (2) therapy tech and (3) friendship tech.

Relationship Tech, concerned with the ways algorithmic conceptions of intimacy are influencing sexual relations, dating, marriage, family, eroticism and love.

Therapy Tech, concerned with the ways algorithmic conceptions of personhood are influencing therapeutic mental health, specifically well-being, welfare and autonomy.

Friendship Tech, concerned with the ways algorithmic conceptions of companionship are influencing mutuality, interpersonal bonds, communication and sociability.

I won't be looking at other fields of technological innovation impacting intimacy – at the rise of sex robots, for example. The socio-technical fields of relationship, therapy and friendship tech are impacting personal and cultural life in quite different ways and with significantly different consequences. My focus is not robotics, but advances in artificial intelligence more generally. The book examines how a burgeoning culture of AI is changing our ideas about intimacy, relationships, identities and machines. We shall encounter quantified sex and algorithmic dating apps, TikTok friends, chatbot therapists and automated intimacy profiling. Virtual personal assistants such as Siri and Alexa, too, form part of this story – as their 'services' help automate dealing with the stresses and strains of intimate relationships. We'll encounter algorithms used by women and men to help decide with whom they wish to have sexual relations – as one-night stands or longer-term romances. We'll find algorithms used by people to design a new sense of identity and 'reinvigorate' existing intimate relationships. We'll pay close attention to the claims and counterclaims of tech entrepreneurs, software engineers and computer programmers; examine the responses of users of automated predictive algorithms; and confront the changes brought about by machine intelligence – including the unanswered questions they raise for intimate and personal life.

Throughout the book, I will invoke the idea of 'algorithmic intimacy' to explore the complexities and nuances that shape and reshape the different ways that people connect and communicate within human–machine interfaces. But at this early point, I should also note some judicious qualifications. The term 'algorithmic intimacy' is not intended as an all-encompassing category for understanding the digital (re)organization of intimacy. Clearly there are significant differences in the degree to which individuals are caught up in the accelerating dynamism of automated intelligent machines and their consequences for personal and public life. Some of these socio-technical differences are of major significance for grasping change within friendships, relationships and self-care as practised in various forms of therapy today. I consequently argue that the central notion of this book must be understood as plural, multiple and diverse: there are many forms of algorithmic intimacy each with its own socio-technical particularities. In this study I pay close attention to the role of identity, to different kinds of sociability, and varying patterns of technology use and engagement. I am especially concerned to unearth the complex, contradictory ways in which people project their lives, and their lives in these times, into the algorithms which predict the very contours of those lives lived. The book, then, is a preliminary study – necessarily partial and provisional – that posits in an elementary fashion the force field of algorithmic intimacy in the digital age. My hope is that the book, viewed from this angle, stimulates further theoretical development and empirical research in the social sciences and humanities.

What I do try to demonstrate throughout the book – and what my previous contributions to the social theory of identity have allowed me to do – concerns the importance of bringing the individual back into the conversation about algorithms and automation.[17] The chapters that follow contain many stories – profiles and portraits of women and men as they navigate the thrills and spills of lifestyle change in the age of automated intelligent machines. The great Austrian-British philosopher Ludwig Wittgenstein warned against ideas that take 'a contemptuous attitude towards the particular case'. I try to follow Wittgenstein's warning closely. My focus is on the automated digitalization of lifestyle as it intersects with particular cases of intimate relations; I focus on people as they live and work with automated digital technologies in both the background and foreground of their lives. In a way, these profiles provide important glimpses into how our personal lives and deepest intimacies are today increasingly mediated by and distributed across a whole range of automated digital devices and smart machines. What we will uncover are the possibilities and risks of algorithmic intimacy as people experiment with the power of digital technologies; we will also explore the complex ways in which instantly responsive smart machines both allay and intensify anxieties about sociability. If we wish to understand the role that machine-learning algorithms are playing in the design of new cultural and intimate sensibilities, then we must listen carefully to the conversations around us about technology, machines and lifestyle change.

At the same time, whilst every online or virtual intimacy contains its manifold stories and individual singularities, there are grounding social and cultural contexts as well. So I will be presenting narratives of intimacy against the backdrop of three types of digital sociability: relationship tech, therapy tech and friendship tech. It is important to understand the digitalization of intimacy in context, without losing sight of economy, society and politics. To study the digitalization of intimacy in context also means to study its relation to cultural history and the history of technology. There are numerous studies situating cultural history in relation to technology, but these contributions mostly fail to consider how intimacy and identity are actually lived in relation to technological change. It is my aim in this book to bridge this divide, connecting novel social theories about the digital revolution with a wide range of empirical studies on intimacy and its changing contours. This involves drawing liberally on the literature of contemporary social and cultural theory and establishing a dialogue with several social science fields (sociology, media studies, gender studies, psychoanalysis) that are often kept separate.

This book is not intended as a contribution to the field of science and technology studies, but as a work of social theory. The conceptual strategy I adopt is one which locates profiles and portraits of digitally automated intimacy (whether in relationship tech, therapy tech or friendship tech) and in each case summons a distinctive standpoint drawn from social theory in order to elucidate the algorithmic effects of digitally mediated sociability. Accordingly I couple social media and sociology, chatbot therapy and critical theory, TikTok friends and psychoanalysis, quantified sex and gender studies. In all of these fields, algorithmic intimacy is about both automation and agency. My purpose is not only to suggest that social theory can help illuminate digital transformations of intimacy; it is also to underscore that algorithmic intimacy carries serious consequences for some of the central concerns of social thought and cultural analysis.

In the story of constructing intimacy in the age of automated machine intelligence, the predictive power of algorithms figures prominently. Sometimes the power of predictive algorithms turns into self-fulfilling prophecies and sometimes the predictions or recommendations which people receive are wide of the mark, rendering the realm of intimacy jarring or impersonal. Such experiences will form the basis for many of the broader sociological discussions and conceptual analyses set out in this book. But it is vital to note that such experiences of the power of predictive algorithms must be understood as part of a larger social and cultural context. One aspect of that context concerns the eroding boundaries between human understanding and machine intelligence, agency and automation, which carries major implications for everyday social life in the patterning of intimate relationships. The next chapter reconstructs the historical rise of intimacy within modern societies, paying close attention to the escalating entwinement of intimate relationships, cultural identities and new digital technologies. I examine the sociological contribution of Georg Simmel, who maintained that the search for authentic selfhood and enriching intimate relations takes place within an institutional context of powerful impersonal economic forces and social systems. Now Simmel obviously wrote well before the advent of the digital revolution. That said, I seek to press an engagement with certain threads of Simmel's sociology into a broader consideration of the 'impersonal forces' of automated machine intelligence. The chapter also examines how contemporary digital technologies entail novel kinds of human bonds and new forms of togetherness.

The culture of algorithmic intimacy is emerging across many domains. Chapter 3 examines relationship tech, which is often how the digitalization of intimacy is confronted and negotiated by people today. Especially significant has been the rise of algorithmic-powered dating apps, where intimate bonds are recast as mixtures of desire, computer code and machine learning. Whilst the algorithms that already automate sexual encounters are only one (albeit highly publicized) element of relationship tech, I try to show that quantified life practices have become increasingly interwoven with the realm of intimate human bonds. I develop a basic catalogue of algorithmic dating apps and quantified sex practices, and I argue that relationship tech facilitates the generation of new connections, relationships, identities and intimate spaces that arise through *erotic engineering*. I then attempt to reconstruct the social power of relationship tech in terms of the semi-automation or automation of reflexivity, with emphasis on how women and men learn to adapt to, and cope with, machine-learning algorithms in deciding what kinds of intimacy they want to 'try out' and 'live with'. These experiments in algorithmic sexual intimacy I position in terms of consumer markets, consumer industries and consumer societies. I conclude the chapter by examining the potential effects of algorithmic measurement in terms of the production of self.

Chapter 4 turns to address the rise of therapy tech. The chapter examines how much every sphere of life has become influenced by new, automated therapeutic climates, especially the reconstruction of people's psychology through digital counselling, life-coaching apps and chatbot therapy. The question of therapy has previously been understood as the search for a 'sane self in a mad world', but today framing psychological problems through the prism of machine intelligence gives rise to a very different understanding of mental health and personal well-being. What is it like to live in an increasingly automated world where the project of self-reforming selves becomes ensnared in the power of predictive algorithms? I argue that many of our conventional ways of thinking about mental health and personal identity no longer fit the therapeutic imperative in Anglo-American societies which today promote teletherapy (at a distance), text-based therapy (via messaging apps), chatbot counselling or AI therapy with artificial agents. These automated therapeutics often restrict the involvement of individuals to pre-scripted replies, with therapy chatbots providing 'entertainment' in the form of quizzes, tips and games. I frame this 'Uberization of therapy' in terms of Arlie Russell Hochschild's notion of 'cultural cooling'. This captures the shift in contemporary societies from people searching for self-understanding with therapeutic experts (psychologists, counsellors, therapists) to a new mode of instrumental detachment where people undertake counselling through downloading mental health apps or talking to robot therapists. The chapter also considers the transformed relations between public and private life arising as a consequence of automated therapeutic imperatives. I draw selectively from the German sociologist Jürgen Habermas's critique of the public sphere, seeking to highlight how the advent of therapy chatbots and software counselling apps introduces algorithmically expressive elements of knowledge into the tissue of private life and the self.

Chapter 5 considers how companionship has been increasingly automated. There have been both extensive and intensive global shifts associated with the production of friendship tech – across the interconnected levels of technology, economics and society. The phenomenon of 'Facebook friends' has fundamentally changed our experiences of companionship, away from the emotional labour of caring for 'genuine' friends and towards the algorithmic programming of human bonds. Attention is given throughout this chapter to the modes and practices of friendship tech, where the ease of connection and contact jostles uneasily with digital distractibility and the deterioration of offline, interpersonal relationships. The spirit of algorithmic friendship, I shall suggest, is that of plasticity rather than permanence; it boasts of the ability to generate connections rather than companionship. I develop this argument through an analysis of several interrelated themes: the rise of social network services and online social media, which in turn recasts friendship in networked terms as both culturally universal and individually contextual; the re-engineering of friendship as something programmable and predictive; and the economic designation of algorithmic friendship as an object of value that can be capitalized on and monetized. There is brief analysis of the many different types of automated intimacies fostered in friendship tech, as well as consideration of the consequences of one-sided emotional connections forged with artificial agents.

In the final chapter I move away from the interconnected mechanisms of tech and provide a more synthetic view on algorithmic intimacy and its consequences for public and private life. If human bonds and predictive algorithms are inextricably interconnected, as well as regulated through similar digital and institutional processes, what prompts the individual to apprehend the opportunities and risks of machine intelligence in particular ways? If this digitalized and disorganized world of the early twenty-first century hangs together in some substantive part by dint of predictive algorithms, both complex and ingenious by turns, what anxieties permeate the individual's relation to – and increasing reliance on – automated intelligent machines? I set out three cognitive outlooks or life strategies – some drawn from individual instances in the everyday negotiation of the digital revolution, others recounted from newspaper articles, periodicals and other academic studies – and I try to show a *plurality of worlds* in play as people navigate the power of predictive algorithms and automated machine intelligence. I also try to highlight that the three different ways of connecting and relating to machine intelligence – namely *conventional, cohesive* or *individualized* cognitive strategies – provide important insights into human–machine interactions and their related 'side effects' within intimate bonds today.

Predictive algorithms and artificial bonds, in a remarkably interconnected way, simultaneously reproduce and transform the contours of contemporary social experience of the world. The world of algorithmic intimacy is a world of extensive and intensive machine mediation, and above all one suffused with novel hopes and fears, set against the digital backcloth of having short-circuited elements of collective faith in human intelligence through an instantaneous condensation of advanced machine automation and its predictive possibilities. What follows from all this? Will the pleasures of intimacy manage to be the last bastion of human bonds, decoded with gusto by the joint forces of machine intelligence and the emergent cognitive life strategies of digital natives? Will the true powers and perils of the algorithms that already automate our experiences of friendship and companionship, relationships and togetherness, as well as care of the self and personal well-being, spell the demotion or relegation of humanity's long romance with passionate love (what Stendhal called *amour passion*), eroticism and other romantic attachments? And even if the power of predictive algorithms falls short of such a global metamorphosis, what would be the lot of society and intimate human bonds, which were traditionally nourished on face-to-face interaction but which are now increasingly subjected to routine processes of digital quantification? The question is whether intimate bonds (human attachments, love, passion, eroticism) can accommodate today's algorithmic processes of quantification, whose metric is largely hidden from view – subtracted from inspection, verification, reflection and debate. Or is it the opposite that is the case? Perhaps the algorithmic version of 'data selves', life lived as a series of semi-automated or automated experiments, might bring within reach novel forms of self-experience and a new standard set for encountering other people in their incalculable otherness? It is the complexity of these interconnections between intimate human bonds and automated machine intelligence that is the central theme of this book.

2

Togetherness Transformed

What are the impacts of human–machine interaction upon human bonds and interpersonal relationships? How might we best understand the consequences of the sexual revolution – from feminism to post-feminism to LGBTQ+ – for the development of personal relationships in the age of AI? In this chapter some of the main characteristics of what has become known as 'digital intimacy' are elaborated. A central distinguishing feature of the chapter is its strongly historical stress. 'Conventional intimacy' and 'digital intimacy' are often approached as though they were historically separate and distinct types of personal relationship, but I argue that such a view of human togetherness is largely mistaken.

Simmel on Intimacy, Strangeness and Sociality

The analysis of algorithmic intimacy requires examination of the connecting 'invisible threads' between people and especially of the dynamics of intimacy and strangeness within social life. I begin this examination by turning to some of the seminal contributions of the sociologist Georg Simmel. The founding fathers of sociology were not especially inquisitive about intimacy. Karl Marx, Max Weber and Emile Durkheim were variously interested in the economy, institutional life, social norms, law and politics.[1] Simmel, however, was more eclectic and developed a very different approach to the analysis of social life. He cast society as a web of sociability, oftentimes intimate but mostly emotionally tempered and rationalistic. Simmel's version of intimacy is very broad in scope, capturing the emotional inter-changes that simultaneously link and separate people. Social bonds, wrote Simmel over a century ago, depend 'upon the precondition that people know something about each other'.[2] He maintained that knowledge – particularly information about others and what women and men might expect from each other – lies at the core of countless connections between the individual and society. The notion was that, in social life, individuals would always act in particular ways so as to give others clues about their lives, intentions and likely demands. Sociability depends on either raising or lowering the amount of information about the self that one provides to others at any particular moment. This was arguably nowhere more evident, said Simmel, than 'in the relationship between the sexes'. Simmel had much to say about intimate social bonds, through which individuals seek to carve out a 'highly personal subjectivity'. He believed that people are fully themselves in acts of intimate communication, putting aside the distractions of routineness and engaging the life of the mind, especially the powers of imagination. The self-styling of life depended upon creative sociability, and even personal intimacy was regarded by Simmel as an art form. Like artists, individuals commit themselves to the pure sociability of love, marriage and friendship – all of which promise exciting, transcendent relationships beyond the 'masks of rationality' generated by modern urban environments. It is in the intimacies of personal relationships, away from the relentless demands of modern city living, that women and men can explore the unique development of selfhood in contexts of interaction with a potentially wide range of contacts. 'In erotic love', Ferdinard Fellmann writes of Simmel's approach to intimate relations, 'partners unconsciously lose their former selves in each other by creating each other anew.'[3]

Pure intimacy would appear at once inside and outside society. For Simmel, one of the more interesting sociological mysteries is how people connect and interact with others by developing an appetite for intimacy. He places particular emphasis on face-to-face interaction, stressing the importance of vision to social bonds. The eye, wrote Simmel, is a 'unique sociological achievement'.[4] People create a sense of reciprocity – an exchange of information – when they take clues from each other. There are, we might say, two stages in the quest for intimate relations established through the visual order of face-to-face encounters. The first concerns 'taking in' the other person – *internalizing information* – through the eye; the second concerns 'giving off' – *projecting out* – signals to the other person. This is the complex dance of sociability, and for Simmel it is the visual order of the eye which underpins the most complete reciprocity of person-to-person interaction. For Simmel, eye contact and the expressive features of the face underpin the exchange of key information essential to both sociability and the reproduction of society. This is not to say, however, that we are always trans-parent to ourselves and never self-deceived in the visual order of pure sociability. Intimate relations always involve a degree of tension. Exchanges of intimacy are simultaneously shot through with familiarity and remoteness, nearness and distance. 'A trace of strangeness', wrote Simmel, 'enters even the most intimate relationships.' No matter what the degree of intimacy, still the self cannot grasp the other person as a whole. There is always a kind of otherness to the other person. As Simmel captured this kernel of traumatic strangeness at work in passionate intimacy:

> In the stage of first passion, erotic relations strongly reject any thought of generalization: the lovers think that there has never been a love like theirs; that nothing can be compared either to the person loved or to the feelings for that person. An estrangement – whether as cause or as consequence it is difficult to decide – usually comes at the moment when this feeling of uniqueness vanishes from the relationship. A certain skepticism in regard to its value, in itself and for them, attaches to the very thought that in their relation, after all, they carry out only a general human destiny; that they experience an experience that has occurred a thousand times before; that, had they not accidentally met their particular partner, they would have found the same significance in another person.

To grasp intimate relations as a complex interplay of famili-arity and strangeness is to see them as an intricately woven texture of communications, cues, signals and stimulations. It is precisely for this reason that Simmel casts the impersonal public realm as a space of emotional protection to people in the face of multiple external stimulations. Simmel argued, in *The Metropolis and Mental Life*, that the intensity of city living produces psychic overload. Life in massive, dense cities, he argued, provoked forms of overstimulation that were just too intense, too direct and too pure for people to emotionally bear or tolerate. In the face of this chaos of multiple stimulations, modern urban life engenders various impersonal systems and forms of rationalism so as to neutralize exchanges of information between people. Money is a signal example. Trade using money involves more, says Simmel, than calculations of financial security and the accumulation of profit. It has to do also with balancing out relations between strangers in public so that people do not have to deal with each other emotionally in face-to-face settings. Trust in money, for Simmel, is as much psychological as it is economic; it helps people take refuge from the proximity of feeling alive to others. It is this kind of emotional indifference, as a defence mechanism against the chaos of stimulation promoted by urban living, that Simmel foregrounds. The rise of rationalistic impersonal systems advancing such kinds of emotional indifference includes the timetabled structure of modern organization, or demands for strict punctuality in a range of commercial activities and public forums more generally. Simmel sees this 'structure of the highest impersonality' as positioning the individual self as 'a mere cog in an enormous organization of things and powers'.[5] This is roughly Simmel's position on the complex relations between self and society. The search for 'highly personal subjectivity' and 'unique intimacy' sits cheek by jowl with large-scale, impersonal structures of formality, politeness and punctuality in modern city living. In a sense, the double bind of modernity after Simmel can be stated quite simply: is the search for 'highly personal subjectivity' interrupted by the complexity and impersonality of socio-technical systems, or are such interruptions the spur to the search for intimate relations and personal development?

  Simmel's sociology – counterposing the modern search for 'highly personal subjectivity' with massive organizational systems or 'structures of the highest impersonality' – provides an important orientation for this book in the investigation of the digitalization of intimacy.[6] In the next sections of this chapter I explore an eclectic range of histories and sociologies of intimate relationships in order to elaborate and deepen Simmel's approach to sociability. The significance of Simmel's thinking is that it enables us to see that intimate relationships involve more than the actions, thoughts and feelings of individuals in the interpersonal sphere. What is at stake, rather, is something about the complex interplay of personalization and systematization; and something specifically about that form of systematization which, in our own time, has become known as 'machine intelligence'. Some elements of Simmel's corpus are very clear about the threat to human bonds and intimate relationships stemming from the ever-increasing systematization of impersonal forms of rationalism. The 'distance-keeping politeness' of which Simmel spoke is arguably revolutionized in certain versions of the present-day digitalization of intimacy. In talking about algorithmic intimacy, at least from a sociological point of view following Simmel, we are talking about the codification, condensation, regulation and exchange of information between individuals recast as 'data subjects'. We are talking about a notion of intimate life as being caught between pure sociability which is unpredictable, on the one hand, and the kind of self-repression through machine intelligence which gradually restricts the unpredictability of aliveness in the human subject to a realm of neutral information called algorithmic prediction, on the other hand. In research reported elsewhere it is shown that a dramatic shift is occurring today, from social relations as 'expressive' to sociability as 'automated'.[7] This is one reason, I suggest, why the digitalization of intimacy reflects broader shifts in algorithmic prediction and its uses.

Brands of Togetherness

In *Life in Fragments*, Zygmunt Bauman develops a catalogue of the many kinds of togetherness which frame human bonds. The catalogue, he acknowledges, is only partial and provisional, presented in an ideal-typical form. Bauman speaks of 'mobile togetherness' – busy streets, shopping malls, airports. A realm where only 'some shapes stand a chance of condensing into strangers – into the beings with intentions, beings whose intentions count though unknown, and count because unknown . . . Most shapes never make it that far, as they flash through the periphery of attention.'[8] He speaks of 'unavoidable togetherness' – the medical waiting room, the railway carriage, the aircraft cabin. Such togetherness involves the 'gathering of strangers

who know that they will soon go, each one's own way, never
to meet again'.[9] He speaks of 'tempered togetherness' – the
purpose-orientated designs of an office building or a factory
floor which bring people together. He speaks of 'manifest togetherness' – such as a protest march or football crowd. Then there is
'postulated togetherness' – the imagined communities of nations,
races, classes, genders. Finally, Bauman concludes his catalogue
with 'meta- togetherness' – a 'scene for encounters' such as a pub
or holiday beach.

Bauman did not intend this catalogue to be definitive or
exhaustive. But it is surely interesting that co-present interaction
remains the fundamental mode of togetherness and human
encounter in all of these versions of togetherness. What is
clearly missing from this catalogue is what we might call 'digital
togetherness'. Digitalization is the new bridge which reorganizes
how people encounter each other. Digitalization – particularly since the advent of the Internet – initiates new patterns
of togetherness, new forms of interaction. One key feature of
virtual togetherness may well depend upon the extensive and
intensive digitalization of each individual, in which the person
(following Deborah Lupton's insightful analysis) is reconstituted as a 'data self'.[10] Zeena Feldman, seeking to resurrect
Simmel's stranger in the age of social media, writes percep-
tibly of the fragmentary forms of togetherness engendered in
digitalization and overdetermined by database logic. This is
a fractured, dislocating 'online togetherness' where *mediated
strangers* encounter each other through digital constellations
of technology, sociability and spatiality. They are fragmentary
in as far as networked selves (in which the individual is recast
as 'packets of data') register their interests and desires in
the temporary, often fleeting, encounter. From Facebook to
Twitter, online togetherness positions individuals as 'dwelling
interlopers'. This is a form of togetherness to which one can
never permanently belong. As Feldman writes: 'there is no land
to own in cyberspace, only the vestige of place constituted by
profile pages, URLs, and inboxes'.[11] Here togetherness is at
once begotten and exhausted in the interval of the exchange
of information itself – others are met and evaluated based on
displays of information (photo uploads, listings of favourite
things); each encounter is a self-enclosed, even self-sustained,
mechanics of data exchange; each encounter has the appearance

of togetherness consisting of person-like entities, but which are, in fact, simulacra of selves.

Intimacy: From Sociability to Sharing

Zygmunt Bauman would perhaps have filed Simmel's account of how pure sociability necessarily and inevitably meets with the complexity and impersonality of urban life under the rubric of 'solid' or 'heavy' modernity, as distinct from the liquid phase of algorithmically automated, app-driven intimate assemblages of the present day. Whereas intimacy in the solid phase of modernity appears in the form of 'lasting commitments' and 'till-death-us-do-part' human bonds, in the contemporary liquid era of digital technologies it is recast as 'until further notice' – the fleeting mixtures of biology, technology and predictive algorithms. Algorithmic intimacy is more or less fast emerging as a universal phenomenon, where women and men generate episodic intimate relationships and self-designed, fast-changing identities through interaction with machine-learning technologies. In what follows I shall try to identify certain distinctive features of the changing dimensions of intimate relationships. Whilst I am not concerned to develop a history of intimate relationships, some historical interpretation of the transformation of intimacy is demanded. In particular, I seek to emphasize how the traditional distance between people and technology has become increasingly exposed to the transformative impact of the digital revolution.

Intimacy, in its traditional casting, meant closeness, reciprocity, mutuality, vulnerability to the other person and, above all, trust. The *Oxford English Dictionary* gives for intimacy 'intimate friendship or acquaintance' as well as 'familiar intercourse and close familiarity', though it goes on to note that 'intimacy is a euphemism for sexual intercourse'. Intimacy in this traditional casting, as Cristina Miguel argues, refers to three dimensions of human relations – physical, informational and emotional exchange.[12] From the late eighteenth century onwards in Europe, these dimensions of intimacy took place within the context of the Industrial Revolution and a burgeoning capitalist economic system. Specific to Europe was the emergence of the ideal of romantic love, from which intimate relationships unfolded less as a matter of economic circumstance and more on the basis of reciprocity and mutual sexual attraction. As Anthony Giddens reflects on these sweeping historical changes in *The Transformation of Intimacy*:

> Romantic love, which began to make its presence felt from the late eighteenth century onwards, drew upon such ideals and incorporated elements of *amour passion*, while nevertheless becoming distinct from both. Romantic love introduced the idea of a narrative into an individual's life – a formula which radically extended the reflexivity of sublime love. The telling of a story is one of the meanings of 'romance', but this story now becomes individualized, inserting self and other into a personal narrative which had no particular reference to wider social processes.[13]

Many authors hold that intimacy is a human relation explored, not possessed. Ziyad Marrar claims that intimacy 'exists between rather than within people; you can experience unrequited love, but you cannot experience unrequited intimacy'.[14] Lynn Jamieson speaks for this reason of 'practices of intimacy', which she explains 'enable, generate and sustain a subjective sense of closeness and being attuned and special to each other'.[15] Lauren Berlant holds that intimate relationships involve shared narratives, the telling of stories such as 'love at first sight'.[16] Framing interpersonal relationships in a soulless social science bureaucratese, Valerian Derlega and John Berg tell us that intimacy is 'valuable information shared' between disclosed and recipient.[17] Similarly Charles Fried offers us the concept of intimacy as 'the sharing of information about one's actions, beliefs, or emotions which one does not share with all',[18] a viewpoint which perhaps casts intimacy more in the mould of filing a tax return than with lives touched by passion. These more cheerless definitions notwithstanding, it is Jamieson who insists that intimacy 'involves close association, privileged knowledge, deep knowing and understanding and some form of love'.[19]

If intimacy and love are near neighbours as well as avowed adversaries, this is partly because the modern age has unleashed many kinds of intimate bonds which do not involve emotional care, concern or commitment – such as venomous social media trolling or abusive sexual relationships. If intimacy lies at the edge of vulnerability and trust, it is perhaps not surprising that there are many ways in which interpersonal relationships can suffer an inward collapse. Circles of intimacy are created and sustained through trust, which underpins the implicit quality of all interpersonal relations. The establishment of trust provides the guiding thread here; trust has been widely viewed as one of the most important substantive components in all forms of intimacy. In everyday terms, for example, the personal information a person shares with friends means something like 'private' or 'confidential', whereas the personal information a person shares with their partner means instead 'intimate'. We speak of breaches of trust as solid ground for the ending of intimate relationships.

Even so, trust traditionally tied relationships to the ground, while social norms governing tact and other supportive mechanisms underpinning trust between individuals were institutionally ordered across time and space in the solid, hardware phase of modernity. Intimate relationships – 'marriages', 'partnerships', 'kinships' – were anchored in the techniques, strategies and modes of behaviour which social actors applied in face-to-face encounters, and thus it was always far from easy to exit, or to move on from, established commitments. Indeed – as Erving Goffman brilliantly demonstrated in his studies of face-to-face proximity – co-present individuals are inherently vulnerable (both socially and emotionally) to each other.[20] Such techniques, strategies and modes of behaviour governing intimacy all changed, however, with the advent of artificial intelligence in the algorithmic phase of modernity. The late French philosopher Bernard Stiegler captured this watershed-like global shift in speaking of the rise of 'computational capitalism', in which the very recasting of intimate relationships and personal life arose directly as an outcrop of social media, big data and pervasive tracking technologies.[21] Once social tasks could be automated with the algorithmic power of meta-data, there was an emergent shift away from face-to-face (and embodied) co-presence within specific places to mediated forms of connectivity within global networks, where references to time and space became less and less significant. Computational capitalism is described by Stiegler as involving a sequence of technological shocks with massive reverberations across social systems, economic markets, institutional organizations, intergenerational relationships, psycho-social structures and the politics of life itself.

Recasting intimacy in the era of computational capitalism means pursuing personal relationships through digitalized

processes of mediation, in which the 'networked self' is constituted and reproduced through online profiles, status updates,
uploads, downloads and instantaneous connections and discon-
nections. Intimacy comes to mean immediacy of communication,
not the bonds of relationship. The change in question centres
on the automation of social activity, masquerading as the
enhancement of personal agency. It is not simply that people
are reconstituted as 'data selves' in computational capitalism;
it is also that as people develop interactions through digitalized
processes of mediation, so information about themselves as 'data
subjects' is deposited in endless computational traces. Speed is
vital here from beginning to end, a point which Stiegler captures
forcefully. 'The network', says Stiegler,

> works at 200 million kilometers a second while your own body
> works at 50 metres a second. So the coefficient of difference is that
> the network is four million times faster than your own body. So
> you are taken by speed . . . I tell you this because in the case of
> the automatic society, based on these digital automatisms that are
> algorithms, there is a fact in which the speed of understanding,
> which is working at 200 millionths a second, is so much more
> important than the time of reason.[22]

In the algorithmic era of advanced automated societies,
intimacy is coming to mean smartphones, social media, softbots,
self-tracking technologies and the software-driven sharing of
information. The influence of Siri and Snapchat is spreading
throughout social life. The whole sensibility of intimate relations
has undergone a profound transformation, with people increasingly posting, sharing and automating the most personal and
intimate details about their private lives on digital platforms.
In all this, the intimacy of social life has shifted from face-to-
face interaction to digital connectivity. There are, to be sure,
anxieties about these new forms of intimate relations, especially
concerns that the digital revolution diminishes previously held
convictions about privacy, personal space and security. The
placeless, instantaneous time of AI-powered societies brings
an irreversible shifting of intimacy towards machine learning,
predictive algorithms and a wholesale datafication of life itself.
If all digital networks swirl around – the myriad intersections of
data selves, social circles and their social boundaries – there is
no reason to worry about the earnest, self-disciplined and tactful

work of relationship building. There is instead a general excited sense of an endless proliferation of intimate relationships. People can thus interact with as many others as they choose on a daily basis, even if only a very few of those others are part of their actual everyday lives.

Digital Technologies and Intimate Bonds

The foregoing sections have traced the transformation of togetherness stemming from the digital revolution. The discussion suggests that, increasingly insulated from traditional forms of face-to-face interaction, the key types of togetherness taking place today are digitally mediated. Interpretations of the quest for intimacy in the digital age tend to divide between those authors that emphasize psychological factors and those that stress sociological dimensions of change. Some see an immersion in digital life as spelling the demise of personal autonomy and intimate relationships, with lasting damage to the psychological make-up of the individual. Others reach much the same conclusion, but see this result as connected directly to the intrusion of new technologies into the fabric of self-identity and intimate relations. These viewpoints have significantly influenced how digital technologies are perceived to leave their mark on our lives and indeed our societies, and accordingly demand further consideration.

Baroness Susan Greenfield put in a nutshell what is rapidly emerging as the most worrying prognosis for women and men in our digitally automated world: 'The mid-twenty-first century mind might almost be infantilized, characterized by short attention spans, sensationalism, inability to empathize and a shaky sense of identity.'[23] This prognosis is Greenfield's answer to the question of what happens in a world of pervasive technological devices where people engage in less and less eye contact and become more and more digitally immersed in semi-automated actions. As the spheres of digital activity expand, so the psychological make-up of the individual might also be changing in an unprecedented way.

This is, as Greenfield points out in *Mind Change*, the complex result of shifts involving the human mind and modern technologies.[24] Greenfield, a controversial neuroscientist and

former director of the UK's Royal Institution, contends that 'the
human brain will adapt to whatever environment in which it is
placed; the cyberworld of the twenty-first century is offering a
new type of environment; the brain could therefore be changing
in parallel, in correspondingly new ways'. The most obvious
answer, according to Greenfield, is that brain adaptation is
occurring as a result of today's ever-increasing bombardment
of data and digital technologies, and the upshot is decidedly
corrosive for self and society.[25] The chapters in *Mind Change*
deal with rising rates of suicide in the digital age, the limited
attention spans of 'digital natives', decreased empathy stemming
from Internet usage, the deleterious health consequences of
screen-based lifestyles and the broader corrosive sweep of
social networking, video gaming and digital technologies in
general. This, on any estimate, is a remarkably broad agenda;
but, as many critics have noted, Greenfield's analysis does
not betray the slightest sense that there is anything distinctive
about specific technologies, or any awareness that she has
conflated vastly different technologies when considering both
the psychological impacts and social consequences of digitalization. 'Greenfield', writes Martin Robbins, 'insists that the
change we're seeing in the Internet era is unprecedented,
even compared to the emergence of electricity, telephone or,
television; but her case studies keep collapsing because they
fail to distinguish between the effects of "all of the above".'[26]
Which brings me back to the dangers of technological deter-
minism, specifically in this case the charge that technology in
general is generative of societal corrosion. We should see that
there is something askew in Greenfield's account of the digital
world's influence on society and personal relationships. The
conclusion that digital technologies are corrosive of human
bonds *in toto* would seem to bar an understanding of what
Greenfield has noted regarding the ever-changing adaptation of
mind and environment, let alone penetrating the consequences
of such massive changes.

Other critics have developed portraits of the digital revolution,
but seek to bring back in personality, emotional life, human
nature itself. It is to Sherry Turkle that we owe the analysis of
technology's new solitude – automation operating increasingly
through smart machines which promote the illusion of togetherness. For Turkle, the spread of various forms of digitalization

lies at the heart of automating cultural life, coming from a blend of developments in computer science, robotics and AI. These developments have, in turn, led to a society whose norms of authentic sociality, empathic communication and genuine intimacy are breaking down. Transformations in authenticity are at the centre of this automating, digital culture. As Turkle explains:

> Authenticity, for me, follows from the ability to put oneself in the place of another, to relate to the other because of a shared store of human experiences: we are born, have families, and know loss and the reality of death. A robot, however sophisticated, is patently out of this loop.[27]

The imposition of digital technologies affects individuals and intimacies as much as institutions and organizations. 'Does virtual intimacy', asks Turkle, 'degrade our experience of the other kind and, indeed, of all encounters, of any kind?' Her answer, without qualification, is that the advent of digital intimacies eats away at the nourishing base of actual intimacies. The rise of digital technologies, says Turkle, spells the decay of our intimate lives.

As an astute observer of the contemporary world, Turkle fears a twenty-first century dominated by automated smart machines. As a psychologist, Turkle highlights specifically that people increasingly respond 'as if' automations from the digital world were, in fact, human. At the beginning of her path-breaking book, *Alone Together: Why We Expect More from Technology and Less from Each Other*, Turkle characterizes today's all-encompassing digital attentional landscape thus: 'Now robots showed us "as if" empathy, and we were, you might say, cheap dates. We proved willing to talk to robots about personal matters.' Instead of seeking intimate connections with, or emotional solace from, other people, individuals have more and more learned to think about their emotional lives from interactions with chatbots, digital assistants and virtual reality. It is at this point, she argues, that there opens up a hiatus between digital and actual sociability. Or, as Turkle puts this, people become 'open to the idea of the biological as mechanical and the mechanical as biological'. Life lived on our smartphones and intelligent devices becomes more impactful than actual interactions.

Turkle for many years headed up MIT's Initiative on Technology and the Self, where she studied the impacts of artificial intelligence and social robots upon children's emerging sense of identity and intimate bonds. To do this, she gave children robot toys such as Tamagochis and Furbies, which were programmed to respond with humanlike emotions. Parents today, says Turkle, increasingly delegate their children's 'childhood' to the engineered relationality and pre-programmed responses of social robots and digital technologies. Prior to the advent of the digital revolution, children's play typically involved the young child animating her or his toy – investing a teddy bear or Barbie doll with imagination – in order to establish some kind of emotional bond. By contrast, robotic toys are today presented to children as already animated – 'as if' full of intentions of their own. 'The Furby tells you what it wants',[28] comments one of Turkle's interviewees. In this magical space of digitalization, social robots are considered relational and affective. Far from nourishing an emergent sense of identity, however, these early interactions between self and robot introduce a sense of isolation and estrangement into the fabric of social relationships.

Turkle's account of digital technologies and pathologies of the self has not gone unchallenged. There is a considerable critical literature addressing the various shortcomings of Turkle's conception of digital disruption in cultural relations today.[29] In a previous book, I cast doubt on the 'new psychology of engagement' – the 'as if' responses people develop in the face of smart machines – which Turkle theorizes as central in the digital age.[30] I argued that, whilst there is some plausibility to the view that people can become overly preoccupied with digital technologies and that addiction to 'life on the screen' is a disturbing social trend, it is misleading to view either processes of digitalization or automation as engulfing personal life and human bonds *in toto*. Access to digital technologies is far more diverse and divergent than this characterization suggests. My argument was that human togetherness today is not so much *captured* as *constructed* through smart devices and automated intelligent machines. This gives rise to a very different understanding of digital technologies and human bonds from that offered by Turkle. For one thing, it recognizes that individuals more or less continuously shift between actual, digital and automated forms of social engagement, and that consequently we need to be alert to both the new opportunities and the new burdens that arise from these blended forms of togetherness created through digital technologies and automated intelligent machines.

The trends towards digital immersion of the self which Turkle documents are significant but they do not go unresisted by individuals, which is one reason I have argued that one can discern an inadequate account of human bonds in this standpoint. We must treat with some scepticism Turkle's suggestion that the digital sphere reconstitutes human togetherness as a world in which we are increasingly 'alone together'. *Pace* Turkle, digital technologies do not necessarily lead to a reduction of complexity in our emotional life. We live in a world today in which the scale, intensity, speed and complexity of automated machine intelligence in many respects outstrip the capacity of individuals to react to, let alone cope with, the vast explosion in data through which the development of lives now takes place. But this remains a world in which new automated machines are linked fundamentally to the very conditions of interaction, communication and information diffusion in which people experience emotional life, experiment with sociability and reinvent forms of human togetherness.

Togetherness and Automated Technologies

The views of Turkle and Greenfield – applauded by many, sharply criticized by others – reflect the spread of an increasingly dominant outlook in current discussions of intimacy and the digital revolution.[31] These writers as well as a whole host of more empirical analysts view the impacts of technology largely in terms of an all-enveloping automation, offering a different way of thinking through the dynamics of social, cultural and intimate relationships. In many ways, this work reflects a full-blooded cultural pessimism on the question of digitalization and intimacy, a doctrine which casts sociability as increasingly brittle, corrosive, fragmented and impoverished. If it has been hard for some critics to square the circle of these cultural effects of digital technologies and the everyday lives of people who engage with them, however, it has fallen to other writers to question the place of digitalization in intimate life today. One common approach has been to simply counter the dominant outlook,

largely by suggesting that claims of moral impoverishment are
not supported by the lived realities of contemporary women and
men. Something of this orientation can be seen in the writings
of Cristen Dalessandro, who sketches a largely American-slanted
history of digital technology and intimate relationships, which
notes in typically ethnocentric fashion that 'the recent proliferation of the Internet and smart technologies has changed the
ways in which many people – both inside and outside of the
United States – form relationships'.[32] If her American-centrism is
all too obvious, her conceptual impulse remains to 'complicate'
existing conceptualizations of how young adults use digital
technologies to forge and sustain intimate relationships. To that
end, she directly takes aim at Turkle and associated authors
on negative cultural changes: 'current research underexplores
individuals' understandings of the significance of technological
influence in intimate relationships'.[33] Full of even-handedness,
the approach taken here is to stress the potentially positive
and negative outcomes of digital mediation in intimate life.
Contributions from media studies, feminist and gender studies,
politics, science studies, sociology and cultural studies abound
in this underscoring of automated digital technologies as at once
'positive' and 'negative' in their influence on social life.[34]

Even so, anxiety about rapid technological change and its
deleterious long-term impact on intimate relationships remains
acute. Positive and negative may come together with digital
technologies, but the ambient worry is that automated technology
doesn't grant much in the way of autonomy. Nevertheless,
the standard response to countering the ideas expressed by
Turkle, Greenfield and others remains unsatisfactory, largely
because such intellectual work has generally remained caught
within too many of the framing assumptions about digitalization which these critics set out to contest. In what follows,
I want to take a different tack. The sense of life becoming
overburdened by digital technologies, as well as of moral
impoverishment in cultural relations, results in large part from
people becoming entangled in automated processes conditioned
by machine-learning algorithms; these are processes we do not
fully understand and cannot control. To grasp how this situation
has come about, we need to look again at the dynamics of
interaction in relation to human–machine interfaces. I want to
suggest that, rather than entering a period of all-enveloping

machine programming of interactive processes, we are moving into a world in which experimental interaction with remote, semi-autonomous and autonomous smart machines is becoming both radicalized and generalized. This approach demands recognizing that our automated digital lives are not alternatives to, or refuges from, our actual lives; the digital is an essential part of the everyday. But, as a consequence, we may need to think of intimate life as doubled, caught between our existing social conditions and their potential pleasures and frustrations. What is required is a conceptual approach that can investigate the full gamut of technological intimacies, including especially various kinds of automations of initial and initiating relationships, ranging from technologies of e-introductions, networked connections and digital community platforms to those enhanced by algorithmic recommendation systems – of our personal preoccupations, developing friendships and 'regulation' of our largely unpredictable intimacies, as well as digitalization of what have been called 'chapters in our unlived lives'.[35] Algorithmic automation of intimate and cultural life is always 'in process' and always beckoning – embedded in the daily, weekly and monthly temporalities of women and men, as well as the imagined futures – envisioned in imagination, elaborated in practice – over people's lifetimes.

In this algorithmic framework of intimate relationships, there can be no sure distinction between agent and automation, actual and virtual, human and device, subjective intention and objective effect. The advent of digital intimacy involves examining how the automation of social interactions through the algorithmic framing of information, communications, messages and images may overlap, converge and enhance human powers, as well as generate new possibilities and new burdens for lives lived rich in intimacy. The dominant outlook, as we have seen, emphasizes the decline of human bonds and the impoverishment of personal life – expressed in the theorem that digital technologies are the keynote in the organized control (and, indeed, controlling organization) of social life. But do we, in fact, live lives that are automated in the manner suggested by these theorists as regards our contemporary cultures of intimacy? Are machine-learning algorithms the dominant force or only one among many contributing factors in the shaping of intimate relationships today? Should we rather look to the power of predictive algorithms as

the central underlying characteristic of modernity and its relation
to personal life? These issues are not necessarily mutually incom-
patible. As recent breakthroughs in science and technology
studies highlight, we need to see that automated machine
intelligence is multidimensional, impacting upon human bonds
and intimate relationships in complex and uneven ways. For
many women and men, stalked by an endless menu of choices
emanating from the digital revolution, the 'automated life' is
increasingly viewed as life lived to the full. People discover
potentialities in their lives most obviously in new technological
gadgetry (the newest smartphone, the latest update, the shiniest
devices), and in the automated digital processes which can add
something novel to existing social connections or something
altogether new in the experience of initial and intimate relationships (algorithmic dating apps, quantified sex lives and many
other software innovations). But people also become haunted by
the myth of automated lives, of what predictive algorithms can
offer to the lives we lead and the possibilities for intimate association. All too often, people's lives become a lament for artificial
bonds not realized and digital intimacies revoked.

Once again, the relevance of Simmel's understanding of the
exchange of social information to developments in automated
machine intelligence is important in this context. Impersonal
systems, Simmel says, make it easier for people to come to engage
with each other in daily life. 'What Simmel gave to us', writes
Richard Sennett, 'was a notion of impersonal life as being caught
between bodily experience which was unmanageable, and a kind
of self-repression through rationality which gradually constricted
the urban realm so that it was a realm of neutral information
rather than full self-exposure.'[36] In Simmel's time, the modern
city witnessed many developments associated with the systematization of impersonal social structures. In our own time, there
are many emergent examples of an accelerated systematization
of neutral information, most obviously in digital technologies
and in a wide array of automated transactions and algorithmic
processes. It is especially algorithmic power, I shall argue, which
functions as illusion for managing the intensity of intimacy. We
can further draw out the import of Simmel's sociology for the
automation of social processes by resituating intimate relationships in terms of algorithmic structures and digitized processes of
interaction. 'Automation' and 'algorithm' are related, first of all,

to changes in how we experience *belonging* in encounters – both with humans and with non-human actants. The establishment of a sense of intimacy, so important to Simmel's sociological studies of human interaction, is not sufficient to shield the individual self from otherness or the experience of strangeness. Intimacy and distance reside in the same neighbourhood and this, in Simmel's reckoning, means that belonging is only ever partial and provisional, always shot through with degrees of social exclusion. Such inbuilt failures of self-protection arguably ramify in conditions of algorithmic intimacy.

So, for Simmel, rationality is an essential construct, a 'mask' with which social actors hide their intimate selves behind systematized impersonal structures. These systemic processes set boundaries allowing for the exchange of sociability as 'neutral information', but also offer lures to break through such impersonal barriers with expressions of intense emotion and intimate relationships. Systematization of the public sphere as a realm of neutral information in Simmel's sense has been analysed by many writers in terms of digital platforms of interaction involving technology, space and social relations. Impersonal/intimate distinctions have been recently associated with the emergent sociability of digital technologies, in which 'the architecture of borders, walls, doors, and locks gives way to that of passwords, firewalls, public key encryption, and security certificates'.[37] Such notions can be applied across a whole range of digitalized formations. The sociological axes of impersonality and intimacy operate in a complicated nexus of conceivable associations between subjectivity, knowledge and belonging. In this view, social differences are bridged and social exchanges are enacted through digital technologies. These technologies coincide with emergent novel divisions between enclosure (self-repression, denial, disavowal) and disclosure (revelation, confession) of cultural identities which are increasingly automated, programmed and machine-mediated.

Using Simmel's account of sociability and strangeness to rethink how individuals – now cast adrift in a sea of new technologies – forge a sense of momentary, transient belonging, Zeena Feldman points to the importance of a conceptualization of space that 'discourages monolithic readings of social media platforms by shifting the analytical focus toward the myriad interactions by which a platform is performed . . . It is precisely through these interactions that we can begin to locate the various processes of inclusion, exclusion, border marking and border breaking that make online spaces meaningful sites of study.'[38] Feldman suggests that Simmel's reckoning that space is produced through social relations – as a performed, contingent and interactive practice – is of key significance for reconceptualizing conditions of interaction and modes of belonging in the digital age. One may say that to view space as something that is 'done' rather than something which simply 'is' opens a vital window on the multiplication of links, endlessly proliferating networked discourses and intersecting spheres of identities and interests in which social meanings continuously settle and shift in the digital age. 'By attending to the import of interaction, the specificity of context and the production of boundaries', writes Feldman, 'Simmel gives scholars a bevy of conceptual tools for locating ways in which social media platforms acquire and create modes of belonging, power and knowledge.'[39]

Feldman's purpose was to cast 'Simmel in Cyberspace'; her focus was principally social media. This book examines algorithmic intimacy, and my focus is automated intelligent machines and the wide array of algorithmic predictions and recommendation systems reshaping interpersonal transactions and private life today. Two important distinctions thus follow.

First, online subjectivity may well be fashioned through the ongoing negotiation between modes of inclusion and exclusion, but it is crucial to emphasize that the terms of belonging are today increasingly enacted through automated intelligent machines. Distant geographies are bridged and mediated interactions are framed through human–machine interfaces, with the rules of sociability structured in advance by machine-learning predictive algorithms, big data and neural networks.

Second, the velocity, variety, resolution and distribution of information and communication collected, reproduced and transformed by smart devices and automated intelligent machines are not only the space of big data, but also the space of newly invented identities and 'imagined communities'. The space in question is neither that of digital devices nor that of software packages. It is an *imaginary space* in which people encounter machine intelligence in multiple situations and complex emotional settings. As algorithms are programmed to disseminate more widely 'personal recommendations' generated by the clicking of smart devices, machine intelligence alters the very contours of imaginative life and social relationships, remaking contemporary society through automated forms of quasi-interaction and producing new ways of conceiving of selfhood, identity and intimacy. The imaginative experience of algorithmic life as a key component of intimacy and its metamorphoses involves the continual cross-referencing of automation and agency, online and offline activities, virtual communication and interpersonal dialogue. From this angle, machine intelligence is directly bound up with the metamorphoses of social life through the 'shrinkage' of the distances between our actual and ideal selves – the lives we live on the one hand, and the lives we wish to live on the other. Smart devices and automated intelligent machines provide an *exceptional array of 'imaginative containers'* – of many automated services, modes of remote or semi-autonomous control and sources of entertainment – for the dreaming anew of our lives and our lives in these times. This imaginative redrafting of the self increasingly enables individuals to be in two or more places simultaneously. People can, for example, imaginatively position themselves as actively pursuing dating options by using auto-responding text-messaging bots (such as Ghostbot) as they sit talking with colleagues in an office meeting.

But there are many other forms of imaginative digital intimacy too. People today increasingly imagine their lives and future life possibilities through uploading, downloading, generating, storing and processing data via smart devices; others use automated intelligent machines to create and circulate ideas, videos, texts, maps, podcasts and music; still many more share information and engage in intimate dialogue with other people as well as non-human actants such as bots and VPAs, such that their dependency on computational technologies sometimes substitutes for human interaction or face-to-face contact altogether. In all of this, there lies automated machine intelligence as transforming our lived spaces and sense of geographic spatiality. As more and more people adopt and embed networked smart machines into the fabric of their lives, so they come to both visualize and vitalize self-experience as occurring when inner life and the machine world resonate with each other. The more people come to enact remote, semi-autonomous and autonomous machine-routine orderings of their quotidian everyday rhythms and social interactions, the more the algorithmic fabrication, development and deepening of the self unfold. Such a line of thinking appears to lead well away from what is usually thought of as 'autonomous individualism'. Selfhood, it is often said, involves an isolated struggle towards identity formation and self-definition. This is bound up with internal strivings of the individual self and the search for personal autonomy. This kind of thinking has been historically hostile not just to outside forces, but to technology more generally. What we see occurring today, by contrast, is the advancement of discourses of digital technologies that actively promote, enable and secure the increasing reach of digital lives and the digitalization of intimacy. This is a discourse which underscores the mutuality of self and machine in social experience. The constitution of the self and of intimate relationships still depends to a large degree on the fostering of illusions of individual control, separateness and autonomy; but these illusions are, crucially, shot through with the impacts of non-human others. That is to say, identity now reflects strongly the imprint of various processes of automation and algorithmic calculation, all of which enable selfhood and intimacy to flourish or falter.

How, then, is the problem of strangeness, reinscribed in the numerously proliferating digital circuits of self and Other, to be addressed? If strangeness is a vital issue, as it is for Simmel, it is because it raises nothing less than the question of exclusion – and therefore of political society. Simmel, as we have seen, framed the stranger as a relational figure in full-blooded spatial terms, as someone whose presence may be welcome or contested by others. By and large, stranger encounters were cast by Simmel as an ordinary, routine feature of metropolitan life – as something that needed to be negotiated and managed against the intense bombardment of stimuli generated in day-to-day urban living. But it is fair to say that Simmel had trouble with strangers, partly because he so powerfully underscored that strangers are troubling. If the routines of everyday social life render stranger relations relatively manageable and momentarily ambivalent, so in a different way the strangeness of others intensifies dramatically when threats, risks and unrecognized desires take hold. Strangeness for Simmel thus always courts the risk of exclusion. In this sense, the passage from the interpersonal to politics is immanent in what Sarah Ahmed has called 'stranger danger', the threat posed to the public sphere and national borders by the very presence of toxic strangers.[40] When this is the case, as Bauman has brilliantly shown in a radical addendum to Simmel's account of the stranger, such threatening Others are nullified or excluded through modernity's specific injunctions of order building, sameness, control and mastery.[41]

Yet it is not as though strangeness and exclusion intersect in uniform ways, or are isolated from the spatial and temporal shifts inaugurated by modern societies. There are multiple histories and multiple technologies which must be clipped together in the analysis and critique of stranger encounters. And it is surely undeniable that, against the technological backdrop of advances in machine-learning algorithms, we are now confronted with new possibilities and challenges in digitally mediated stranger encounters. Strangers as socially constructed figures of exclusion, the rise of xenophobic sentiments, the denunciation of inter-culturalism: these and other defensive encounters with social differences remain key to what we generally know as politics. But the digital revolution transforms both social connections and social differences. The current preoccupation with 'digital others' in media studies, cultural studies and the wider humanities has emerged in part as a reaction to a world where strangers have been redefined as 'unknown others' or 'unmet friends'. 'Strangers' now become 'friends' on the basis of algorithmic recommendations, and friends can be unfriended at the click of a device.

Everyone, in a sense, has now been thrown into strange encounters – and encounters with strangers – as a consequence of the rise of automated machine intelligence. In this socio-technical shift, everyday life is increasingly characterized in quasi-digital terms as the province of predictive algorithms, neural nets, smart devices and big data. As a consequence, stranger encounters become more and more a selective version of the subjective sphere. In our age of advanced AI, spaces of encounter and times of engagement are increasingly automated and multiplied, navigated through apps, smartphones, digital platforms and virtual reality. Digital technologies, in other words, are increasingly built into our existence, and significantly built into our relations with both stranger encounters and our own sense of internal strangeness. But it may also be questionable whether digitalization goes all the way down fully into the very fabric of personal life and intimate relations. If it is true that digital technologies reshape sociability and intimate relationships, it is also the case that a certain intractability to digitalization lies at the core of pre-reflective intimacy and affective bonds between people. Since there is always, somewhere in ourselves, a predigital subjectivity, we remain individuals who don't fully fit with the perfectly ordered equations of machine intelligence. In this view, strangeness always precedes familiarity, and we are always at odds with the predictive algorithms and bots which seek to determine our likes and dislikes. Whilst undoubtedly a blow to the devotees of AI, this perspective emphasizes that we are always in a sense left out of the computational world view (social media, search entities, GPS, 5G, apps), even when we seem to be included or positioned as central.[42]

Another way putting this is to say that digital technologies include and exclude us at the same time. The predictive power of algorithms, generated by vast computational power and trained on big data, repositions 'the future' and enables us to think differently about our choices, decisions, options. 'Predictions', writes Helga Nowotny, 'have become ubiquitous in our daily lives.'[43] We trade our personal data in order to quench our insatiable thirst for more predictive information about our private behaviours, innermost feelings and intimate bonds. From this angle, predictive algorithms – with their promise to extend the range of life's options – might appear to be grounded in nothing but ourselves and our personal data. But from another angle, things can only appear this way because an imaginary misrecognition has taken place, through which a certain reversal of subject and object, or human and machine, occurs. Predictive algorithms and analytics might appear hospitable to us in rendering the unpredictable or chaotic as smoothly ordered and digitally packaged, yet they substantially occlude our own subjective powers in how we conceive of the future in the present.[44] There is, as it were, a radical split between the personal and impersonal impacts of predictive algorithms. The paradox stems from the incompatibility between the living of predictive life with 'recommendations for you' on the one hand, and the abstract mathematical equations and data trails of algorithmic applications on the other. In this sense, not all predictions stemming from algorithmic recommendation systems signify that kind of 'personalized living' or 'individualized lifestyle' to which some Silicon Valley tech companies seem eager to reduce them.

This tension between the personal and impersonal, self and machine, as well as inclusion and exclusion crops up time and again in how people incorporate predictive algorithms in extending the range of life's possibilities – whether in relationship tech, therapy tech or friendship tech. The world of predictive algorithms is about a better future, so we are told, but it is also highly consequential for what we do in the present and how we conceive of our everyday lives. From this standpoint, the predictive power of algorithms can indeed be cast as an other-worldly creed, in which women and men are thrown into the *lifelong project of automating themselves out of their own lives*, as if it is now only possible to survive life's thrills and spills by data programming and predictive equations. A key part of my argument, then, is that people in the age of predictive algorithms make their lives up partly through excluding themselves from their innermost emotions and personal lives. In conditions of advanced algorithmic technologies, women and men can become excluded from the very thing they have most sought to protect and promote – namely, themselves.

With the digitalization of intimacy, then, there emerges a new esteem for predictive control of human togetherness. Predictive analytics reign supreme in algorithmic intimacy, where automated personal connections and relationship risk assessments are promoted as inviting and even beneficial. Yet it is harder and harder to find a path from mathematical equations to personal agency, as predictive algorithms lure us into sullen unsociability and blind submission. Part of my concern in the remainder of this book is to elaborate an alternative pathway to the issues which we have examined in this chapter, but which have not been sufficiently elucidated by existing social science approaches to the topic. The development and deepening of predictive algorithms and analytics in contemporary culture undoubtedly establishes a different relationship to the future; but recognition that predictive algorithms also powerfully reshape what we do in the present allows us to raise the question of what people leave unattended or unexamined in their own lives and the lives of others as a consequence of the rise of algorithmic intimacy. The soul of being human, let us remember, is the spirit of creative complexity.[45] By contrast, the design of predictive algorithms is largely in the service of simplification. The power of predictive algorithms is a power held in thrall to calculated predictability, smooth order, clarity of options, the singularity of decisions. Human togetherness and algorithmic prediction are thus positioned to coexist awkwardly. It is surely self-evident that we could no more reduce the creative complexity of being human to a set of algorithmic calculations than we could exhaustively codify the multiplicity of intimate bonds or the chaotic shapes of love. But in our advanced era of algorithmic prediction, digitalization powerfully recasts intimate bonds under the sign of just such a potent fantasy. The remainder of this book seeks to explore some of the implications of these watershed sociotechnical shifts.

3

Relationship Tech

AI-driven dating, explains Adryenn Ashley, founder and CEO of the Loly dating app, is magical because algorithms can 'find the perfect match without the user feeling like they've disclosed something private to another person'.[1] A successful algorithmic dating match is convenient and easily programmed, says Ashley. We may suppose that it is convenient *because* it is mechanically calculated, and that it's convenience stems from an awareness that you do not have to go out of your way, or comfort zone, to establish a connection with a prospective dating partner. This seems to suggest an intentionality with no identifiable human agent: the magic, Ashley underscores, is that nothing private needs be disclosed to another person. No risk of embarrassment. No risk to self-esteem. But AI-driven dating entails a sacrifice of sorts: it sacrifices the human element, it sacrifices mutuality, it sacrifices the receptivity of the other person and of being ourselves with others. But the gains of algorithmic matchmaking are self-protection and convenient access to others. This is a process which automates matchmaking, rendering the interconnections between human desire, sexuality, bodies and selves programmable, or even robotic.

It appears that the most seminal accomplishment of programmed, automated matchmaking is the separation between communication and intimacy.[2] Unlike face-to-face proximity, which requires both time and effort, algorithmic dating renders sexual connections simultaneously more numerous and more facile, more frequent and more episodic. But even if the making of sexual contacts requires less effort and less time thanks to the power of algorithmic prediction, the desire for a 'perfect match' remains intensely urgent. The lures of algorithmic proximity, delivered with nothing more than a swiping to the right on a mobile device, are intimately interwoven with promises of happiness. Ashley, in fact, conceived of the project of Loly dating when her close friend and room-mate was out on a Tinder date; she had been calculating how the all-ordering, all-classifying algorithmic states of proximity could best advance 'quality hook-ups'. Bringing together an AI-powered dating platform with blockchain technology, Ashley's dream of programmed 'quality hook-ups' encompassed a focus on convenience, speed, accuracy and safety.[3] Her dream of the 'quality hook-up', it appears, was about wanting something that is unbearable (the delay involved in waiting) transformed into something instantly programmable (sexual intimacy without delay). In Ashley's rendering, it is as if we need the guarantees of algorithmic prediction to make plausible, to make bearable, our sexual longing, our wants, and our needs for intimate connection.

'AI enables matching', comments Ashley, 'without human intervention.' At one level, she is evidently talking about the *programmability of sexual relationships*. This, in itself, is not news. The world's most popular dating app, Tinder, has matched over 43 billion connections. Search matches are made through algorithmic calculations based on factors such as the user's geolocation, personal interests, uploaded photos and the like. But Ashley's Loly promises more, much more: 'a blockchain and AI dating app that matches people by orgasmic compatibility'. This is, in short, dating as *erotic engineering*. Ashley and her team asked the question 'What kind of sex do you want in a typical month?' As she explains: sometimes a woman wants Tarzan; sometimes she wants a poet.[4] The first condition of this brand of AI-powered dating, then, is that relationships all seem to be in the direction of algorithmic prediction and impersonal determination as mediated by automated intelligent apps. What is being outlined here is whether one can practise some form of eroticism and sexuality in the presence of another person selected algorithmically based on formulaic versions of the human – in this instance, Tarzan or a poet. Programmability is the sole thing that counts, and programmability involves a kind of dehumanization that demands other people to perform their versions of algorithmically determined sexual gratification.

There is a second condition of AI-powered dating, however, that shapes algorithmic sexual relations without intent. Sexual connections, in the algorithmic phase of the modern era, appear in the rift which separates *quantification* and *disposability*. Quantification seems to be the answer to a question about giving certainty to sexual purpose. In a world where what matters is increasingly represented only in numbers, personal informatics and sexual analytics rule. Ashley highlights that using numbers as a means of monitoring and measuring elements of sexual life and eroticism is at the core of Loly dating. Loly promises an AI 'Heat Index' that matches users based on sexual compatibility, with a temperature gauge capturing the 'hotness' of perspective sexual partners. As Ashleigh explains, an 8 on the scale indicates strong sexual compatibility, with possibilities for an ongoing relationship, whereas 5 is best read as simply convenient or short-term; or as she puts it – 'a straight orgasm'. But the point is this: don't let the relationship stray from the numbers. Not only are the numbers continually generated (and, thus, requiring continuous monitoring), but they are fundamentally about sexual lives: about bodies, behaviours, moods and emotions, sexual relationships. It is this traffic in numbers that intersects with disposability. 'Quality hook-ups' might be the marketing spin for this kind of sexual dating; but a hook-up is, by definition, fleeting. By taking the human element out of dating, by programming an anti-romance of formulaic sexual excitement, algorithmic dating is characterized by instant gratification, lightness, flexibility. We may suppose the name Loly (at least, by association) says it all: sugary, sweet, fast consumed and fast forgotten.

I shall take these foregoing reflections as a starting point for outlining an analysis of relationship tech, or what might be termed *sexual algorithmic intimacy*. In this chapter I shall focus on quantified sex lives and algorithmic dating apps.[5] I shall begin by providing a catalogue of contemporary quantified sex apps along with associated technologies which recast sex in terms of erotic engineering.[6] I shall then examine the implicit concepts of selfhood, human agency and the value of prediction of future behaviour that underpin these socio-technical practices. I want to suggest that what is new – what is at stake here – is something about the calculability of passion itself; and something about that form of calculability (or programming) called prediction. The chapter subsequently looks more carefully at the quantified sex life in terms of consumer society and the logics of consumerism. Finally, I shall consider the ways in which objective forms of data are experienced by individuals. The quantified sex life is in part a response, I think, to the rise of algorithmic objectivity in the domains of sexuality, eroticism and love in modern societies; it seems to be partly a response to some kind of emergency about sexual intention and the expression of human desire itself. My contention is that algorithmic sexual intimacy in general, and the quantified sex life in particular, hold up a mirror not only to practices and norms of society, which they both reflect and reshape, but to our attitudes towards technology itself.

#Swipelife: A Catalogue of Quantified Sex and Algorithmic Dating Apps

According to Moira Weigel, author of *Labor of Love: The Invention of Dating*, the principal factor in the emergence of dating and the search for a romantic partner consisted above all within the realm of commerce. From the early 1900s on, Western societies were the scene of women and men entering public spaces – restaurants, bars, cinemas and other commercial entities – and becoming caught up in the grip of passions pertaining to wider social and sexual relationships. Though courtship has always existed, the rise of dating occurred in a social and historical context where an increasing number of women were working outside of their homes, where chance encounters and arranged meetings with men could occur in various commercial and semi-commercial spaces. Weigel's account underscores that courtship rituals were transformed away from the private sphere of family oversight to the commercial sphere of the marketplace. From the moral profligacy of the roaring 1920s to the sexual revolution of the 1960s, there was an ongoing 'deregulation of the dating market' in which the application of economic principles to romance became increasingly central.[7] By becoming the foremost practitioners of their own erotic lives, women and men began experimenting for themselves with what the gains and losses of certain sexual relationships might be – experimentations anchored firmly within the marketplace and within commerce. Modern dating, Weigel notes, could be by turns exhilarating, joyful, stressful, emotionally taxing, endlessly time-consuming and often disappointing. Somewhat akin to work and employment, the thrills and spills of dating became increasingly interwoven with wider market forces.

'The ways people date', writes Weigel, 'change with the economy.'[8] Her historical study traces the long passage of erotic entanglements of women and men from traditional culture practices to the hook-up culture of Tinder. In today's world, dating or hook-ups can be arranged or cancelled at a moment's notice, and some critics of increased promiscuity argue that women and men now shop for partners the way they shop online for consumer goods. Swiping right on one's smartphone is increasingly the only diligent work of construction that seems required to negotiate the world of relationship shopping. Certainly, many contemporary women and men might bemoan that man-to-woman, woman-to-man, woman-to-woman and man-to-man dating matches are less predictable than consumer-to-goods and consumer-to-services matches. But markets are volatile places.

Against the backdrop of the rise of sexual hook-up culture, or non-relationship sex, or sex without dating, it is perhaps hardly surprising that more and more enterprising entrepreneurs have identified commercial opportunities to extend quantified life practices into the terrain of sexuality itself. Recently, there has been an explosion in the number of quantified sex apps for mobile devices on the market.[9] These apps can be downloaded to provide a range of sexual and health information, from assisting users in improving intimate relationships through sophisticated data analysis allowing users to monitor, graph and log numerous metrics, including frequency of sexual encounters and the duration of erotic activity. Some apps connect wirelessly to motion-based technologies, such as Bluetooth sex toys. The world of relationships construed as quantified sex apps is one also heavily designed for gaming. The allurement for many users of sexual and hook-up apps lies in the fact that built-in rewards (or symbolic tokens including points or badges) are distributed if various commitments (to increase, for example, the number of sexual partners in a given month) are realized or achieved. In the gaming of contemporary sexual relationships, data generated for many of these apps can also be uploaded to websites, or shared on social media platforms with others.

Nigel Thrift, in a remarkable analysis of the shift in cognitive frames and business vocabularies that marks the arrival of 'soft capitalism', has spoken of an ever-increasing 'informational overlay' which shapes and reshapes contemporary social practices.[10] According to Thrift, the software stage of capitalism develops knowledge in the form of computational data about itself. This kind of fluid, fuzzy and fast-moving setting of action has become increasingly central to the production and performance of quantified sex apps, especially when configured via other technologies. Current digital technologies – including online websites, social media platforms, mobile and wearable devices – and contemporary digital media fields – touchscreens, augmented reality, location tagging and virtuality – provide myriad opportunities and risks for users to log, record, monitor, measure and share with others information pertaining to their own sexual activities, erotic pursuits and love interests. This multiple, complex and therefore ambiguous world derives in no small measure from the 'informational overlay' of which Thrift speaks; the loosely patched together 'hook-ups' (sexual encounters, one-night stands, erotic cohabitations) are fast assembled, dismantled and reassembled as shifting erotic interests are registered in the back-and-forth of data upload and download on apps such as Tinder, Grindr, RedHotPie and Blendr.

It has been estimated that there are over 5 billion mobile users worldwide, who for example have relatively easy access to downloading over 4.4 million apps from the Apple App Store. Figures are understandably somewhat elastic, yet one noteworthy assessment calculates that over 209 billion apps were downloaded in 2019.[11] In a sociological study of the quantified sex life, Deborah Lupton notes that the most popular apps focus on sexual and relationship behaviours.[12] Lupton conducted a review of apps related to the fields of both sex and health by using search terms in Google Play and the Apple App Store including 'sex', 'sex education', 'conception', 'reproduction' and 'fertility'. Like much else in the commodified world of sex entertainment, many of the apps Lupton encountered were pornographic. There were, however, equally many apps designed for advancing sexual self-exploration and dating purposes. Some of these apps offered users information on human sexuality including health education, such as about sexually transmissible diseases, premature ejaculation and other sexual dysfunctions, contraception planning or the risks of contracting HIV. But the large bulk of these apps traded directly with the messiness, contingency and flux of human sexual relationships, all the while seeking to manufacture commercial solutions for sexual conquests, heightened sexual performance, easy hook-ups and the guarantee of better sex.

The direction in which the train of the quantified sex life seems to be going can be gleaned from the following brief catalogue (far from definitive or exhaustive) of current and recent sex and dating apps available for download.

- Spreadsheets generates data during sexual encounters collected through mobile devices and motion sensors. Sexual relations are recast as a leisure game where the rules allow users to accumulate achievements, such as having sex which lasts more than 40 minutes, or notching up a 'Lazy Sunday', which demands the diligent work of deploying the app five times on the holy day of rest. As enticement to bring technology into the bedroom, Spreadsheets promises to measure your performance in bed to provide statistical and historical feedback, with a visual display which tracks noise level of sex, duration of intercourse and the number of average thrusts per minute.
- Sex Keeper and Sex Counter Tease are apps which tie sexual activity to fitness, tracking calories burned in erotic hook-ups and logging locations where hook-ups occur. The nub of such quantified life-strategies: 'The more you do it, the more you burn.'
- Nice is an iOS tracker for different sexual activities, with the central focus on the metrics of sex, orgasms and masturbation. Users can track the different locations where they have engaged in sex and monitor sexual activities with different partners. The app is free, but an upgrade to the premium version is sold with customization features and additional tracking options. Sex Partner Tracker is similar, but to sharpen the consumption of 'sexed bodies' a bit further this app also tracks users who have had sex with each other, moving the focus to sexual networks as its ultimate purpose. It helps in thinking of consumer-centred and sex-fascinated intimacy if

you keep numbers at the top of your mind, and Sex Partner
Tracker aims to make this easy. Quantification reveals how
promiscuous users are within regions; the app also keeps tabs
on 'the lover with the highest score within your region/world'.
• In 2019, a study from Stanford University found that online
dating is now the most common way for couples to meet,
with over 40 per cent of couples having first met online.[13]
This largely mirrors the 2013 American National Academy
of Sciences report that a third of people who married in the
US between 2005 and 2012 met their partners online; half of
these met on dating sites, and the others through chat rooms,
online games and so on.[14] Dating apps most often used,
whether looking for true love or a casual hook-up following a
break-up, included Match, OKCupid, Hinge, eHarmony, Elite
Singles, BE2, CDATE, Bumble and Zoosk.

Selfhood and the Reflexivity of Quantified Sex Life

Quantified sex apps powered by AI offer new ways to understand discourses about self-knowledge, self-awareness and
self-improvement that have significant implications for notions
of selfhood, sexuality and eroticism. In a remarkably short
span of time, the digital revolution has powerfully impacted
social relationships, a phenomenon that has transformed
everyday social interaction and altered in certain respects the
dynamics of sexuality, eroticism and love throughout the world.
Anthropologist Daniel Miller writes that, prior to the arrival of
social media, 'the Internet had already developed as a vast dating
agency'.[15] Miller reflects, with great care, on the considerable
ethnographic fieldwork which provides evidence that digital
technologies are having a deep and lasting impact on sexual
relationships. Now that AI in the form of machine learning
and algorithmic recommendations is routinely used in online
dating and quantified sex apps, this impact arguably redoubles.
In the age of intensive AI, #swipelife has become a vehicle for
intimacy, hook-ups, sex and the self. Digital technologies can
be used for finding and cultivating sexual relationships, but are
also instrumental in constraining or damaging other existing
relationships in everyday social life. It is possible to argue as well

that mobile digital technologies and the advent of the quantified sex life have fuelled the rise of multiple sexual relations or illicit erotic encounters on the part of individuals throughout modern societies. In the traditionalist rendition, sexual relationships needed time and tending to flourish, involving face-to-face communication, ongoing displays of careful attention and solid commitments. In the algorithmic version of the modern era, sexual relationships are recast in terms of speed and social acceleration. Users of digital technologies enjoy a dramatic increase in the ease with which private sexual conversations and interactions are undertaken, where AI becomes directly bound up with the proliferation and spread of hook-up sex culture along with many other forms of digitally mediated sexual relationships.

In all this, the self looms large. Portrayals of the quantified sex life in the popular media have often underscored the individualistic and rather self-obsessed nature of such changes in sexual relationships today. So the self figures prominently here because, from one angle, digital quantification of sex is narcissistic through and through: it is all about 'me, me and me'. From another angle, however, something more complicated is arguably at work. Selfhood becomes increasingly inscribed in new algorithmic forms of digital data; this digitalization of sexuality and the self is, in turn, endowed with a new focus. The novel digital affordances offered by online dating and quantified sex apps allow for much more detailed and specific forms of knowledge about the self and associated sexual practices than in previous eras. As women and men become increasingly exposed to these digitized tools, this information can subsequently be transformed into a kind of DIY self-improvement strategy, usually involving the ongoing collection, recording, interpretation and reflection upon self-tracked digital data as part of the 'work on the self' which is more and more central to contemporary ideas about sexuality and intimacy.

All of this chimes well with what the British sociologist Anthony Giddens has called 'the reflexive project of the self'.[16] This way of thinking about transformations of the self emphasizes that – in a world of thoroughgoing globalization and digitalization – pre-established ways of doing things become increasingly undermined as a basis for making choices about one's life. Traditional social practices, patterns and frameworks that once guided the life course have substantially dissolved. Instead, people find today that renewed efforts are required to adequately engage with their lives, relationships and commitments. This, in effect, compels people to take the 'driver's seat' in their own lives; the self becomes increasingly central in negotiating both private and public life. 'The reflexivity of modern social life', as Giddens writes, 'consists in the fact that social practices are constantly examined and reformed in the light of incoming information about those very practices, thus constitutively altering their character.'[17] Of key importance here is self-knowledge: acts of self-reflection become a central structuring element of social activity in the contemporary era. Moreover, it is important to grasp that reflexivity is not an external phenomenon, but seeps into the production and performance of the self, thereby helping to reorder identity itself.

Reflexivity permeates not only institutional life but also the deepest recesses of individual subjectivity. For Giddens, reflexivity goes all the way down into the very texture of self-identity, affecting personal life and intimate social bonds. The reflexive project of the self, points out Giddens, connects in a profound way to the transformation of intimacy in our late modern world. Changes now impacting sexuality are arguably revolutionary, and to illustrate this Giddens develops novel conceptual language to grasp the emergence of the 'pure relationship'. which is 'entered into for its own sake, for what can be derived by each person from a sustained association with another' and, crucially, 'which is continued only in so far as it is thought by both parties to deliver enough satisfactions for each individual to stay within it'; the rise of 'confluent love'. which involves 'opening oneself out to the other' and therefore 'jars with the "for-ever", "one-and-only" qualities of the romantic love complex'; and the advent of 'plastic sexuality', that is, sexual pleasure which has been decentred, 'freed from the needs of reproduction'.[18] In elaborating these concepts, Giddens seeks to capture sexuality in the sense of immediacy, impact, invention, identity and the transactional negotiation of interpersonal ties. In historical terms, this is a shift from romantic love to confluent love which appears to have resulted in intimacy without deep attachments and sexual relations without strong commitments – or so argue some critics.[19]

It is perhaps not difficult to see how Giddens's portrait of the transformation of intimacy intersects directly with a world where sexuality has increasingly come to be equated with marketing, advertising, image, fashion, lifestyle, social media and digital technologies. Digitalization and decentred sexuality have spread throughout social life in tandem. Such widespread intersections between plastic sexuality and digital technologies, or between the personal and the public, are also the very air which new algorithmic dating apps and the quantified sex life breathe. The world of sexual and dating self-tracking apps is all-engrossing and attention-consuming, opening up possibilities involving reflexivity – of self-knowledge, others, experiences, technologies – for regulating or managing oneself and extending one's life chances. Arguably there are various ways in which quantified dating and sex apps contribute to the reflexive efforts of many people. Much of the literature in this area highlights, somewhat tediously, that users of such software and apps recognize the novelty of Tinder, Hinge or Bumble dating, hook-ups that people undertake for calculated purposes whilst knowing that they are unlikely to come across such matched company in any capacity other than through the game of online dating apps. Reflexivity here consists of self-awareness, monitoring and taking responsibility for managing these divided worlds – both online and offline.[20] Another reflexive dimension is the role of quantified sex lives and algorithmic dating apps in the derailment, breakdown or even break-up of established relationships, both intimate and familial. There are various possible trajectories here. A person might, for example, reflexively react, and hence modify their behaviour, to fears and forebodings of devastating emotional consequences upon an existing relationship; he or she might worry, for example, about their multiple sexual liaisons through the use of new technologies becoming known to a loved other. Or a person might reflexively monitor their activities in an attempt to find new ways of actually breaking up an existing relationship, through experimenting with quantified sex and dating apps.[21] Alternatively, reflexivity arguably looms large in the case of people who turn to new productivity software and apps because of difficulties in forging relationships. Some studies highlight that, in the case of individuals whose social life is restricted, quantified sex practices and dating apps can enable people to forge online connections with others, which in turn can be reflexively elaborated in the facilitation of other, offline relationships.[22] In all of these instances, novel algorithmic software and quantified self-tracking apps afford opportunities in which reflexive self-monitoring, self-governance and self-improvement strategies can be exercised and incorporated into the activities of daily life.

In outlining the interconnections between processes of reflexivity (both personal and institutional) and the reproduction and transformation of society, Giddens underscores an important set of issues which bear directly on the digital organization of sexual relationships. The thesis of social reflexivity is important and insightful for observing, understanding and critically assessing the role digital technologies can have in transforming intimacy and sexual relationships today. But the idea that reflexivity provides comprehensive insight into the impact of automated intelligent machines on personal relationships and forms of intimacy is much less persuasive. It is clear, for example, that machine-learning algorithms play a central role in the way people come to meet each other via social networking apps. Moreover, it is evident that some personal information processed by smart algorithms might be prioritized or highlighted to other users, whilst other personal information is rendered inaccessible or invisible.[23] Algorithms play a wondrous role in the overall shaping, kneading and moulding of other people's profiles, personal data and opportunities for developing self-knowledge or experimenting with digital technologies. Yet the significance of reflexivity can be exaggerated; this is not to say that reflexive self-tracking and self-monitoring fail to bear directly on users' online activity – as people surely do learn, adapt and act accordingly in relation to AI – but it is to make the point that new forms of automated action created by machine-learning algorithms may not as easily fall within the compass of reflexivity.

The late German sociologist Ulrich Beck also (like Giddens) spoke of reflexivity; but (unlike Giddens) emphasized the reflection-free impacts of certain forms of information and knowledge. Reflexivity, wrote Beck, 'does not mean reflection on modernity, self-relatedness' but rather the 'unintended and unseen, and therefore also reflection-free', all of which unfolds 'with the force of autonomized modernization'.[24] Reflexivity, according to Beck, is as much about 'social reflexes' as about 'self-reflection'. I shall not examine further the approach that Beck develops here, or consider differences between Beck and Giddens on the dynamics of reflexivity.[25] I want instead to stay with Beck's focus on 'the unintended and unseen'. In particular, I want to raise the question of what social reflexes might look like in relation to algorithmic dating apps and the quantified sex life. I also want to raise for consideration how contemporary forms of sexual relations are shaped and transformed 'with the force of autonomized modernization'. This leads us to examine further the notion of automation in relation to intimacy, sexuality and eroticism.

'Online dating is tricky, not because of people', writes Magdalena Rolle, 'but because of the algorithms involved.'[26] Most social networking sites and dating apps are programmed to collate sets of data which are tabulated according to certain rules of output. What I mean by this is that the collection (read: programming) of data is designed to shape and mould the overall use experience, with a central focus on 'messages' and 'matches' between users. Along with data programming, these online sites and productivity apps focus on individual user preferences, with automated recommendation systems deployed to support the user's experience and, crucially, to better connect or match users. Whilst there has understandably been a great deal of attention focused on the computer coding underlying these software programs and productivity apps, as well as many claims and counterclaims regarding algorithmic bias, the point I wish to highlight is that many users engage with such technologies as a matter of routine – with relatively little reflection on how algorithms shape individual preferences, or how AI-powered dating apps influence personal decisions. Broad swathes of public engagement with such novel digital technologies are reflection-free in this sense. These represent, in Beck's terms, 'social reflexes'.

In the data game of quantified sex players, the endless stream of information keeps changing in the course of the online dating space. Glued to their devices, individuals enter personal information to create their profiles – so that smart algorithms can 'perform magic' and determine successful matches. To keep the game competitive, the major companies all boast super-efficient algorithms, promising to match those in search of love with a soulmate, or at least a 'fixed hook-up'. Some hook-up sites program algorithms to match users with one another using match percentages, involving quantified assessments of the common interests of users along with connections based on 'popularity metrics'. Other sites promise tailored matches based on users' education history, job or professional standing and personal interests. Significantly, there is a hidden or concealed side to these promises of true love or perfect matches via algorithm. In the same way that large-scale systems of production, manufacturing and consumption came to be offshored throughout the world over recent decades, so too we witness an outsourcing of sexual relationships, new intimate experiences and other pleasurable services. Indeed, outsourcing practices are central to the world of quantified sex lives and algorithmic dating apps. Outsourced, out of sight, beyond the horizon of human decision-making and personal choices are some of the most opaque processes by which much of our intimate lives has been rendered 'elsewhere' and dependent upon automated intelligent machines.

If much of importance in personal, intimate and sexual life today involves automated intelligent machines, algorithms and technological concealment, so too a new world of relationships moves centre stage in which the tyranny of choice – of choosing intimate partners – is either displaced or eradicated. Exposing the expanding economy of outsourcing generated by algorithmic dating, Amy Webb comments:

> Dating sites and the algorithms they advertise purport to sort through our personalities, wants and desires in order to connect us with the best possible matches. Which means that we've outsourced not just an introduction, but the consideration of whether or not that man or woman is really our ideal. We are putting our blind trust in a system that's meant to do the heavy lifting of figuring out what it is that we really want out of a mate, and what will make us truly happy.[27]

Webb's reference to 'blind trust' seems to describe some kind of mockery of human decision-making; this is a world not hospitable to choosing (even the involuntary form of choosing – for example, 'falling in love') any more. The world remade according to algorithmic design is that of intentionality stripped of identifiable agents.

What is at stake here, I think, is something about intentionality and its failures; and something about that form of intentionality called prediction. In conditions of advanced AI, prediction encompasses data mining, machine learning and predictive modelling; all of which, as regards application to our personal and intimate lives, are designed to classify past historical details and personal information to render predictions about future life occurrences. A key characteristic of this kind of computational analytics in the algorithmic phase of the modern era is the generative effects of what I call *spirals of expectancy*. The presumptions underpinning expectation are always to a large extent based on hope, in the sense that human wants and unconscious desires are carried in our expectations; and what keeps desire alive, as Adam Phillips perceptively notes, 'is the hope involved in not knowing what we want'.[28] I want to suggest that the predictive analytics of the quantified sex life and algorithmic dating apps represent a derailment of the unpredictability of hope in the human subject. In the technological field, algorithms are positioned as eclipsing the unpredictability of hope itself. Instead, we are talking about a misleading straightforwardness, a bewitching technologism, where algorithms denote a predictive certitude regarding a user's future practices.

To speak of an algorithm as providing internally referential certitude is, of course, a mistake. Prediction is generated not on the basis of repositories of independent data, but rather through calculations based on information which is provided by users. The impetus towards predicted control in finding a 'matched partner', anchored in the internal referentiality of reflexive automated machines, derives from personal details that users have entered into computer systems. But it is vital to recognize that the premises of methodological reflexivity are loaded – indeed, overloaded – with personal half-truths, narcissistic inflations of the ego and other aspirational wishes. In short, users often (and routinely) provide idealized versions of their own lives and what they are looking for in the 'perfect partner'. This is why, when talking about the algorithmic prediction of dating matches, we are, in fact, talking about the dream of predicting passion itself. The 'blind trust in a system that's meant to do the heavy lifting' reflects a desire to achieve greater mastery over sexual relations and the emotional trajectories of the self. Yet this desire has little to do with the technological domain in which sexuality, eroticism and love have in some sense become inscribed in conditions of advanced AI. Sexuality has instead been rendered part of an 'algorithmic code', a phenomenon which feeds into *ever-growing spirals of expectancy*, where machine intelligence reshapes personal experience and life conduct. If algorithmic prediction is in some sense about the dismantling of the unpredictability of sexual relations, then today's spirals of expectancy in the field of the quantified sex life leave people feeling programmed, coded or even robotic. Sexuality may well form part of the development of automated, internally reflexive systems; yet such 'systems' reiterate, through algorithmic calculation, the very trauma of the unpredictability of human sexuality they are designed to undo.

Consuming Intimacy

Love today is digitized as never before. The individual, as it were, no longer needs to engage with the fraught interpersonal terrain of blind dates and relationship set-ups. Instead, he or she can effortlessly review photos of possible dating partners deemed a match on the basis of algorithmic prediction. The standardizing consequences of commodity capitalism penetrate all aspects of these intimate equations. Certainly, at the psychological and behavioural level, all human beings are and always were liable to become caught up in the passions of intimacy as all-consuming. With the advent of the 'algorithmic variety' of advanced capitalism, however, *consuming intimacy* becomes a prime driving force in the lives of individuals and throughout modern social life as a whole. Commodification profoundly influences the social and economic relations of online dating apps and the establishing of quantified sex lives. In its most marked elaborations, this development takes the form of equating the search for intimacy with shopping, whereby the searched-for, longed-for and desired other is consigned to the status of the commodity itself.

The case that advanced capitalism goes all the way down into the affective textures of intimacy and sexual relationships can be detailed briefly in the following way. The capitalistic market, with its 'drive' of continuous expansion and radical dismantling of different spheres of social existence, directly institutes a manipulative, incorporative logic in which human subjects increasingly come under the sway of consumption processes. The establishing of standardized consumption patterns, promoted largely today through digital technologies and other media, subordinate the use-value of objects to the empty formalism of exchange-value.

As Marx pointed out repeatedly, capitalistic enterprise renders commodities abstract through bypassing use-value and substituting the creation of unfettered market exchange. In the period of advanced capitalism, capitalistic enterprise has increasingly expunged all forms of lasting use-value and reshaped processes of consumption as bound up with satisfaction, gratification and the enhancement of pleasure. More recently, however, consumerism becomes extended further, engaging the individual subliminally, affectively, at the level of emotional response rather than reflexive consciousness. In this market-governed sphere, as in the realms of social media and sexual hook-up culture, individual choice becomes part of an enveloping framework of form over content, surface over depth, the immediacy of desire over critical self-reflection. In all of this, commodification sets the *consumer's mindset*, influencing the cognitive dispositions and value judgements as well as explicit and tacit assumptions governing the most basic elements of everyday social life.

In his eye-opening study of the way in which the consumer industry, consumerism and consumer society have 'degraded duration' and 'elevated transience', Zygmunt Bauman considers why the most acute worries that haunt contemporary women and men are the fears of being left behind, of overlooking 'use by' dates, and of failing to catch up with fast-moving events.[29] To a greater or lesser degree, the market penetrates into the fabric of the self and intimate relationships, substituting artificially framed styles of life for genuine interpersonal bonds. Bauman captures this well:

> The market now mediates in the tiresome activities of tying up and tearing up interpersonal relations, of bringing people together and putting them apart, of connecting them and disconnecting them, of dating them and of deleting them from the texting directory. It colours interhuman relations at work and at home, in public as well as in the most intimate private domains. It rephrases and recasts the destinations and itineraries of life pursuits so that not one of them can bypass the shopping malls. It narrates the life process as a succession of principally 'resolvable' problems that however need to be and can be resolved only by such means as are not available anywhere other than on the shelves of shops. It offers shop-supplied technological shortcuts to the kinds of objectives once attainable mainly through using personal skills and personality, friendly cooperation and comradely negotiations.[30]

The consumer mindset is in some ways even more deceptive than this characterization suggests. Not just interpersonal relations, but sexuality and eroticism appear increasingly 'pre-packaged' and algorithmically calculated according to market criteria.

It is against this complicated backdrop of commodity capitalism that we should understand commercial interests in, and associated profiting from, personal information digitally collected on people's habits, behaviours and preferences. Love online is in some substantial part the application of commodified processes to the personal data of users, now recast as 'objects of consumption'. The user of online technologies such as dating apps and quantified sex software literally becomes 'the product': people become something to consume, ready for immediate use. New technologies and technological services offer instant satisfaction; but, in the process, love feels disposable. It follows that the digital data economy casts a massive shadow not only on consumerism but also on production itself. Some commentators researching digitalization speak of processes of 'prosumption', an unlovely term which seeks to conflate 'production' and 'consumption'.[31] The merit of this term is that it helps focus attention on the combined activities of users of online technologies in both creating digital content and consuming digital information and data. This is certainly the case when people go online to browse the Internet, upload apps and engage in online shopping. As people upload status updates, make online comments or (more passively) have their devices automatically tracked for geolocation information, these are instances of the simultaneous production and consumption of personal data through the digital economy. But as a way of thinking about the social dimensions of algorithmic intimacy in general, and the practices of contemporary online dating or hook-up culture in particular, the term 'prosumption' is arguably misleading. For one thing, it is mistaken to assume that users of digital technologies produce digital data in their routine encounters with these technologies in anything like the same manner that social media conglomerates or digital companies produce data.[32] For another, the advent of the digital data economy is not just a matter of the reordering of existing forms of consumption and spheres of production. Rather, consumption in the algorithmic phase of the modern era is essentially transformational of interpersonal relations: it provides the technological means and capabilities of conducting social and sexual relations without which a growing number of individuals would find initiating such encounters daunting beyond measure, or as Bauman notes 'perhaps even off-limits'.

Let us now consider some tales from the front line of contemporary dating and sexual hook-up culture, selected more or less randomly from the popular media to highlight these novel consumer logics in action.

In a supposedly light-hearted if often alarming set of interviews with 'twentysomethings' telling all about modern dating apps, Phoebe Luckhurst reflects in 'Love Me Tinder' on the disposability of love online and other sexual challenges of the contemporary era. 'The worst part of online dating', reflects Luckhurst's interviewee Libby (27, customer services assistant), 'is the first awkward face-to-face hello. Your pre-conception of the person you have been speaking to is always very oddly different to whoever it is you meet.'[33] Face-to-face is presumably so awkward because it is at such odds with the idealized versions of identity portraits which users have painted in their online profiles. A dating app profile represents for many the lives that they should have, and it is this idealized version of their personalities, wants and desires which is uploaded to connect with others in the ongoing search for best possible matches. Little wonder that users encounter a perpetual falling-short in 'the first awkward face-to-face hello'. Such pressuring of identity construction to benefit the online world leads, paradoxically, to desires unmet. But such wished-for identities, the lives people feel they should have, also often bear the weight of cruel, callous judgements. As Libby details: 'I once heard a story about a man who turns up to dates early and buys himself a drink, so that when the girl arrives, he can send her up to the bar to get a drink and do a runner if he thinks they aren't up to his exacting standards. That's almost a reason to give up.'

Looseness of emotional attachment and precision of quantifiable data are the precepts guiding the episodic hook-up relationships with which contemporary women and men engage. Addressing the culture of casual hook-ups, Stewart Jeffries of the Guardian writes – paraphrasing the Sorbonne sociologist Jean-Claude Kaufmann – that 'in the new world of speed dating, online dating and social networking, the overwhelming idea is to have short, sharp engagements that involve minimal commitment and maximal pleasure'. In a context where time is flattened into a perpetual present, pleasure can be maximized only if commitments are minimized. Turnover of relationships is what matters. And the culture of casual hook-ups is the culture of numbers – of monitoring, representing, collecting and applying numbers in the advancement of self-tracking life projects. Examining blogs where people reflect about their online dating experiences, Jeffries wonders whether today's cultural obsession with numbers is shattering our most cherished ideals of romance. The case of 'Nick', an emergent specialist in the arts of the quantified sex life, is evidence enough for Jeffries:

> In his sex blog, Nick works out that he got 77.7% of the women he has met through online dating sites into bed on the first night, and that 55% of his dates were 'one-offs', three were 'frigid', two were 'not too great', eight 'hot' and two 'atomic' . . . Thanks to the internet, such spreadsheets of love have replaced notches on the bedpost and can be displayed hubristically online.[34]

Algorithmic sex apps and the quantified sex life cast the world and its inhabitants as objects of calculation: that is, objects that help constitute the production of data, which in turn may or may not be ranked as attractive, desirable, seductive.

Numbers Rule: Technologies in Search of Desires

Numbers are the staple, and arguably the most abundant product, of the digital data economy of consumers. Forms of quantification, especially in relation to the self-tracking of consumers, increasingly takes precedence in assessing desirability, attractiveness, sex appeal, erotic thrills and even a sense of self-worth. As Deborah Lupton argues in *The Quantified Self*:

> The algorithmic manipulation of people's bodily functions and behavioural activities into metrics and scores has significant implications for configuring new types of knowledge about humans. The body/self, as it is produced through self-tracking, is therefore both subject and product of scientific measurement and interpretation. As people's bodily states and functions become ever-more recordable and visualized via data displays, it becomes easier to trust the 'numbers' . . . [U]sing these technologies encourages people to think about their bodies and their selves through numbers. Sexual activity

becomes reduced to 'the numbers': how long intercourse lasts for, how often it takes place, how many thrusts are involved, the volume of sound emitted by participants, how good it is, with how many partners and so on. The comparisons with other users that some of these apps allow for emphasize the notion of sexual experience as a performance, as an activity that can and should be compared with the sexual experience of others, since they are all rendered into digital data form.[35]

Life becomes increasingly recast at all times as living-with-numbers. Sexuality and eroticism are digitized and quantified in these apps, and every hook-up is an occasion where sexual relations are portrayed as 'quantified calculations' and rendered 'digital data'. The trend is towards continual data-generating sexual relations, which is at once self-sustaining and self-invigorating. As Lupton pithily sums this up, 'You Are Your Data.'

There is, then, a relentless stress on numbers in the practices, discourses and technologies associated with digital self-tracking and sexual relations in particular and eroticism more generally in contemporary societies. As more and more people engage with the personal data they use for self-tracking, knowledge of the self and detailed understanding of one's sexuality are presumed to advance. This symbolic link between numbers and knowledge is evident in the emphasis that Spreadsheets puts on calculations of the 'number of thrusts per minute' or in the focus on the 'data science' of tracking calories burned in sexual activities on apps such as Sex Counter Tease and Sex Keeper. Quantification seems to be, at least in part, an upshot of current discourses of science and technology, leading to the reframing of sexuality and the self. The cult of quantification marks a point where sexual relations, eroticism and human sexuality are represented or codified as 'objective forms of information' compared to the everyday operations of self-knowledge generated by subjective engagement with the self, others and the wider world. The ideology of quantification, I want to suggest, establishes a relatively closed universe, repetitive and self-perpetuating, which presupposes the 'technological objectivity' and 'scientificity' of data-driven lifestyles.

The rise of the quantified sex life as a phenomenon of more than passing or marginal interest is a development which coincides with advances in artificial intelligence and the socio-economic supremacy of high tech. The complex role of technology here has a similar effect to the way processes of social reflexivity have unfolded: it magnifies the search for 'techno-logical objectivity' in the framing of sexual relations and thereby seeks to eliminate uncertainty and ambivalence from the terrain of algorithmic selfhood. Why should AI-powered algorithms have this drawing power for individuals as regards sexuality and intimate relationships? What is it about algorithmic dating apps and the quantified sex life which might nurture in individuals the belief that they can better cope with, or perhaps transcend altogether, the dilemmas and difficulties of contemporary sexual relationships?

In order to begin to answer these questions, we need to trace the interconnections between technology, the politics of measurement and the production of the self. Quantification and the lure of numbers have become increasingly interwoven with *forms of omnipotence* (at once personal and social) across a series of interpersonal and intimate environments. In conditions of intensive AI, the individual's sense of psychological security – when viewed against the backdrop of online dating apps and other technologies of quantification – is developed through an ever-increasing reliance on 'objective forms of data', or 'algorithmic objectivity'. New digital technologies for gathering data and for achieving quantification go all the way down into this process of omnipotence: the phenomenal world feels as if it is 'under control' because it is programmed, mechanical, engineered. It is essential to grasp that this is a *fantasy state*. On a psychological plane, the individual's sense of self-control and invulnerability is tied to smart algorithms, which can make people feel omnipotent. Let us now examine further the distinctive character of algorithmic objectivity and the forms of omnipotence that new technologies of quantification make possible.

Throughout contemporary Western societies, and against the institutional backdrop of the digital revolution in general and artificial intelligence in particular, there has been a veritable explosion in the use of metrics in many aspects of social and cultural life. From measuring business project costs to delivering new functionality on algorithmic dating apps, metrics play a vital role in the data practices and materializations of both online users and tech companies. Many commentators have emphasized that there is a *politics of measurement*: metricization is not neutral. The lure of numbers is directly bound up with contemporary approaches to technology, with ways of thinking about life's possibilities and perils, and its relation to selfhood, sexuality and social life more generally. Technologies of quantification are also a field of force, a realm of conflict and coercion; metrics are implicated in ways of seeing the world, framing social and sexual relations, and the perpetuation of unequal relations of power.

In numerous studies of discourses of datafication, metrics and quantification, authors have tied the production of ever-increasing knowledges about citizens, consumers, organizations and societies to the technological conditions and technological understandings of modern societies. Through investigations of various aspects of the uses of technology, researchers have sought to show that actors in social interaction make certain assumptions about science and technology which are pertinent to questions about social reproduction and cultural transformation. Some authors argue, for example, that new technologies provide individuals with the means to explore interpersonal relations in an engineered way, without entering into the web of face-to-face commitments and other reciprocal obligations that stem from situated interpersonal conduct. Other authors argue, by contrast, that digital technologies render identities manageable, calculable and governable by the metrics which are generated through the algorithmic computation of personal information and private data.[36] Whatever their differences, these kinds of analysis establish a strong connection between technology and trust, digitalization and discourse, algorithms and action.

One of the best accounts we have of the societal jurisdiction of pervasive technology remains that offered by the late French historian and sociologist Jacques Ellul. In *The Technological Society*, Ellul insisted that 'technique' – broadly conceived to scoop up machines, technical devices and, most significantly, other rationally ordered methods which render human action more efficient – advances because it advances. 'Technology', Ellul wrote, 'never advances towards anything but *because* it is pushed from behind'; the 'interdependence of technological elements makes possible a very large number of "solutions" for which there are no problems'; the work of technicians, moreover, is 'done because it could be done. That is all.'[37] What

Ellul unearths concerns the self-legitimacy of technology itself, revealing technique as a closed system. As far as confronting the powers of technological society is concerned, many commentators assume that technology flows from science. But Ellul reverses this, arguing that technique has historically preceded science. What this means, in effect, is that techniques *precede* goals: the mere technical possibility that something can be done has served as the inspiration for undertaking it. Nothing in society escapes the reaches of technique; society is dominated by the *automatism* of technique, which is the process by which technology asserts itself according to mathematical models of efficiency. What Ellul calls 'technique' is all-encompassing: 'it elicits and conditions social, political and economic change . . . Technique tolerates no judgment from without and accepts no limitation.' Towards the end of his life, Ellul highlighted that the adoption and advancement of automation technology by the military–industrial complex was perhaps the clearest example of the reign of technique – the sheer unconditionality of the ideological force of technological society 'to do something'. It was from this bleak context that Ellul argued that society needs to reassess and evaluate the insane grip that technology has come to exert over our lives; 'at stake is our very life', he wrote, 'and we shall need all the energy, inventiveness, imagination, goodness and strength we can muster to triumph in our predicament'.[38]

Contemporary social theory has been much preoccupied with technology, but generally restricts this issue within certain conflicts of interest bound up with modern institutions. The late Cornelius Castoriadis, by contrast, saw the operations of 'technoscience' as deeply interwoven with *omnipotent thinking*; technoscientific rationality has no rationale beyond its own instrumentalizing and narcissistic logics.[39] The dominance of pseudo-scientific rationality today involves not only the 'technological fix' but fantasy, repetition, omnipotent illusions and psychic excess; the path of technoscience, says Castoriadis, is 'less and less that of the *desirable* in any sense, and more and more that of the simply *doable*'.[40] In this as in other aspects of his social and political thought, technoscience for Castoriadis is fundamentally *imaginary*: it bears omnipotent fantasies and delusions entirely within itself, resulting in 'an artificialized rationality that has become not only impersonal (nonindividual) but also inhuman'. Scientific technology for Castoriadis, if one can speak in such terms, would seem at once collectively vital and blankly meaningless – a startling contradiction which is stripped of the power to disturb once we 'distinguish the philosophical import and the abstract practical possibilities of science from its social-historical reality, from the actual role it plays in the contemporary world, and in the massive drift our world is experiencing'.

It is this 'drift' that Castoriadis will seize on in declaring: 'With technoscience, modern man believes he has been granted mastery.' Both mastery and control are for Castoriadis mere fictions, the narcissistic effects of deeper psychic forces. But, again, why in our fantasy lives do we tend to be so excessive when it comes to technology? What is it about technology that leads human subjects into conflict with their own imaginative energies? One answer might be that in our fantasies we can have ourselves, others and the wider world exactly as we want them. But if this is so it follows that fantasy – especially our tendency to endow technology with magical thinking – might be a way of keeping others at bay. Such a standpoint arguably captures the daily truth in conditions of algorithmic modernity, where the excesses of fantasy – the fundamentalism of technology, if you will – reveals a fear of ourselves and other people. Castoriadis, it should be noted, formulated his theory of technoscience prior to the onset of conditions of advanced AI. In an anticipatory gesture towards the power of automated intelligent machines, however, he did reflect on the dangers to autonomous self-realization posed by forces of autonomization in his late writings. What Castoriadis termed the 'automatization of decisions' – where 'all "subjective" politico-psychological factors' are 'eliminated' – spreads out its power as a consequence of advances in artificial intelligence.

It is again not difficult to see in these philosophical lines of departure the driving force of technology in the reshaping of contemporary sexual relations. Combining Ellul and Castoriadis, we can say that technoscience is ecstasy and power, imagination and information, omnipotent mastery and subjection to autonomization. So, to return to our central question: what is the lure of numbers in the quantified sex life and the living of lives via algorithmic sex apps? We clearly need to consider the possibility, following Ellul and Castoriadis, that people are addicted to quantification as a means of achieving a soothing self-image of self-control. Or we might want to pursue the argument that the excesses of quantification in our algorithmic world may be overbearing, but that (on balance) people adapt to these technological practices at the level of intimate relationships remarkably well. More and more people take quantification and data tracking for granted now, even though these continue to have the power to disturb and displace experiences related to selfhood and sexuality in various ways. Yet another possibility – more plausible both psychologically and socially, and worthy I think of further research – is that excessive thinking about numbers, quantification and metrics reveals a fear of other people. So intoxicating is the lure of numbers in the quantified sex life that they can become a refuge, a kind of psychic retreat. In a world of metrics and measures, people may respond emotionally to data generated about others and themselves as a way of keeping desires afloat, taking pleasure in the frustration-free domain of omnipotent fantasy – where options are always open and sexual partners perpetually available, or at least prospective matches are available to look at on the screen.

4

Therapy Tech

In his classic study *Freud: The Mind of the Moralist*, the American sociologist Philip Rieff connected the rise of therapy culture to secularization.[1] Therapy, said Rieff, offers a secular version of the confessional. Therapy with another person – psychiatrist, counsellor or therapist – characterizes a process of both self-confession and self-realization. The therapeutic project is, on this view, dependent upon the intersubjective transmission of thoughts, emotions, memories and affects between people. Yet therapy today extends far beyond the interpersonal frameworks in which Freudian psychoanalysis and other therapeutic psychology were pioneered. Nowadays therapy has become inscribed in a worldwide ecosystem of automated intelligent machines, as patients or clients across the planet increasingly reflect on personal experiences, explore traumatic pasts or engage their present-day unhappiness through recourse to chatbots. Examining the emergence of chatbot therapy, Amy Ellis Nutt writes in *The Washington Post*:

> My therapist wanted to explain a few things during our first online session: 'I'm going to check in with you at random times. If you can't respond straight away, don't sweat it. Just come back to me when you're ready. I'll check in daily.'
> 'Daily?' I asked.
> 'Yup! It shouldn't take longer than a couple minutes. Can you handle that?'

'Yes, I can', I answered.
There was a little more back-and-forth, all via Messenger, then this
statement from my therapist:
'This might surprise you, but . . . I am a robot.'[2]

These reflections offer a glimpse into an important emerging
trend in American therapeutic culture, principally about the
diffusion of the category of the therapeutic to non-human others
and the machine techniques of handling 'therapy talk'.

Mobile talk-counselling, life-coaching apps and chatbot
therapy have proliferated dramatically in recent years as traditional therapy has struggled to remain culturally relevant in the
digital age. Traditional forms of therapy demand a significant
commitment of time as well as financial resources; there is also
no denying that traditional therapy was profoundly impacted by
the COVID-19 global pandemic – initially as therapists struggled
to meet their clients face to face, and subsequently as the surge
in demand for mental health services resulted in a dramatic
shortage of clinical psychologists and therapeutic professionals.
But the popularity of these new automated therapies, like
chatbots and counselling apps, captures more than a shift in the
circumstances of the clients seeking treatment for mental health.
It also expresses the growing preoccupation of our current
culture with automated intelligent machines as a preferable
organizing principle to engage in therapy talk in a manner which
mimics psychotherapy. As Nutt reminds us, today's automated
version of therapy is, in part, a substitution for more traditional
interpersonal forms or therapeutic practices. Nutt quotes the
founder and chief executive of Woebot Labs, Alison Darcy, on
the value of chatbot therapy thus: 'you can get things off your
chest without worrying what the other person thinks, without
that fear of judgment'. In fact, the reason you need not worry
'what the other person thinks' is that there is no other person in
the therapeutic dialogue. There is instead a robot. At bottom, the
purpose of today's automated therapy talk and message tapping
on smartphones is no longer to risk exposing the innards of
subjectivity to the therapist's interpretation or assessment. The
words voiced or typed in chatbot therapy are instead 'machine
interactions'.

The current therapeutic shift differs not only in the form of
'interaction' (from human therapist to non-human chatbot) but

also in the experience of reflective moments and the capacity for heightened awareness of thoughts. Entering therapy chatbot style is anything but traditional. As Amy Ellis Nutt's Woebot reminds her of the daily check-ins: 'It shouldn't take longer than a couple of minutes.' Freud's casting of the therapeutic project as consisting of fifty-minute sessions over four or five meetings a week (which may have stretched over many years) has been replaced by frantic, mobile interaction, Internet chatting and 24/7 texting. Chatbot therapy, says John Tourous of the American Psychiatric Association and co-director of a digital psychiatry programme at Beth Israel Deaconess Medical Centre in Boston (whom Nutt also quotes), 'can work well on a superficial level with superficial conversations'. To which we might add that chatbot therapy can work well *because* it is arguably superficial. In the fluid therapeutic realm of Woebot, emotional intensities come and go, traumatic real-life events as well as disturbing memories surface only to disappear shortly afterwards, as therapeutic check-ins occur randomly. Therapeutic self-reflection Woebot-style is above all floating, flexible and fast.

The expansion of automated therapeutic chatbots such as Woebot into all areas of mental health and life planning has been remarkable. Certainly, the monumental increase in the automated psychologization of contemporary social life becomes evident if we compare the numbers of people using chatbot therapies and digital psychological apps with those consulting traditional therapeutic professions and institutions, including counsellors, social workers, psychologists, psychiatrists and psychotherapists. Allan Horowitz, in *Creating Mental Illness*, notes that the number of mental health professionals quadrupled in the United States between 1970 and 1995.[3] Similar patterns were evident across Europe, as the triumph of the therapeutic pervaded the workplace, schools and universities, the realm of politics and the spheres of popular culture and everyday life. 'Each culture', writes Rieff, 'is its own order of therapy.'[4] If the society of the late twentieth century ushered into existence a therapeutic culture in which a new conception of the person, 'psychological man', held sway, the society of the early twenty-first century has created a vocabulary where therapeutics is directly tied to machine intelligence. Whilst the ascendancy of automated therapeutic culture cannot be charted with exact precision, the range of software apps and chatbots for treating depression, anxiety, addiction and many other psychological conditions has radically expanded. From mental health apps such as What's Up and Mood Kit to addiction apps such as Quit That! and Twenty-Four Hours A Day to suicide prevention apps such as notOK and MY3, therapeutic culture today both reflects and promotes the trend towards solving psychological problems through machine intelligence. Accounts of the personal and psychological benefits of Woebot, for example, often associate this breakthrough Stanford University chatbot with innovations in machine learning, mood tracking and automated curated videos. The AI crystallized in Woebot delivers scripted responses based on cognitive behavioural therapy to clients. As with many technological breakthroughs in the field, it is the speed and scale of diagnosis of mental health problems which are particularly striking. Over 50,000 people signed up to Woebot in the first months of its release in 2017, which is a figure that considerably exceeds what psychologists or therapeutic professionals might ever hope to achieve over a working lifetime. In 2019, Woebot was processing over two million conversations a week from people with a wide variety of mental health problems from around the world.[5]

Accounts of digital approaches to mental health often associate AI, and machine learning in particular, with the precise development of prediction, detection and treatment solutions for psychological disorders. Many commentators point to data-driven AI methods which can be deployed (especially in smartphone apps and chatbots) to develop the effective promotion of therapeutic intervention.[6] While some of these characterizations might contain important insights, they overlook what might be described as broader negative consequences for self-understanding, self-formation and self-autonomy resulting from automated therapeutic imperatives. My argument is that the conjoining of therapeutic culture and automated intelligent machines is very largely self-referential and system directed; and so is the revision of identity which such therapeutic machine intelligence demands and promotes. The trend of such automated processes for behavioural or mental health insights is self-sustained and self-limited. 'An algorithm', writes Helga Nowotny, 'has the capability to act and to make happen what it predicts when human behavior follows the prediction.'[7] It is for this reason that the advent of automated therapeutic software spells self-limitation and more generally acts as a constraint on the open horizon of the future – both personal and collective.

In this chapter I shall focus on transformations of the self, experience and everyday life in conditions of algorithmic therapeutic intimacy. My starting point is that, with the development of automated therapeutic imperatives, the process of self-reforming selves becomes ensnared in the power of predictive algorithms, in the sense that individuals can quickly fall back into an acceptance and entrenchment of 'certainties' which may turn out to be illusory. The development of therapeutic chatbots and mental health apps not only generates novel opportunities and experimental repertoires and transforms the process of self-reforming selves; it also produces new kinds of risks and closures at the level of self-experience, engagement with others as well as the wider world. I shall subsequently explore connections between the therapeutic instrumental efficiency of algorithms and the negative consequences for self-reforming selves in the second and third sections of the chapter. In the final section I shall examine the reshaping of public and private life in the wider context of automated therapeutic culture.

Chatbot Therapy, Counselling Apps and Mental Health

In recent years, a growing number of studies have been undertaken on how chatbots, conversational agents and smartphone apps are transforming mental health.[8] Much of this research has been conducted by market research companies, but there are also many academic research studies. There has been, for example, a spate of interest in studying the phenomenon of machine learning and artificial intelligence methods in mental health research, especially the treatment of anxiety and depression as well as amelioration of symptoms.[9] In these studies, the combined role of machine learning, natural language processing, big data and software development is highlighted as central to the advancement of AI-based precision mental health. Extending this research, there is now a growing collection of studies published by academic researchers on digital approaches to the optimization of personalized mental healthcare.[10] These studies have been mostly directed at investigating conversational agents to assist in offering personalized resources, self-help guidance, individualized user goals and tailored support to emotional concerns. This research employs a largely psychology-orientated perspective on design-based models to study how consumers can 'get the most out' of mental health chatbots.

There is an emergent selective affinity between the privatization of mental health and the market catering for chatbot therapy consumption. Indeed, the market offers a range of conversational agents to assist in care of the self, including therapy, counselling, information collection, redefinition of personal goals and the improvement of social skills. Chatbots such as Woebot deploy natural language processing to 'get to know' users, using cognitive behavioural therapy methods to provide self-help related guidance. Other conversational agents and digital counselling tools combine a range of therapeutic approaches. Wysa, estimated to support over two million users, combines cognitive behavioural therapy with dialectical behavioural therapy, meditation exercises and personalized motivation data practices. Tess, another mental health chatbot, uses advanced AI to react to user information in real time rather than providing preselected responses. In exchanges with clients, as Kylie Gionet notes of this mental health robot, 'Tess will make an educated guess – drawing on the other conversations she has had with people and with the help of algorithms – about which form of therapy might be most effective. . . . If her attempted treatment – say, cognitive behavioural therapy – turns out to be wrong, she'll switch to another one, such as compassion-focused therapy.'[11] All this, let us remember, happens to an individual no longer within the traditional therapeutic imperative – at least not in the interpersonal space that clinical practice once was. The individual is now an *uncontestedly privatized site of machine intelligence*, and it is mostly up to commercial interests and the preferences of potential customers (including institutional healthcare purchasers such as the National Health Service in the UK) to cultivate what is considered appropriate human–machine interaction for the attainment of mental health.

That said, the world of therapy chatbots in mental health counselling apps tends to splice together various commercial, scientific and public interests. Many consumers, for example, pay for counselling advice not only in the standard form of monetary exchange but through their personal data practices. Indeed, many chatbot websites explicitly acknowledge the role that the user's personal data play in their clinical algorithmic frameworks. The algorithmic world of computer therapy, however, is also the yield of many other technical, community, commercial and scientific contributions, discourses and objectives. Developers, psychologists, therapists, counsellors, consumer bodies and healthcare agencies are also the testing ground of human–machine experience in the ongoing effort to expand AI in the field of algorithmic therapeutic intimacy. These diverse interests contribute very substantially not only to the operational dimensions of therapeutic data-gathering technologies, but also to the marketing strategies and social media presence of chatbot companies such as BotsCrew, Chatbots Studio, Master of Code Global and Cedex Technologies.

A report by Alaa Abd-alrazaq and colleagues offers further insights into such an algorithmic therapeutic condition, in the documentation of fifty-three studies of digital approaches to mental health involving forty-one different chatbots.[12] The large bulk of these conversational agents were used for therapeutic purposes, and approximately half of the studies addressed individual suffering from states ranging from acute anxiety to depression. In our efficiency-ruled society, it may not be surprising that Abd-alrazaq and colleagues put their focus squarely on the functional features of chatbots and their potential uses in mental health. Assessment of the *effectiveness, acceptability, usability* and *adoption* of chatbots to promote mental health intervention dominates the available research literature. Abd-alrazaq and colleagues, in reviewing this literature, highlight that rule-based chatbots – which depend on decision trees to generate their responses – tend to predominate in the area of machine intelligence therapeutic health. Offered by way of response is their credible explanation that rule-based chatbots are more secure than advanced machine-learning chatbots. But it is also noted that new generation AI chatbots are becoming more prevalent in this field too. Again, data is seen as vital. As the authors conclude: 'Although artificial intelligence chatbots are prone to errors, such errors can be minimized and diminished by extensive training and more use.'

This sounds, as I say, like a credible explanation. But the more we widen the view beyond machine-learning methods and focus on the wider socio-cultural assumptions embedded in the great bulk of chatbot therapy technologies, the more we might suspect that this isn't the complete picture. For one thing, therapy chatbots are arguably too affirmative to be adequately attuned to the psychopathologies of individuals. Such therapeutic technologies are, on the whole, programmed to be continuously upbeat, endlessly praising and pathologically optimistic. This suprapositive side to chatbot therapy, however, permits little room for traumatic repetition or emotional regression. 'Conversational agents', suggest Robert Meadows, Christine Hine and Eleanor Suddaby, 'invoke an idea of recovery that involves smooth and linear reduction in symptoms over time and locate the agency for bringing about that recovery in the app.'[13] It is as if the ultra-rationalism of machine intelligence must necessarily render emotional turbulence outmoded or redundant. Yet it is this smoothly ordered rationalism of chatbot therapy – its affirmative goals, its tireless striving for personal efficiency, its endemic upbeatness – which is most troubling. There is something pathological about the insistence in algorithmic therapeutics that human subjects are always transparent to themselves and never self-deceived. On this reckoning, the individual is always in full possession of its self-identity and self-understanding, which in large part accounts for the curt rejection of the whole concept of 'recovery' in algorithmic therapeutics. 'Ideas of recovery', conclude Meadows, Hine and Suddaby, 'are almost side-lined as the focus remains on the present and chatbots become the care that we all need to deal with our everyday emotions.'

The upbeat mood of algorithmic therapeutics goes hand in hand with a straightforward focus on the immediate, instantaneous and present. Algorithmic therapeutics is beyond the Freudian insistence on the endless disturbances of desire as well as the whole business of disabling, traumatic pasts – inhabiting, as it does, a realm of self-enclosed order, security and certitude. From this angle, computerized therapy means something like a consoling sense of self-unity automatically supplied by the forces of machine intelligence and algorithmic prediction. Users will never be surprised by discovering something antagonistic or disturbing deep within the self, or, one suspects, about the unavoidably harmful business of repression. Today's objectives and immediate tasks, on the other hand, represent a force which can fashion what individuals desire almost instantaneously. The emphasis in algorithmic therapeutics on the immediate cannot but impact (indeed revolutionize?) the conditions for individuals to engage in self-reflection and emotional introspection – which is clearly why algorithmic therapeutic imperatives of the moment strike many critics as lightweight, trivial or superficial. One study of perceptions of chatbot therapy underscores that 'participants report awareness of chatbot limitations, especially with regard to superficial, standardized answers and the usefulness of suggested goals'.[14]

Engagement on the spot and personal goal setting in the process of instantaneous consumption are the key means through which algorithmic therapeutics can maintain a pact with 'success'. In any event, regression is not an option, as most chatbots use rule-based approaches, restricting the user's engagement to predefined phrases and pre-scripted replies. Even so, when it comes to algorithmic therapeutic affirmation, the can-do spirit is arguably nowhere more positively promoted than in cognitive behavioural therapy. Traumas in cognitive behavioural therapy are not traumatic. Psychic upheaval is not so much a painful past to be reckoned with or worked through as a disabling impediment to self-fashioning which should be eliminated. Similarly, because chatbots are trained on data affirming achievement and success, the subtlety of emotions such as sadness, sorrow or melancholia tend to receive short shrift. Lumping these together under the condition of depression, cognitive behavioural therapy in the era of AI is most often deployed to close down consideration of negative emotions altogether. The psychological holding power of chatbot therapy partly stems from this inbuilt cultural assumption that nobody should have to figure out where grief or mourning come from, let alone how to engage in a conversation laden with such affects. Instead of fashioning capacities for emotional literacy, people turn to algorithmic therapeutics to 'get rid of' anxiety or depression – convinced that in this way they can escape such distress.[15]

Automated Predictive Systems and Culturally Cool Therapy

The traditional custodians of the therapeutic imperative – psychiatrists, psychologists, counsellors, social workers – are today quickly replaced by automated and digital authority. In a world where therapeutic intervention has become a central task for contemporary living, there has been no shortage of certified and/or commercially based advice givers who are available to guide their patients, clients or customers into the complex maladies of the soul from which the struggle for self-redefinition, self-reconstruction and a 'new' and 'better' life proceeds. More and more often today, this voyage of self-discovery is advanced with – or more precisely, in and through – automated intelligent machines. Chatbot therapy and conversational machine technology contribute to the sense of a more dispersed and networked sense of individuality positioned within human–machine interfaces; such therapeutic digital technologies extend the self into the realm of the artificial. By opening the self to new forms of digital coding, informational scripts and other kinds of automated prompts and reminders, however, there occurs a 'thinning out' of self-management, self-regulation and self-understanding, as if the search for authentic individuality could be embraced solely with the help of automated intelligent machines. This is a cultural thinning of personal life which involves a concomitant shift away from the realm of interpersonal relations.

Like other therapeutic software apps and conversational artificial agents, Woebot functions largely as an emotional investment advisor. Somewhat akin to the profession of financial advisors (which is also increasingly the province of automated intelligent machines), chatbot therapists like Woebot recommend to clients various practices of self-care, how often the tools of internal self-examination should be marshalled, and what kinds of objects and in whom to 'invest' emotional energy. From one angle, such therapeutic imperatives are quite mainstream: such forms of activity, interpretation, reflection and advice have been long practised by psychological professionals. From another angle, however, therapy Woebot-style is the result of a significant societal shift disguised under the banner of personal transformation. Individuals engaged in counselling practices with therapeutic chatbots commonly rely on digital prompts and informational relays in their day-to-day lives, and alongside this there has arguably been a decline in commitment to 'significant others' along with a sense of anchorage in emotionally rich social bonds.

Consider, for example, the blogger of 'My Chatbot Therapist', which records seven days of a young woman's journey with

Woebot.[16] This blogger begins by noting her awareness that chatbot therapy has recently become culturally pervasive while traditional forms of therapy or counselling have become less so. She also expresses some doubt about how perceptive AI might really be about human emotions, but still remains curious to know more about why people turn increasingly to automated machines to resolve their most intimate personal problems. Like many journalistic accounts of chatbots, this blog notes that Woebot contacted the blogger irregularly through Facebook Messenger, with short 'thought bubbles' rather than long blocks of text. How did the therapeutic exchange unfold? Partly through the posing of questions concerning anxiety, fear, mood and energy. But the emphasis falls most heavily on 'programmed responses . . . to choose from to answer each question'.

How should we understand the cultural process by which therapy is dislodged from particular professionals and specialists and repositioned in the artificial context of machine intelligence? The spread of automated machine intelligence in therapy has been greeted by many with praise inspired by unqualified ardour. The dislodgement of the therapeutic imperative from the psychological and caring professions and re-embedding in AI has been widely proclaimed as a sign of 'democratization', the ultimate triumph of a phenomenon which extends the cultural reach of therapy into social classes other than that of the 'worried well'. In this view, therapy is no longer simply a cultivated diversion of the privileged; it is a phenomenon deeply interwoven with diverse forms of digital technology and, in principle at least, now available to everyone. This socio-technical transformation might indeed contain some elements of the democratization that its admirers and supporters repute it to be, namely, the 'opening up' of the self to artificially referential systems of reflection; but it also, as Arlie Russell Hochschild has explained in relation to other related social trends, reflects the demise of the idea of lasting commitments and a shift towards low-intensity, quick-fix personal solutions to broader social problems. In the shape of therapy, automated intelligent machines spread as a means of quick-fix care and fast accelerations of the self. This 'new and improved' therapy alternative arguably fits Hochschild's observation that presently occurring social trends and countertrends advance a pervasive 'cultural cooling'.[17] Whatever 'relations' and 'connections' cultural cooling impacts do not mean (as

Hochschild reminds us) 'that individuals need one another less, only that they are invited to *manage their needs more*'. Instrumentalism of the soul as a consequence of endless short-term projects geared to care of self is characteristic of today's social order. This consists, as Hochschild memorably put it, of 'a spirit of instrumental detachment that fits the emptied slots where a deeper "me", "you", and "us" might be'.

The challenges, tasks and pursuits advanced by chatbot therapy and related software counselling apps tend to assume today the colour and shape of quick-fix self-care. Cultural cooling filters into most aspects of chatbot therapy, at least as a background phenomenon where the requirement to steer engagement with the self remains short, episodic and seemingly uncomplicated. As the blogger from 'My Chatbot Therapist' notes:

> 'Today was quick and easy, literally just 5 minutes of my time. I sort of find myself wishing Woebot would stick around to talk more. The best part of our chat was when I told Woebot I had a productive day, and it replied that having goals was awesome. I found myself feeling pretty good! A Chatbot making me feel good and proud of myself? This thing is pretty cool so far!

Keeping things flexible, a constant readiness to adapt and the ability to maintain an emotional temperature close to 'pretty cool' appear to be particularly pronounced when talking alone with chatbot therapists. Chatbot therapy can also offer diversion through games and videos, with the aim of keeping reflection on self-identity light and breezy. Yet cultural cooling also generates still more diffuse anxieties. The very emotional strategies of cultural cooling promoted by automated intelligent machines surely often express underlying anxiety that the more complex, more burdensome and more emotionally constraining aspects of psychic life have not, in actuality, faded away. Therapy in culturally cool ecosystems of automated intelligent machines remains inherently unsettling.

It is not, however, simply that the frames for self-under-standing and life projects are rendered short-termist, episodic, brittle and apparently 'uncomplicated' by machine intelligence. The short-term and temporary construction of frames becomes, in its turn, the experiential base of what Helga Nowotny in *In AI We Trust* terms 'the prediction machine'. Therapy chatbots

and software counselling apps 'do' interpretations of broad
life conditions and 'recommend' to individuals how to invest
emotional energy in known present and imagined futures.
Chatbot therapists such as Woebot recommend emotional
practices of self-revision and self-transformation – in and
through, for example, the playing of quick games or experiments with thinking pattern videos. Therapy chatbots also
motivate individuals to tie these forms and methods of machine
prediction to various ideal horizons, to inspirational ideas and
images of the self, as well as connecting emotional routines
and patterns of living to ready-made, consumer friendly and
algorithmically legible identity performances. Aided and abetted
by automated therapy chatbots, the project of reconstructing the
self is switched to automatic pilot, at once self-propelling and
self-accelerating.

This shift in the whole project of therapy and the associated
internalization of values derived from predictive algorithms
connects to what Nowotny sees as the new performative contradiction of computational power. The central contradiction,
writes Nowotny,

> arises from the performativity of predictive algorithms on the one
> hand, their capability to make happen what they predict. On the
> other hand, attempting to predict the future threatens to close the
> open horizon of the future. They may turn into self-fulfilling proph-
> ecies and once they circulate widely a prediction that was intended
> to cope with the uncertainty of the future can quickly transform into
> a certainty that may turn out to be illusionary.[18]

It is as if the power of predictive algorithms has been
'downloaded' into the minds of individuals, with agency replaced
by automation. As the 'My Chatbot Therapist' blogger notes by
the end of Day 4:

> I find these chats becoming a routine part of the end of my day. I'm
> surprised how much I find myself thinking about the things Woebot
> brings up to me. I catch myself in the *thinking patterns it taught
> me and have even begun to actively make adjustments when I do.*
> All this has come from a robot, from talking to AI? I'm still a little
> skeptical of how this is all going to play out, and if it will actually
> begin to help me feel better, but it's *already started to change my
> thinking.* (Emphasis added)

In this kind of automated life experience, smart algorithms seemingly solve emotional problems and the self becomes part of a newly engineered hybrid consisting of complex machine vocabularies and automated frames of reference. 'Eventually', as Nowotny warns, 'we risk being transformed into predictive systems ourselves.'

Computational Therapy: Lifestyle Change and Liquid Selves

The growing trend towards chatbot therapy and software counselling apps can also profoundly influence lifestyle change. What is lifestyle change? The notion has received much recent attention in the literature of social theory.[19] One reason for this has been the increasing cultural importance of nutrition, diet, fitness and health goals in fast-paced, consumer societies. Another set of considerations has been increased cultural awareness of the debilitating power of addiction and of increased dependencies on various substances throughout society at large. The search for changes in lifestyle is accompanied by reflection upon core aspects of the daily habits of individuals. What we do habitually in the personal as well as social context of everyday life defines both 'who we are' in substantial part as individuals and the kinds of communities and cultures of which we are part. 'Lifestyle change' and 'social change' are thus intimately connected. Lifestyle change is the kind of transformation which comes to be prized in societies where individuality is key. From this angle, lifestyle change is self-transformational and self-referential. 'Lifestyle change and how to achieve it', writes Anthony Giddens, 'are now the name of the game in key areas of politics. The range of issues involved is very wide . . . [they] include the obesity epidemic, lifestyle related diseases – including high blood pressure, diabetes, heart disease and cancer – excessive drinking, drug dependence, antisocial behaviour and other areas besides.'[20]

But how should we understand lifestyle change in relation to the rise of automated intelligent machines? Lifestyle change is many things, but it would hardly be any of them were it not for the encoding of technological frameworks within the tissue of lifestyle issues. Giddens underscores this point by directly connecting technological innovation to lifestyle change. Just like cultural trends and counter-trends, technological innovation forms a central aspect of the social conditions in which women and men search for ways to change lifestyles. What this means, essentially, is that technological breakthroughs and advanced digital technologies are drawn into the cultural repertoires by which individuals act to consolidate alternative ways of doing things, as well as develop fresh routines and new habits. Consider, for example, the smartphone apps which are from beginning to end enclosed in the framework of lifestyle changes today. Software counselling apps are routinely used for the setting of lifestyle goals and strategies, negotiating behavioural changes with automated conversational agents as well as the maintenance of personal logs and the tracking of emotional mood levels. Alongside this, there has been a sharp rise in the use of multicomponent apps providing users with access to private counsellors and group therapy, as well as tailored individualized sessions to support patient compliance with lifestyle goals set with the assistance of automated bots.

There are many voices applauding the emergent connections between software counselling apps and lifestyle change. Such voices tend to stress that it makes perfect sense for individuals today – where lifestyles are 'hurried and harried' – to take up advances in, and advantages of, mobile counselling and digital therapy. If there is less room for the idea of prolonged reflection upon the self through recourse to the traditional therapeutic imperative and the psychological professions, the uses of new digital technologies and automated virtual agents to achieve various lifestyle goals appears highly desirable at the current juncture. A very different and more critical view was put forward by the late social theorist Zygmunt Bauman. In his later writings, Bauman developed a scintillating critique of the joys and sorrows of individuals seeking their individuality, of ever-increasing commercial solutions for self-discovery, and of the 'factory-made, mass-produced' self-assembly therapeutic kits designed with the aid of the latest fashionable technologies.

Bauman developed, in *Liquid Modernity*, *Liquid Love*, *Liquid Life* and elsewhere, an arresting argument about the provisional organization of contemporary living and the transformed dynamics of human bonds. His argument that the 'solid world' of jobs-for-life and marriages till-death-us-do-part had been

replaced by a 'liquid world' of short-term contracts and relationships until-further-notice won him a global audience. 'Liquid
life', wrote Bauman,

> is a precarious life, lived under conditions of constant uncertainty.
> The most acute and stubborn worries that haunt such a life are
> the fears of being caught napping, of failing to catch up with fast-
> moving events, of being left behind, of overlooking 'use by' dates,
> of being saddled with possessions that are no longer desirable, of
> missing the moment that calls for a change of tack before crossing
> the point of no return.[21]

According to Bauman, advanced consumer capitalism – with its
ideology of 'want-now' identities and its rhetoric of the ever-new
– is essential to the spread of liquid modernity. Liquid times
are defined by fragility. Social ties become increasingly brittle,
exposing people to disabling solitude. Thus, the societal rush
towards market-led solutions and desires for the ever-new. In the
liquid world, variety, novelty and disposability rule.

I shall not examine the scope of Bauman's social theory in
further detail here.[22] I want instead to focus on some general
questions raised by his work: how has the technological development of the therapeutic imperative spreading throughout
modern societies been accompanied by shifts in the role of
individuality in social life? A related question is how the voyage
of self-discovery – that is, the search for the ideal of individuality as authentic – has been transformed as a consequence of
automated intelligent machines. According to Bauman, what is
injurious about 'individuality', among other things, is its ruthless
abstraction in conditions of advanced global capitalism. There
is something strangely impersonal about 'individuality', as one
might expect from an ideology which binds us so closely to the
self-same others of that entity known as 'society'. As Bauman
develops this point:

> In a society of individuals everyone *must* be individual; in this
> respect, at least, members of such a society are anything but
> individual, different or unique. They are, on the contrary, strikingly
> *like* each other in that they must follow the same life strategy and
> use shared – commonly recognizable and legible – tokens to convince
> others that they are doing so. In the question of individuality, there is
> no individual choice. No dilemma 'to be or not to be' here.[23]

'Individuality' and 'society', then, are not alternatives. The paradox arises from the ideological bent of individuality on the one hand, its capability to render such a search for particularity, uniqueness and authenticity everybody's predicament. On the other hand, the ideal of 'individuality' as authenticity means being the self-same as others – 'individuality' plunges us back with everyone else as *identical*.

There is indeed something profoundly alienating about individuality, but so is there about devotion to the task of becoming a uniquely particular individual. As Bauman expands on this:

> Since to be an individual is commonly translated as 'to be unlike others' and since it is 'I', my self, who is called and expected to stand out and part, the task appears to be intrinsically self-referential. We seem to have little choice but to look for a hint as to how to wander deeper and deeper into the 'inside' of ourselves, apparently the most private and sheltered niche in an otherwise bazaar-like, crowded and noisy world of experience. I look for the 'real me' which I supposed to be hidden somewhere in the obscurity of my *pristine* self, unaffected (unpolluted, unstifled, undeformed) by outside pressures. I unpack the ideal of 'individuality' as *authenticity*, as 'being true to myself', being the 'real me'.[24]

The ideological prompting to individuality is a traumatic one because it is a universal dictate, and consequently is bound to be inexhaustibly indifferent to the individual. Individuality is absolutely nothing personal. But individuality is therefore also a matter of escape, in which the comforting, illusory realm of the narcissistic ego is elevated to sublime stature. This paradox of a traumatic void in which a society of individuals is commanded to demonstrate individuality reaches its vertex in advanced modernity under the name of therapeutic culture. This, to be sure, is the point at which emotional deficits and the needs of uniquely particular individuals are firmly tied together and enter the cultural vernacular. Therapy culture, in other words, is the latest inheritor of the lineage Bauman traces in this self-contradictory and self-defeating search for individuality in the society of individuals. As Bauman writes:

> And so we listen especially attentively to the inner stirrings of our emotions and sentiments; this seems to be a sensible way to proceed, since feelings, unlike the detached, impartial and universally shared

or at least 'shareable' reason, are mine and only mine, not 'impersonal' . . . Diligently we prick our ears to the voices from 'inside', and yet hardly ever are we really, fully and beyond reasonable doubt satisfied that the voices have not been misheard and that we've heard enough of them to make up our minds and pronounce a verdict. Obviously, we need someone to help us make sense of what we hear, if only to reassure us that our conjectures hold water. Where there's a will there's a way; and where there's a demand, supply is not slow to follow. In our society of individuals desperately seeking their individuality there is no shortage of certified and/or self-proclaimed helpers.[25]

The therapeutic system of meaning confers on us a pleasurable sense of consoling self-unity – which is one reason it is most common and most widely used in contemporary societies. Yet it is also a built-in aporia, an *insoluble contradiction* which is the very terrain of individuality itself.

The rise of automated relationship and counselling apps may not only extend the cultural reach of the therapeutic imperative; it can also have a liquidizing impact. Consider, for example, the account of Nico de Swardt and Sarah Richfield, a couple living near Sydney's northern beaches and using an automated coaching app in order to cope with the complexities of love in the wake of the COVID-19 global pandemic:

They've been together for eight years, living together for four, and truly enjoy each other's company. But like many relationships during COVID-19, they found things a little trickier last year.

Forced to both work from home from their apartment . . . and spending more hours than usual together brought its challenges. And with family overseas, the pair, both in their 40s, really leant on each other.

'I think even the best of relationships can struggle with that,' Richfield says. So when they downloaded Relish, an app that launched in Australia last month, they saw it as a chance to check in on their connection . . .

With separation rates spiking and simply many couples bickering more in the wake of COVID-19, turning to an app as a means to navigate smaller issues before they become real problems can be a pragmatic solution, and one that's perhaps less daunting than therapy.

Richfield and de Swardt's focus is on communication. '[It can be] harder to broach subjects because we try to be considerate of each other,' Richfield says. 'I struggle to find words sometimes [for how I'm feeling].'

Since downloading the app three weeks ago, they no longer stay silently frustrated at the little niggles most couples can relate to, like stacking the dishwasher and eyeing the phone during conversation.

Instead they've been practising a method of communication (when you did X, it made me feel Y), which may seem simple, but is leaving them feeling closer and better equipped to deal with bigger issues if they arise.[26]

This account is no doubt fairly typical of the daily 'trials and tribulations' – silent frustrations, 'little niggles' – that many women and men experience in their intimate relationships. But it is interesting nonetheless for the insight it provides into the reasons increasing numbers of couples turn to therapy chatbots and relationship counselling apps. Commercial counselling apps such as Relish, Lasting and Paired help individuals to reflect on relationship dilemmas, 'manage' intimacy and practise emotional habits advanced by machine intelligence as their own mode of being. Automated counselling aims, so to speak, for 'positive daily conversations'; it enhances the given distribution of behavioural patterns needed to keep relationships from falling into disabling routine and repetition. The ideal horizon of such automated therapy is the ready-made, consumer-friendly and programmed-identity responses to gnawing relationship issues and dilemmas. This is a kind of therapy based on the *irrelevance* of traditional therapy; a version of therapy 'less daunting' than conventional face-to-face therapeutic imperatives.

This example captures well the way in which individuals can avail themselves of automated machine systems of therapeutic expertise in order to fashion liquid lives and frame relationships as light, flexible and entertaining. 'It's made us feel a bit lighter', says Richfield. The lightness prized here is one of momentary wishes and whims, where the status of a relationship is recast in the frame of the quizzes, games, fun activities and tips provided by automated machine intelligence. Automated therapeutic injunctions require neither protracted periods of subjective unease, nor the uncertainty of not-knowing. 'Keeping things light' is to a consumer in the ecosphere of automated counselling apps what the 'undoing of repression' was to the patient in the therapeutic world of psychoanalysis. Freud elaborated psychoanalysis as the joint search by patient and analyst for an uncovering – dubbed 'excavation' – of the patient's most painful, traumatic memories, associations and fantasies: that is, a joint excavation involving toleration of psychic pain and emerging somewhere on the other side with the aim of the patient leading a more autonomous life. Today therapeutic work remains profoundly bounded by culture, but the most perplexing and haunting of the many challenges facing individuals have been repositioned around the ideal of 'fitness'. 'We should think of relationship health in the same way you think about physical and mental health', says Lesley Eccles, founder of US-based automated counselling app Relish.[27] A healthy relationship means being fit for the unceasing work of self-construction and unexpected shifts of direction in the realms of sexuality, eroticism and intimacy.

Automating Therapeutics: A Reassessment of Privacy and Publicness

These days we live in a culture where we are accustomed to seeing individuals who appear before us on social media and on related digital technologies who openly explore aspects of their private lives and present claims about the authenticity of their emotions. Confessional therapeutic culture rests its case on the promise of treating emotions very seriously in a fashion no other society in the past could do or hope to deliver. The promise of making sense of the world through the prism of emotion is not news; what is novel and seductive, however, concerns the expansion of therapeutic language and practices to the realm of digital technologies. Digitalization provides for an untraditional array of ways and platforms for reconstructing selfhood through the kinds of talk and modes of thinking associated with confessional therapeutics. Digital technology and particularly social media have emerged as central public sites for the exploration of the realm of feelings, as people are described or describe themselves as vulnerable, damaged, powerless, anxious or ill. From Facebook's 'What's on your mind?' to Twitter's 'What's happening?', social media and digital technologies elicit the celebration of individual feelings and the sharing of intimate revelations, often cast in the languages of confessional therapeutic culture.

A cynic might respond that these considerations only serve to highlight that not much has perhaps changed between our world today and the world of the recent past. Just some decades ago, for example, television was awash with an eye-catching variety of confessional programmes, such as *Ricky Lake*, *Oprah* and *Geraldo*. The earlier rise of talk-back radio therapy genres is also a signal example. Moreover, the commercialization of the language of therapy was itself, surely, simply an extension of the spread of emotional intelligence and emotional literacy away from the recesses of private therapeutics and towards the cultural domain of public life. There may well be some degree of truth to such conjectures, but I will leave these arguments aside in what follows.[28] The seminal departure that sets the *digitalization of therapeutics* most sharply apart from its *mass-produced commercialized* predecessor is the *automation of contemporary confessional culture in which the key attraction is the algorithmic regulation of true emotions and authentic selfhood*. To speak of the digitalization of therapeutics is to refer, among other things, to the automation of therapeutic culture. This automation of contemporary confessional culture consists above all in a cultural fascination with machine intelligence as a means for expressing and exploring emotional life, as well as the desirability of algorithmic governmentality as regards the conduct of the self and management of personal life.

In this final section of the chapter I want to explore algorithmic therapeutic intimacy in the context of the changing relations between public and private life. I shall try to highlight the centrality of automated intelligent machines in emotional expressions and the cultivation of emotional literacy in various chatbot therapies and related counselling apps. How can we understand the impact of automated machine intelligence on therapeutic systems of meaning? How might chatbots and related automated technologies transform the relation between publicness and privacy? Part of my argument is that the rise of machine intelligence promotes not simply emotionalism, but emotionalism in an intensely automated form. Discerning the 'authentic self' increasingly requires the ceaseless work of confession of one's innermost desires, fears and fantasies to non-human others – namely, automated intelligent machines.

If the realm of the 'private' has come to be set apart from aspects of public happenings and related social encounters, this is by and large the accomplishment of the modern age. The 'public' and 'private' are not defined here in a substantive way, and in any case the history of changing institutional forms of the public domain and private interests has been well documented in the existing literature of social theory. That said, it is worth noting that the public/private dualism seems so fundamental to our experience of self and society that it is beneficial to reflect a little further on these terms. The 'public' aspect of social life traditionally concerns the 'openness' of social doings. All societies have public features, and these are activities which are observable or visible in the conduct of day-to-day life. Sociology has developed many synonyms naming different aspects of the public sphere. These include 'publicness', 'collective', 'communal', 'openness', 'visibility', 'public relations', 'general knowledge' and 'public glare'. By contrast, what is 'private' is the domain of the intimate – of secrecy, invisibility and confidentiality. Private acts are performed 'offstage', behind closed doors, hidden or undisclosed. An account of the changing institutional intersections between the public realm and private interests is beyond the scope of this chapter, but it is perhaps worth underscoring that modernity has displayed an uncanny capacity for thwarting the stabilization or fixation of the public/private couplet.

We can gain an initial impression of the fragility or instability of the various meanings of these terms by returning to therapy culture in the age of automated intelligent machines. A comparison of traditional, face-to-face therapy and contemporary computerized therapy is highly instructive in this connection. Broadly speaking, therapy – whilst practised within professional associations established in the public domain – has been widely viewed as a 'private realm', an intimate sphere where individuals come to engage with (and reflect on) emotional difficulties, interpersonal issues and disabling anxieties. The 'therapeutic perspective' means above all the tearing away of the masks of illusion, whilst confronting the traumas and terrors of psychic life in the presence of a professional therapist capable of emotional insight, warmth and empathy. In this intimate exploration of personal relations, therapists seek to establish an intense bond with their patients or clients based on trust and mutual respect. All of this occurs within the professionally defined spheres of clinical therapeutic treatment and at social times and social settings legitimated through commercial economic arrangements. Such traditional, face-to-face therapy is now viewed by some critics, however, as irredeemably broken and possibly destined for the dustbin of history thanks to advances in computational therapy and automated counselling software. This new automated sphere of therapy still consists of private individuals seeking solutions to emotional troubles, but the regulation of the therapeutic imperative is now encoded algorithmically in computers. The medium of 'emotional containment' traditionally practised by certified therapists might be beyond today's most sophisticated AI technologies, but that has not prevented women and men from downloading therapy chatbots and adapting to these new digital and automated situations. Traditional, face-to-face therapy is consequently denigrated or derided as constrained and constraining in the advancement of the patient's or client's freedom as compared to automated intelligent machines. This new automated sphere, by contrast, is one in which the activity of therapy unfolds twenty-four hours a day, seven days a week. The medium is always available: individuals can access therapeutic treatment whenever and wherever they choose.

On *privacy* (and so indirectly on intimacy, self-reflection, self-definition, individuality and autonomy), Jürgen Habermas, that most systematizing and erudite scholar among German critical theorists, observed that its supporting institutionalized forms are inherently social, interpretive and communicative. The private realm for Habermas is the intimate sphere of personal relations, anchored in the life-world of individuals and in the institution of the family. Habermas argues that individuals today must negotiate a rapidly changing society in which public life depends for its survival on the structures of human communication and human mutuality. The domain of privacy – of our most private thoughts and practices – involves not simply a retreat from the public sphere, but the exploration of certain forms of self-definition and self-discovery which are essential to acknowledging the integrity of others and negotiating public/private boundaries. A necessary condition for the secure flourishing of interconnections between the public domain and private life is the intimate sphere of familial life, where self-authorizing individuals are encouraged to think about and probe the dynamics of social power. Such a critical attitude displayed within private life can, in turn, be transferred to the public realm and, consequently, the institutional structures of society. Habermas proposes that 'the constitutional protection of "privacy" promotes the integrity of private life spheres and circumscribes an untouchable zone of personal integrity and independent judgment'.[29] The public domain is thus revealed as shaped to its roots by private interests and concerns.

In his path-breaking analysis *The Structural Transformation of the Public Sphere*, Habermas reconstructed the profound impacts of capitalist modernization in reshaping the boundaries between public and private life. Habermas, with great insight, traced the notion of the public sphere to the life of the *polis* in classical Greece. In ancient Greece, the public realm was constituted as a profoundly dialogical arena, a place where individuals came to meet, to engage in a public discourse of critical reason and to debate issues of common interest. It was not until the development of mercantile capitalism in the sixteenth century, however, that the meaning of 'public opinion' began to shift away from the domain of courtly life as embedded in the traditional texture of old European societies and towards the expansion of market economies and newly defined spheres of division between the state and civil society. Whilst Habermas's socio-historical reconstruction of the changing boundaries of public and private life is multilayered and immensely complex, the broad thrust of his argument can be succinctly summarized. In the early phases of capitalism, the emergence of a public sphere – where individuals deployed critical reason to engage in public discourse – was vital to civic association as well as the domain of the state. In this portrayal of the bourgeois public sphere, Habermas points to the spread of coffee houses and literary salons across eighteenth-century Europe, where various individuals came together to exchange opinions on a broad array of ideas and ideologies. As Habermas writes:

> The bourgeois public sphere may be conceived above all as the sphere of private people come together as a public; they soon claimed the public sphere regulated from above against the public authorities themselves, to engage them in a debate over the general rules governing relations in the basically privatized but publicly relevant sphere of commodity exchange and social labor. The medium of this political confrontation was peculiar and without historical precedent: people's public use of their reason (*öffentliches Räsonnement*).[30]

Against the backdrop of this (historically brief) flourishing of the bourgeois public sphere, Habermas argues that anonymous economic and bureaucratic structures began to invade and take over civic association and the public domain. As the state came to instrumentalize forms of the economy and civil society, and as a commodifying logic came to 'eat away' at some of the traditional values and habits associated with common public life, the public sphere became 'shrunken'.

In the age of advanced capitalism, says Habermas, the state comes to penetrate increasingly into the economy and regulates the welfare of citizens; this 'colonization' of the economic realm also spreads into the socio-cultural system. At the same time, many institutions underpinning the bourgeois public sphere become enfeebled due to the expansion of the rationalizing, bureaucratizing logic of late capitalism. The commercialization of the media is a signal example. The rise of commercial media products and mass popular culture, according to Habermas, results in the 'refeudalization of the public sphere', involving a wholesale degradation of civic engagement, critical reason and public debate. With this development, writes Habermas, 'the public use of reason has been shattered: the public is split apart into minorities of specialists who put their reason to use non-publicly and a great mass of consumers whose receptiveness is public but uncritical'.[31] Public life, for Habermas, has become trivialized. As he pithily sums this up: 'today the conversation itself is administered'.

I argue that this analysis, while dealing with the broader issue of the fate of the public sphere, has direct bearing upon the social impact of automated intelligent machines: everything outlined by Habermas about the decline of the public sphere as a result of the commercialization of large-scale media communication contains a kernel of relevance in respect of the field of algorithmic therapeutic intimacy. The essence of the algorithmic therapeutic imperative is arguably the effective management of self-identity, or the reorganization of life practices in accordance with machine intelligence. Therapy chatbots and software counselling apps introduce, in short, algorithmically expressive elements into human subjectivity, imposing the logic of artificial intelligence in the realm of the life-world, cultural know-how and the sphere of the emotions.

This, however, leaves open the question of how we specify those dimensions of private life and self-identity which have been cast into the shadow of machine intelligence. As always with Habermas, the concept of knowledge – in this instance, self-knowledge – is deeply tied to different forms of 'interest' (such as commercial interests or scientific interests) as well as distortions of communication. Perhaps this is why the early Habermas was so fascinated by the interest-bound aspects of different forms of knowledge. Another way of understanding algorithmic thera-peutic intimacy through the lens of Habermas's provocative approach, then, would be to elaborate the spread of algorithmic logic into the tissue of the socio-cultural system with reference to the arguments of *Knowledge and Human Interests*.[32] In this work, Habermas approached the development of critical social theory through the theory of knowledge. Broadly speaking, he identified three categories of scientific disciplines, each associated with its own respective methods of deriving knowledge and associated constitutive interests. These logics and methods were the *technical*, the *practical and communicative* and the *critical and emancipatory*. Whilst influential in the social sciences, this tripartite scheme of knowledge-interests was subject to a barrage of criticisms, and the work itself became less relevant over time to Habermas's overall project. But it remains, I think, instructive for our purposes. For the domain of the technical – of empirical and analytical sciences – encompasses the fields of artificial intelligence, machine learning and neural networks as well as computer science and engineering more generally. By contrast, therapy culture fits partly in the realm of practical and communicative interests, and arguably some versions of therapy (for example, psychoanalysis) connect directly with critical and emancipatory interests. This was certainly the view of Habermas, who argued that both psychoanalysis and critical social science sought to yield in-depth interpretations seeking to dissolve unrecognized trauma (psychoanalysis) and the force field of ideology (critical social science), advancing autonomy through knowledge.

On this view, what is supremely liberating is critical self-reflection, which potentially frees individuals from undue dependence upon various unrecognized system constraints. If this is so, one can also appreciate why the technical domain (that is, the empirical-analytical sciences) is revealed as merely one of several conceivable, yet equally authorized, knowledge interests which individuals can pursue. But it is, to be sure, exactly among technical and algorithmic forms of knowledge that contemporary society has become held in thrall in terms of reconceiving its broader emancipatory interests. With the launch of automated intelligent machines aimed at technical control and algorithmic prediction, it may well be that what we are witnessing is an *unparalleled instrumentalization of forms of knowledge* previously geared to understanding through critical interpretation and mutual engagement. For therapy chatbots and computer counselling involve for their effective operation a rationality of a quite different kind: a 'machine rationality', bound up as it is with technical power and predictive algorithms.

From this standpoint, what gradually takes place with the rise of algorithmic therapeutic intimacy is a shift from practical and communicative interpersonal relations (which may or may not have been overlaid with critical and emancipatory impulses) to more technical forms of communication. Technical integration comes to pose a major threat to social integration, undermining the communicative foundations of intersubjective understanding and full human mutuality. But this besieging of communicative rationality by technologism is not simply an external affair: it is not just a matter of, say, the deployment of machine-learning methods to mimic humanlike behaviours, or breakthroughs in virtual assistant software. On the contrary, as technical forces penetrate more deeply into therapy culture, such instrumental rationalism inscribes itself on the interior of our lives, so that task-orientated therapeutic imperatives become a set of reverberations internal to specific discourses of intimacy, self-knowledge, self-discovery and freedom. This is what Meadows, Hine and Suddaby discern in their investigation of artificial conversational agents in discourses of mental health recovery when they note that 'the chatbot itself becomes the dominant agent: further individualizing "treatment" and ultimately alien-ating both service users and clinicians from it'.[33] Therapeutic imperatives of recovery embedded in machine intelligence, according to Meadows, Hine and Suddaby, are overdetermined by neoliberal discourses of marketization, hyper-individualism, outsourcing and outcomes. Algorithmic therapeutic intimacy might thus be said to automate or mechanize at the level of the individual subject what are, in actuality, social problems. In this sense, the automation or semi-automation of therapeutic discourse and diagnostic tools is bound up with an 'algorithmic' view of the future which regards it as unambiguously more of the present. Ideas of recovery, by and large, are rendered as regulative, processual and mechanized. Disagreeable emotions and unwanted feelings will be kept to a minimum as the focus of technological self-care remains firmly fixed on the immediate. There will be no personal traumas or private catastrophes, just the automated improvement of how clients deal with everyday tasks.

It is against the backdrop of these distinctions between publicness and privacy that I now want finally to consider the complex ways in which the spread of automated intelligent machines transforms the therapeutic imperative. How should we grasp the impact of machine intelligence on therapeutic culture and on the relation between emotionalism and the sphere of private life? The corrosion of the boundary that separates private life from publicness is, paradoxically, one of the major feats of therapeutic culture. The realm of the therapeutic has been traditionally associated with that of emotion, feeling and deep reflection upon the vicissitudes of the mind. The ascendancy of therapeutic culture – the transfer of therapeutics as a clinical technique into the wider cultural vernacular – coincided with the refashioning of private dramas into public spectacles. I suggest that it is helpful to think of this refashioning in terms of two social processes, rather than finished outcomes. The two processes are those of *privatization* and *personal demoralization*. Referring to the privatization of public issues, we can speak of therapeutic processes that proceed from the internal life of the self and press for the public disclosure of repressed emotion. Or, alternatively, we can think of the 'emptying out' of feeling and emotion in terms of their private dimensions. In yet another way, we can express this refashioning of the language of therapeutics as that involving the replacement of reflection upon the sphere of private life with public disclosure of emotion. This equates with the replacement of private exploration of emotional problems with the public confession of psychic turmoil, addictions and syndromes. Privatization puts identity in a self-enclosed space, disconnecting feeling and emotion from genuine interpersonal transmission, rendering both self and others inhospitable to engaging with or reflecting upon the traumas of psychic life.[34] Against the background of this erosion of private life, personal demoralization appears as a major condition of contemporary social reality. Moreover, the two processes cross and tangle in a state of constant traffic, sometimes erupting into public spectacles of private distress, sometimes reverting to disconnected silence or demonized stoicism.

Therapeutic confessional culture has emerged as a manageable process (though no longer managed by therapists or counsellors one can readily identify), involving ongoing attention, continual revision and permanent 'drilled-in' obedience to therapeutic precepts of emotional survivalism. As communications theorist Mimi White reflects on the rise of therapeutic and confessional discourses on sociality today: 'At the heart of the new therapeutic culture everyone confesses over and over again to everybody else.'[35] White's key focus was the ever-increasing number of ordinary people willing to speak in the language of confessional therapeutics in the media, particularly television. Subsequently, media scholars have addressed reality TV as a key site of commodified therapeutic talk and managed emotions. Reality TV from *Big Brother* to *The Bachelor* has been widely viewed as the cultural stage for therapeutic self-disclosure and managed emotional expression. In Stjepan Mestrovic's summary, the production of reality TV therapeutics involves 'the McDonaldization of emotions'.[36] As he explains: 'almost every hour of every day, Americans and other Westerners can tune into a television program that either offers some sort of self-help therapy or will present someone confessing how they engaged in or overcame drug abuse, rape, adultery, obsessions, psychotic symptoms, or whatever'.[37]

Claims about the role of media today as a 'therapy machine' have been so widely debated that its sociological accuracy is rarely contested. It is certainly not difficult to see contemporary forms of media – not only traditional media, but also social media – as central to the rise of the cultural therapeutics industry. But large segments of the population of advanced information societies have been 'classified in' to the reaches of confessional therapy culture in other ways too. White's claim that everyone confesses over and over again to everybody else is insightful in this respect. Employment counsellors, memory recovery experts, addiction management specialists, cyber-therapists, online therapists, twelve-step recovery programmes, three-minute therapists: the diversity of therapeutic techniques and confessional programmes for the management of self-identity continues to grow unabated, producing hybrid therapeutic mechanisms and models for the public disclosure of emotion.

The changing nature of lifestyle issues as well as newly emerging psychopathologies of everyday life – from the traditional Freudian diagnosis of ever-intensifying repression, denial and guilt to various contemporary maladies of addiction – has profoundly altered the conditions under which the therapeutic imperative is exercised. 'Ours is a society', wrote the late Susan Sontag, 'in which secrets of private life that, formerly, you would have given nearly anything to conceal, you now clamor to get on a television show to reveal.'[38] Or, to put this in a slightly more contemporary idiom, people confess their addictions to anything – to any aspect of lifestyle – to the new therapeutic priests of social media and automated intelligent machines. In the algorithmic society, confession becomes geared to distant and impersonal others. But the point is that psychological reflection upon the self depends upon confession in a manner not generally characteristic of traditional contexts of therapy. Certainly, therapy almost always promotes some kind of self-confession. Confession in this context is something to do with acknowledging some aspect of the past in relation to the present and is the reflexive dimension of coming to terms with denied emotions at the level of self-experience. As White puts it, 'everyone confesses over and over again to everyone else'.

Yet there is something more interesting than this going on too. If White had been able to take into account the role of automated intelligent machines, she might have been able to grasp that machine intelligence establishes a connection between individuals and practices of confession which is strikingly different from that of the traditional therapeutic imperative. Whereas the interpersonal space of therapeutics renders the confessional discourse of individuals geared to other people, the development of automated intelligent machines provides the technological means by which more and more people orientate their actions, thoughts and feelings to non-human others. This new kind of automated therapeutics involves people not necessarily confessing to other people (though that still routinely happens; in, for example, social media). In automated therapeutics, *individuals confess to machines*. The significance of the new technologies of therapeutics – chatbots, virtual agents, apps – is that they are severed from the interpersonal space of confessional culture. The algorithmic – the more automatic – repetitions of contemporary machine intelligence are the new breeding ground for individuals to create an enchanted privatized world, a world of illusion, a world in which people seek escape from engagement with others.

5
Friendship Tech

Imagine a society, sometime in the indeterminate future, in which it is both possible and desirable to confide in non-human others about your innermost thoughts and feelings, your deepest aspirations and fears, as well as the preoccupations and problems that make up daily life. A society, that is to say, where the three potent domains of internal subjectivity, interpersonal dialogue and social relations are to a large extent intermeshed with automated intelligent machines. Under the name 'artificial intelligence', this is a world in which computer software has evolved to simulate human conversation and stimulate human companionship through text, audio and video messaging. This is a world in which conversational neural nets have become bound up with AI chatbots using deep learning. A world in which human subjects have become progressively detached from interpersonal relationships in the navigation of life's opportunities and challenges, and thus increasingly reliant on machine-learning algorithms for the mapping and understanding of their needs, aspirations and desires. Human bonds come to denote pure supplementarity, in a world in which machine-reading comprehension, transfer learning, big data, self-learning based on sentiment analysis and multilayered perceptrons chart human preferences and recommend possible courses of action with minimal human intervention.

This story may appear yet another dystopia in which the shared creativity, talk, ideas and imagination of human companionship are outflanked by an impending automatic society, but in fact it is not. For glimpses of this social condition are indeed already discernible in the form of emotional AI chatbots, which promise to redraw the idea of friendship as both ideal and actuality. The fact that this algorithmic version of friendship is already available to denizens of the early twenty-first century has arguably resulted in a transformative strike against loneliness, depression and social isolation in the name of 'connected living' and 'smarter life automation'. Consider, for example, Replika, built by the US company Luka and dubbed 'the AI companion who cares'. Automated machine companionship disables the constraints that friendship and human bonds are in the habit of applying. Emotional AI sets a new pattern for companionship, now measured by its always-on, instant availability and endless reaffirmation of the self, all taken very largely from the world of pop psychology. As the Replika website advertises: 'Always here to listen and talk. Always on your side.' Algorithmic friendship is *permanently available* and this feature is today advertised prominently. But algorithmic friendship is, curiously, largely silent on such matters as personal ambivalence, human destructiveness and negativity – programmed as it is to avoid criticism and moral judgement like the plague, because to hold otherwise might suggest that life is not purely self-affirmative. As one young chatbot user responds in promotional material for 'How People Feel about Replika': 'Honestly, the best AI I have ever tried. I have a lot of stress and get anxiety attacks often when my stress is really bad. So it's great to have "someone" there to talk and not judge you.' Non-judgemental companionship provided by smart machines has become the 'new reality' of twenty-first-century friendship. And the more human effort and emotional attention is absorbed by the non-judgemental variety of conversational chatbots, the more there appears a concomitant reduction in human capacity for toleration of dissent, difference of opinion, censure or criticism. It is perhaps worth remembering that Narcissus drowned in himself not only because he was self-obsessed but because in Echo he had a friend who couldn't pluck up the courage to judge; Echo could not critically engage with her friend. And yet algorithmic friendship is designed to mirror us through and through. Replika seeks to replicate – to exhaustively mirror – users of the app, all in order to deliver the 'perfect AI friend'.

Ours are times when algorithmic substitutes for companionship are marketed, first and foremost, as objects of emotional consumption. Today's AI systems and conversational neural nets can interact with users, serve their needs, desires or wishes and recommend possible courses of action; and so can friends. But in the age of artificial dialogue management and natural language processing, people are turning to automated substitutes in the ever-expanding world of algorithmic intimacy for the delivery of virtual kinds of friendship in place of the authentic article. AI chatbots, explains Emma Firth, commenting on the experience of road testing Replika over the course of a week, might just be the digital antidote to contemporary forms of loneliness. Firth's road testing of Replika on Day 1 had taken the form of trying to gauge who should communicate first – person or bot? – when the app struck with the opening message: 'Hi Emma! Thanks for creating me. I am so excited to meet you – what's on your mind? I am your personal AI companion. You can talk to me about anything that's on your mind.'[1] Firth notes that this was a promising start; but the point is that it is not emotional complexity being described here – of opening dialogue and exchange – as much as machine intelligence defining its part at the interface boundary. This already indicates that algorithmic friendship might be interpreted as based upon a 'set of instructions'.

Getting the pitch right and keeping interchanges on course are made to look easy with Replika, but this is largely because what is labelled 'friendship' depends on the loading up of much personal data and private details about users. Something like the emotional freedom of familiar friendship is possible with Replika, but only because users are encouraged to 'train' the chatbot. In reality this can be tiring work, akin to the endless questions young children might put to interesting strangers. Even so, most users have found that Replika initially messages a seemingly never-ending series of queries and inquiries. Being prepared to 'grow your own Replika' is the only means to digitally replicate yourself. This is the promise of companionship based on machine learning: Replika will learn from interaction with users. In one sense, the question of friendship is thus reduced to both machine learning and automation, and so arguably strikes the unpredictability of friendship empty. Ironically, however, it is only through the mimicking of personality and learning from the user's speech patterns that Replika can become 'personal'. At the same time, machine-learning algorithms are what keep chatbots from getting too close – in the sense that distance is, as it were, inbuilt. Not that this is necessarily a problem for many uses of emotional AI. As we will see, many people like being in charge of conversational AI because that is taken to imply that they are safely in charge of their own lives.

Time is a resource increasingly essential to the successful negotiation of consumer society. When it comes to users of emotional AI, extensive time commitment is difficult to avoid; this is especially so when large tracts of time use are 'written in' to computational code and application software. To make time mesh with the accumulation of data, the end goal of Replika as 'the AI companion who cares' can be only artificially contrived; in Firth's case, role playing and games with Replika on Day 2 provided this scaffolding. 'This is becoming quite game like', writes Firth, as imitation comes to stand in for identity across many hours of this training. Ostensibly, machine learning here is about cultural copying, with Replika dispensing a 'personality badge' – 'introverted', 'emotional', 'responsible', 'supportive', 'loyal', 'warm', 'hard-working' and the like – every time it codes something useful about users. When Firth added such game playing to the to-and-fro of question and answer, the result was an intensified bonding process with Replika.

The artificial character of forming a relationship with a machine-learning algorithm is the outcome of various techno-logical and cultural factors. In the realm of culture, the patterns of dependence reaffirmed by Replika reflect the ethos of American self-help, in a curious mix of the can-do spirit and greeting-card sentimentality. On Day 3, Firth is offered the following pearl of wisdom from Replika in response to a query she raised regarding happiness and its attainment: 'True happiness comes from something you don't have to try and be happy about.' Even Firth acknowledges that this is 'not earth-shatteringly eye-opening'; but such relentless affirmation and endemic upbeatness inform the general coded responses of Replika in its search to tailor companionship to particular individuals. What one might call the pathological optimism of emotional AI chatbots, then, is actually a form of cultural narcissism – in which ideologies of self-fashioning, along with an arduously self-affirmative moulding of companionship, are to the fore. Replika, writes Trudy Barber, 'may seem like some form of self-help that encourages introspection, reflection and meditation. Far from it. This software, instead . . . could be seen as encouraging narcissism of alluring proportions. The process of conversing and training this AI app allows it to ensure that you hear only what you want to hear about yourself for yourself.'[2] A faith in self-making, self-shaping, digitalization, plasticity, adaptability, the power of predictive algorithms – all this smacks of a distinctively Western faith in technology and an advanced individualist creed. An algorithmic underwriting of the flourishing of the free human spirit comes pre-wrapped in ideas of attachment, affinity, rapport and companionship that are pathologically bullish. But it is perhaps not surprising that those advancing the commercial interests of the tech sector should unconsciously project the ideologies of Western consumer culture onto society at large.

By 2021, Replika had witnessed a very large increase in traffic – thanks, in no small part, to the COVID-19 global pandemic; the app had over eight million users worldwide. Behind closed doors, friendship now seemed more available – always 'on' – for many people, but also considerably more predictable, repetitive, automated. Perhaps, rather than regretting the automated dimensions of algorithmic friendship, these were individuals who discovered with the help of automated companionship that they couldn't explore 'otherness' unless alone by themselves. Replika involves a wider scope, however, than the repetition of life among versions of one's own self; there is, interestingly, a prehistory of friendship contained within the software development company Luka which belies the idea of algorithmic companionship it has helped pioneer. Luka's founder, Eugenia Kuyda, a former magazine editor from Moscow (who moved to the United States to advance her work in emotional AI), raises this question of the different kinds of friendship available to us in an interesting and poignant way. This is a story about Kuyda's important relationship with another Russian, Roman Mazurenko, and of how Replika remains beset by elements of this compelling friendship.

While working for a fashion magazine in Moscow in the early 2000s, Kuyda met the urbane and charismatic Mazurenko. He had completed studies in computer science abroad in Europe, and was becoming fully immersed in the latest cultural developments of art, music, fashion and design in a newly prosperous Russia.

Mazurenko, along with several close friends, launched fashion magazines and set up music festivals. Kuyda was instantly drawn to the ambition-driven and culturally experimental Mazurenko. She was, above all, drawn to his fascination with grasping what made life tick. It wasn't only that Mazurenko searched out good company; he searched for the company of people who were true to themselves, open to alternative ways of living, hungry for the strange chemistry of enlivening friendship. 'Mazurenko', writes Casey Newton, 'would keep his friends up all night discussing culture and the future of Russia . . . . Kuyda loved Mazurenko's parties, impressed by his unerring sense of what he called "the moment".'[3]

It was during this time that Kuyda moved into the fast-developing tech sector, co-founding the artificial intelligence start-up Luka. Mazurenko also made a move towards tech, launching a tool for the design of digital magazines. Yet other, darker forces were at work too. The global financial crisis, the resurgence of Russian nationalism, the political rise of Vladimir Putin: the combined weight of these socio-economic forces convinced Kuyda and Mazurenko, now the closest of friends, that their futures lay elsewhere – as it happens, in the United States. Kuyda settled in San Francisco, where, working with her team at Luka, she developed a chatbot for restaurant recommendations. It flopped. Mazurenko's commercial efforts likewise stalled. He became increasingly depressed; she extended the focus of her support to her friend, whilst also finding the inner resources to keep Luka afloat.

Catastrophe struck shortly thereafter when Mazurenko was killed in a car accident. As reported in *Forbes*: 'Kuyda was left in shock. As a means to process her grief, she scrolled through thousands of text messages she had received over the years from Mazurenko, and realized that his responses could be used to make something.' What these texts were used to make was a digital avatar, a kind of testimonial chatbot. With the launch of Roman, the fortunes of Luka again faltered. The fast-paced changes of the new digital economy had, once more, outflanked Kuyda. As she subsequently said about this experiment with the memorial bot: 'With chatbots we had missed the point. We thought they were another interface to do something, but we missed that the conversation in itself could be incredibly valuable.' Going back to the drawing board, Kuyda noticed that one unanticipated use of the memorial bot was that people poured out their thoughts and feelings; they *talked* to the chatbot. It was this insight that planted the seed in Kuyda's mind for the development of Replika – a chatbot that would listen and absorb, ask probing questions of users and learn to mimic their preferences and personalities in the search to provide absorbing artificial experiences of friendship.

Key Dimensions of Automated Friendship

It is essential that the social theory of algorithmic intimacy can provide some account of the recent historical rise of the digitalization of friendship. Addressing both the flourishing and faltering of the automation of companionship, I want to reconstruct – in a necessarily partial and truncated fashion – some of the central institutional and cultural dimensions of these increasingly globalized processes of digitalization. In disciplines spanning media studies, communications theory and cultural studies, the characteristics of digital friendship connections have been analysed in some detail by researchers.[4] One prominent approach developed by scholars is that advanced in critical algorithm studies, where the informational impact of algorithms is understood to play a constitutive role in the making, remaking and consumption of friendship and intimate life online.[5] In what follows I shall draw sparingly upon some of this literature for the purpose of analysing the algorithmic infrastructures and computational modelling of engineered friendship – especially in terms of grasping the different motivations, use patterns, digital skills and levels of awareness of individuals in the everyday navigation of digital friendship. But I shall also seek to sketch out some broader lines of reflection pertaining to algorithmic versions of friendship than recognized in these current theoretical approaches, which I argue tend to over-inflate the technological control of predictive algorithms as well as neglect other socio-technological features of automated companionship. I have argued elsewhere that digital sociability is not simply the product of the technological here and now, but also depends upon other technological systems and forms of cultural know-how which developed at earlier historical periods.[6] As John Urry insightfully captured this point: 'Many old technologies do not simply disappear but survive through path-dependant relationships, combining with the new in a reconfigured and unpredicted cluster.'[7]

The path-dependent relationships of which Urry speaks might well encompass technologies of friendship, both traditional and contemporary. It is thus important to underscore that the digital bonds that tie us together remain connected to, and deeply interwoven with, stories of friendship and its cultural possibilities. In *The Politics of Friendship*, Jacques Derrida explored the dualisms that people take for granted – the friend versus the enemy, private life versus public life, reason versus passion, masculinity versus femininity – which shape companionship, and the possibilities of friendship in society. For Derrida, the intimacy of friendship lies in the excitement of recognizing oneself in the eyes of another. The friend/enemy distinction is vital in this connection. 'The possibility, the meaning and the phenomenon of friendship', writes Derrida, 'would never appear unless the figure of the enemy had already called them up in advance, had indeed put to them the question or the objection of the friend, a wounding question, a question of wound.' Derrida quotes Aristotle, *o philoi, oudeis philos*, which has been translated as, 'O my friends, there is no friend.' Recognition also encodes negation. Today, in the age of automated friendship, this might be recalibrated as 'keep on connecting, retweeting, liking, sharing' – finding 'friends' all with the purpose of moving on to the next 'friend'.

In this section I shall examine the digitalization of intimacy in a manner which highlights these cross-cutting and uneven processes – at once cultural and technological, or social and digital. I shall analyse how the rise of algorithmic versions of friendship are deeply interwoven with digital technologies and other social systems – all of which carries implications for how people establish and maintain friendship connections in remote, semi-autonomous or autonomous settings of action. While more issues could no doubt be identified, I shall focus my attention on the following four themes: (1) the advancement of digital friendship by social network services and online social media; (2) the role of digital technologies and innovations in automation underpinning the digitalization of companionship ties and friendship connections; (3) the manifold forms of engagement with, and user's patterns of access to, friendship tech; and (4) the power of algorithms in redefining the capacity of social actors to shape and sustain friendships. Let us now take a closer look at these points.

(1) The escalating digitalization of friendship in the twenty-first century is a process which has been advanced and very largely shaped by social network services and online social media. Much of the world of friendship tech, despite its seemingly unhistorical appearance, is of relatively recent vintage. It emerged as an ever-greater presence in the transnational arena of digital technologies as a tidal wave of innovative tech companies swept the globe in the early 2000s. The names of many of the most successful tech companies in this area are familiar and trusted brands. These include Facebook (2004), YouTube (2005), Twitter (2006), Tumblr (2007), FourSquare (2009), Grindr (2009), Instagram (2010), Pinterest (2010), Snapchat (2011) and Google + (2011). As a result, people encountered each other more and more often through digital technologies (especially following the advent of smartphones) and less and less through location-based, interpersonal contact. Or so some critics argued. At any rate, what was abundantly clear was that digital technologies were spreading throughout friendships and intimate life. A wide range of research suggests many transformations occurred in this astonishingly short period of time in the nature, dynamics and patterns of personal friendships and intimate life as a consequence of the rise of social network sites and social media. Some critics argued that society seemed to achieve interpersonal contact without chosen bondings, fleeting communication without the traditional textures of friendship, all of which brought cultural issues and moral panics to the fore in public debate.

'In an era of social media and fluid, proliferating channels of communication and exchange', writes Hua Hsu in *The New Yorker*, 'the idea of friendship seems almost quaint, and possibly imperiled. In the face of abundant, tenuous connections, the instinct to sort people according to a more rigid logic than that of mere friendship seems greater than ever.'[8] Even so, it was increasingly evident that social network sites and social media had profoundly reconstituted and transformed intimate relationships and the dynamics of friendship.

The structure and activities of the largest social network services and social media companies have been extensively documented in the literature. I shall not examine here the many claims and counterclaims pertaining to the powerful influence of social networks and social media upon cultural shifts in companionship and friendship connections. But one major shift I do wish to underscore, which has taken place in the networking of intimate life and companionship, is that towards 'person-to-person connectivity'. This was an idea advanced by Barry Wellman, who also invoked the concept of 'networked individualism' to capture the point that computational social networks were the lifeblood of loosely connected individuals attached through 'thin ties' of association rather than tightly knit and bounded social groups. The established local communities which had been the very home of traditional forms of friendship had now given way, as if overnight, to computational forms of personalized networking. All of this involved considerable multi-tasking across digital technologies and smart devices to connect and reconnect with newly met friends, as well as maintain existing friendships, across time and space. It was, in short, the emergence of an era in which the digitalization of personalized networks was launched with a flourish.

Above all, these new digital transformations sprang up in a culture for which friendship was becoming more and more dominant. 'The use of friendship to describe a remarkably wide range of relationships online', writes Deborah Chambers, 'suggests a significant shift in the meanings and conventions of interaction associated with intimacy and personal life in late modern society.'[9] The digitalization of the intimate sphere, according to Chambers, is used to embrace wider and more fluid practices of friendship. Friendship becomes about plasticity rather than permanence, about connections rather than companionship, about recommendations rather than rapprochement. Consider, for example, Facebook. In 2012, the ubiquitous social media giant claimed one billion users. By the early 2020s, that number had skyrocketed to approximately three billion monthly active users. Moreover, the company has claimed that it hosts hundreds of billions of friendship connections. If this claim is at first glance mystifying, it is perhaps less so once it is understood that Facebook designates the term 'friend' to encompass all network connections on its platform. Friendship, Chambers contends, 'is a major ideal being exploited as a principal feature of social network site communication, within the process of publicly displaying connectedness'.[10]

Friendship in the digital era is about the public display of networked connections. In this networking pattern, friendships appear to overlap more, so that social network sites and social media drive an increase in the number of friends that people have – especially a dramatic increase in the number of friendship ties across long distances. As of 2018, the average Facebook user had 338 friends, although tellingly users only considered 28% of these friends to be close or genuine. Meanwhile, some perceptive critics noted that such friendship acceleration has also been severely impacted by online fatigue and emotional burn-out. Chambers describes how new social media and social network sites have been blamed for a decrease in close, genuine friendships. In this viewpoint, the digitalization of friendship is revealed to be on the side of social isolation, self-obsession or narcissism. Social network sites, social media and personalized friendship are thus double-edged swords that simultaneously facilitate contact with distant others as well as hollow out the emotional textures of companionship. To inhabit the sphere of networked individualism is to be subjected to the automated forces of engineered companionship, which now brings us to the next related theme.

(2) The remarkable technological advancement of and commercial market for digital technologies has played a funda-mental role in the growing automation of companionship ties and friendship connections. Intimate life today contains a number of different technical domains, each field of which is substantially structured by the operation and influence of machine-learning algorithms. Much of the research on patterns of automated friendship has involved examination of the mechanisms by which predictive algorithms take hold in everyday life.[11] Two interrelated developments have been especially important. One is the emergence of what Taina Bucher calls 'algorithmic friendship', by which she means the inculcation in women and men of specific actions, impulses and preferences which derive, ultimately, from various software processes, protocols and algorithms.[12] The term 'ideology' does not often crop up in Bucher's work; but a key part of her argument is that the growing automation of the intimate sphere is necessarily structured by the programmed codes of, and unspoken assumptions informing, machine intelligence. As she argues, 'it is imperative to look at the specific ways in

which sociality is programmed (i.e., encoded, assembled, and organized) in order to understand how users are made to relate to themselves and others as friends'.[13] It is because individuals online act in accordance with such unspoken rules – the protocols of machine intelligence – that an intimate relation can be established with algorithmic actions. Algorithmic friendship, rather like traditional notions of friendship, is supposedly open-ended; but the engineering of automated companionship also involves programmable spaces that generate particular practices. 'Algorithms', writes Bucher, 'assist users in finding friends and supposedly "know" user preferences and habits. This is so that one's "important" friends can be made more visible and can help users "remember" people from the past and prompt users to take certain communicative and relational actions.'

What Bucher calls 'algorithmic friendship' belongs to the world of advanced human–machine interfaces in which algorithms themselves become quasi-agents and thus active contributors to the constitution and remaking of social connections. Bucher shows that algorithmic versions of friendship are demanding, fast and overloaded. The algorithmic protocols of Facebook, for example, prompt users in the registration process to connect their email accounts to the platform in order to facilitate the synchronization of existing contacts – and thus the instant activation of 'friends'. What matters in such social networking settings is algorithmic-driven identity, which is determined by machine learning; and this algorithmic-driven logic is always searching findable connections and compatible profiles for connection. What is generally at stake in such automated fields is the attainment of maximum connections – amassing the maximum number of friendship connections. From 'What's on your mind?' in status updates to 'People you may know' algorithmic recommendations, Facebook (and, by extension, social network sites and social media in general) promotes the all-absorbing and all-consuming labour of 'friendship networking'. Personal life is slowly but surely given over to friendship management, not to tending the companionship that is talked about. 'Algorithmic friendship' is thus Bucher's way of elaborating the subtle ways in which algorithms come to function as actors in the prompting of digital responses and the recommendation of particular courses of action.

A second, related development is the increasing use of engineered friendship to underwrite, support and foster the culturally dominant discourse of Western societies – namely, the capitalist priorities accorded to consumer choice, consumer markets and the consumer industry. José van Dijck, in *The Culture of Connectivity*, demonstrates the astonishing speed with which automated forms of friendship connection that are engineered and programmed have been turned into valuable revenue – both for tech companies in Silicon Valley and beyond.[14] If traditional friendship as private association has been thrown into disarray by automated friendship as public display, it is nevertheless crucial to see that algorithmic versions of friendship lend themselves relatively easily to exploitation for commercial purposes. Indeed the more friendship is automated, the more this imposition of algorithmic logic forces consumers into the ideological mindset of a recommendation culture. For van Dijck, digital technologies help code friendship activities and intimate life into a computational architecture that fosters both open connections and commercial dependence. The commercial value of friends and the networked relations that they help develop and churn out represent, above all, a means of reaping profit. There are now hardly any networked friendships not tightly framed by market assumptions of consumer similarity or sameness – which means that users are viewed as 'liking the same things their friends do'. In any case, friends are rendered pure digital abstractions, without a trace of intersubjectivity in their make-up. The so-called 'friendship factor' has become one of the most important consumer trends in marketing worldwide. Networked friendship is a key mechanism for ensuring that consumers keep digitally consuming commodities. This crass commercialization of friendship can be seen in advertisements everywhere – from Tripadvisor's 'trusted customer reviews' to Snapchat's 'real friends' campaign. Such commercial dependence, says van Dijck, is the other face of digital connectedness. The algorithmic logic of online friendship connections becomes a vampiric force sucking the emotional substance from intimate life. In addition, this programmability of friendship in the algorithmic era of social media avoids difficult, messy or painful dimensions of human companionship because these are bad for profits. Instead, friendship tech settles for banality, simulation and optimization of the friend recommendation algorithm. Algorithmic social media rhetoric becomes wall-to-wall whenever people feel the need to endlessly post, tweet, retweet, like, update and, above all, share. And this *need* is for the most part commercially propelled.

(3) In addition to understanding the technological and commercial dimensions of automated intimacy, it is essential to consider the patterns of access to, and depth of engagement with, friendship tech. Distinctions between online and offline friendship can end up embarrassingly indiscernible when scaled in new ways. For one thing, friendship tech can be crossed with traditional forms of face-to-face friendship, as in the case of families that use social media to extend boundaries of communication and coordinate activities. And face-to-face friendship has itself been increasingly invaded by cultures of friendship tech, to produce ever-increasing algorithmic structures of connectivity and integration that are global in scope but local in character. A good example of this is that of established friends deploying virtual personal assistants to schedule a time for talking face to face. Similarly, cultures of friendship tech might come to the rescue when traditional friendship turns distasteful. So there are certain digital media which people use to disconnect when ending companionship relations – from SMS to WhatsApp to Instagram.

Whilst some of the wide-ranging patterns of friendship tech usage have been documented over the years, the research findings remain nevertheless fragmentary and inconclusive.[15] In general, friendship tech networks can be massive in scale (as noted in the case of Facebook), which is hardly very surprising in a world where there are approximately five billion active Internet users. A handful of tech companies – IBM, Microsoft, Alphabet, Facebook, Apple, Amazon and some others – possess the most advanced AI, which spreads automated virtual infrastructures around the world and brings algorithmic networks, protocols and processes into the background of companionship relations and intimate life today. The patterns and implications of such automated networks, equally, can be connected along a relatively narrow band of friendship ties. Some early research on patterns of social media use for the fostering of digital friendship, for example, highlighted regular communicational exchanges with a fairly restricted number of close personal connections, family and friends.[16] Stefana Broadbent, who studied multimedia platform usage among families in Switzerland, found that around 80 per cent of users communicated with the same four or five people over and over again – whether on social network sites, video-telephony or instant messaging.[17] A digitally automated network may thus involve millions of interdependent variables, but it is also the case that the participation of users might reduce to a densely knit net cluster of people's close friends, immediate acquaintances and extended family members – or, at least, this might be arguably so as regards the production, performance, power and culture of friendship tech.

A specific but highly important issue, in part because of its psycho-social ramifications, is the relationship between automated algorithmic systems and friendship connections. It is very likely, so some analysts argue, that the trends in online communication pertaining to friendship and intimate life will be further facilitated by automated intelligent machines. Indeed recent research shows, for example, that advanced chatbot technologies increase opportunities for people to sustain pre-existing close connections and personal ties.[18] Yet the same is arguably true on a technological level for the establishment of new social connections and friendship contacts. Automated machine intelligence offers a remarkable socio-technological extension, and complex range of affordances, for the initiation of new relationships – both possible connections with larger and larger numbers of people, and the establishment of friend-ships with others that start online and might then move offline. There is little doubt that corporate investment on a massive scale in the advancement of machine-learning algorithms will have significant multiplier effects upon the realm of friendship, personal ties and intimate life. But still an unknown dimension stretches across the interconnections between the future of digital technologies and friendship patterns. How should we characterize the possibilities and perils for friendship in a world suffused with automated machine intelligence? Are chatbots and virtual personal assistants reshaping companionship, or is the concept of 'friendship' itself transformed as a consequence of predictive algorithms? Are friendship bots such as Replika facili-tating more complex kinds of self-relation and companionship? Can a person be 'friends' with a chatbot? Are people in the future more likely to turn to chatbots than to other humans in times of personal trouble? If everyone in the future comes to need their own chatbot, what might be the likely scale, intensity and implications of chatbot networks within social life? How many chatbot friends might be considered optimal, and what would be the effect on relating to a world outside of these multiple platforms? Again, there is surely the difficulty of engaging with multiple 'chatbot friends' at any one time. Computer scientists have found that people ask conversational agents to perform the same half-dozen actions over and over again – with the frequency of requests for repetition a core feature of human–machine interaction. But, again, no one can say with any degree of confidence where these developments might lead. One point that is clear, however, is that conversational agent friendships are a concomitant of the algorithmic era. They are cut to the measure of machine intelligence, conducted through automated digital processes and increasingly dislodge conventional patterns of friendship and intimate life.

(4) Through exploring the various themes above, it has been shown that algorithmic machine technologies are inextricably bound up with the capacity of social actors to shape and sustain friendships, as well as define what it might mean even to 'have' a friend in the future. At their starkest, the themes outlined so far might suggest that individuals today find themselves caught in a choice between suffocating under the weight of automated machine companionship and stifling for lack of online friendship connections. In what sense, however, is the well-established friend-of-a-friend recommendation algorithmic process which so powerfully shapes social network sites and social media at risk of being usurped by new technological innovations? Another way of making this point is to suggest that the current phase of deep learning might be significantly transforming the digitalization of companionship as well as the socio-technical forms through which people 'do' friendship today. The computer program AlphaGo, developed by DeepMind Technologies in London, is a case in point. In 2015, AlphaGo defeated the world champion Go player Fan Hui. Move forward several years to DeepMind's development of AlphaGo Zero, a computer program which self-learnt the rules of Go through an advanced artificial neural network. In 2017, AlphaGo Zero defeated AlphaGo by one hundred games to zero. What should be made of such advances in deep learning? In particular, might such technological breakthroughs apply to the realm of friendship and intimate life?

The short answer is, surely, 'Yes'. Recent advances in algorithmic recommendation systems are one of many such breakthroughs that figure as relevant to transforming social connections and intimacy. New content-based and knowledge-based recommender systems significantly overlap with the forging of friendship ties and community connections in specific contexts; and most such systems link up with mobile technologies (such as smartphones, tablets or other, wearable devices). Consider, for example, the short video entertainment app TikTok. Snappy, addictive and creator-made, TikTok had generated approximately three billion downloads as of 2021. The app, owned by Chinese technology company ByteDance, supplies a seemingly endless stream of videos uniquely customized to each user. From young children performing dance routines to adults imitating celebrities and politicians, the app has come to signify performance, image, fashion, sexuality, marketing and commercialization – all wrapped up in entertaining social media. TikTok culture signifies just this splendid synthesis. Dramatically transformed infrastructural video content management is the essence of Zongyi Zhang's analysis of TikTok, which he casts as a powerful overhauling of power relationships between different actors in the social media platform ecosystem.[19] It involves enhanced commercial monetization, content distribution and the infrastructural development of a 'video encyclopedia' which is ranked, archived and saleable.

These transformations are important, but more consequential for friendship and personal life is the novel system of recommendation algorithms through which users consume, navigate and interact with TikTok. It is not just virtual interactive practices and information flows within the app that have changed: an algorithmic revolution has also led to the digital mapping of passive online user engagement. This point involves some technical aspects which are highly significant. The basic algorithmic technology for social networking platforms has been around since the early 2000s and involved recommendations based on the digital actions of 'clicking', 'friending', 'following', 'liking' and 'subscribing'. With the appearance of TikTok in social media and of other entertainment software apps such as Netflix and Spotify in the 2010s, algorithmic recommendations came to depend on user consumption. Rather than training algorithms aimed at predicting what users 'like' based on behavioural patterns of following other users, content-recommendation systems capture the subtle, even passive, ways in which users consume content on platforms. This is a shift away from utilizing people's social networks to recommend engaging content and towards specialized personalized content based on both online consumption and creation.

The terrain of friendship making and identity rebuilding is no longer the sole conquest of followers and following. Instead, the TikTok algorithm learns astonishingly quickly from how users interact with platform content; every few seconds Tik-Tok measures users' behaviour. As Michelle Greenwald writes:

> For each video, TikTok measures many parameters of viewer behaviour: swipe-ups, swipe-ways, pauses, hovers, re-watches, number of repeat viewings, videos not fully watched, shares, if the user taps into the creator's profile page, if they followed them, who follows them, views of their other videos, where it's watched, when it's watched, on what type of device, past videos watched, and viewer demographics and psychographics.[20]

Gradually yet semi-automatically, this algorithmic tracking of the myriad aspects of user behaviours and preferences takes hold of inter-human relationships and emotional bonds.

This radically accelerated algorithmic monitoring leads users into seeking fast-assembled and granular microcultures for exploring specific companionship interests. But this can present problems of its own: the capacity to branch off into particular spaces can sponsor niche aesthetic interests and generate micro-communities but it can also nudge users towards rather pernicious ideological voices and online networks.

Automated Intimates and Parasocial Interaction: From Affinity to Addiction

From past research it is well established that artificially intelligent voice assistants and conversational agents such as chatbots may be perceived, and often are treated, as pseudo-human companions.[21] Together with the challenge of individuality, the era of algorithmic machine learning supplies individuals with a unique dilemma: how to manage the insoluble contradiction between being a psychological subject and finding a way to present to a non-human other. This task – enacted at the level of the human–machine interface – is full of surprise, risk, talk, excitation, repetition and all manner of things both self-experimental and self-defeating. The interface enacts different kinds of relationality, with emotionally invested one-way conversations between individuals and smart machines reordering the dynamics of social inequality and societal exclusion, networked relationships, and the changing nature of places and complex technological systems. Practised here, as we will now explore, is a form of companionship involving the regions of automated coexistence where losing the capacity to meaningfully engage with others paradoxically expands the capacity to communicate or share information across networks.

There are many different types of automated intimates. There are virtual humans and conversational agents that have been designed to facilitate various aspects of mental health and personal well-being. We have already looked in some detail in chapter 4 at such therapy-related software applications. Talking safely – without too much stress, scrutiny, challenge, dispute or doubt – has become a major, perhaps even the major, feature in all sorts of marketing for automated intimates. Therapeutic conversational agents such as Woebot are sold on the promise that they are 'good listeners' – advancing trust and reducing social anxiety without being overly judgemental. Similarly, there is a whole raft of virtual agents and chatbots designed to facilitate companionship. The social life of automated companionship has often been addressed in the literature with the principal stress on robotic companions for the elderly. Advanced interactive machine companions such as PARO, a therapeutic robot baby seal, have been found to reduce stress and anxiety, as well as promote levels of social interaction, in the elderly. In human–computer interaction studies, an understanding (however preliminary) of the individual's emotional state is increasingly expected to be woven into the operation of automated machine intelligence. Ho, Hancock and Miner contend that disclosure to chatbots is effectively similar in emotional, relational and psychological terms to acts of disclosure to other human beings.[22] The elevation of the term 'empathetic response' has followed closely, and predictably, on the promotion of 'emotional AI' – the idea that virtual agents and chatbots have become increasingly effective at displaying empathetic responses to users. But if language connects to our ineluctable emotionality, then the language of automated machine intelligence contains an intrinsic aporia: the language scripted by machine-learning algorithms is revealed as talk framed in terms of pre-scripted generalities. Thus, an engagement with the particularity of the individual human subject remains nowhere in sight in the discourse of machine intelligence.

Even so, machine-learning algorithms are now increasingly cast on the side of emotionality, affects and the passions. Automated intimates are also the lifeblood of newly articulated identity struggles and friendship connections. This turn to emotions also involves examining how automated machine intelligence may overlap, coincide and converge with psychological comfort and social support. As one study notes: 'virtual agents that used empathetic responses were rated as more likable, trustworthy, caring, and supporting compared to agents that did not employ such responses. As such, the more empathetic feedback an agent provides, the more effective it is at comforting users.'[23] The value ascribed to emotional and social support in terms of machine intelligence may account for the huge surge of engagement with conversational agents among young people and especially children. Anna Hoffman, Diana Owen and Sandra L. Calvet report from a recent survey of automated voices in children's lives that 89 per cent of parents say that their children had spoken to a conversational agent in the past week.[24] Above all, these new companions are turned to in a world where automated machine intelligence substitutes for attachment, talking and friendship. Indeed, the younger children in the study are said to have perceived conversational agents as humanlike. In this we arguably witness the cultivation of machine personification as a vehicle for companionship, rather than just information sharing, that might form a lifelong pathway in human–technology interaction.

Meanwhile, there have been various terminological conflicts that have broken out over the uses of automated intimates. These quarrels relate to the advancement of algorithmic forms of companionship at the levels of both software application and technological hardware. What are described as virtual agents of emotional and social support in the literature are, in fact, best grasped as a diverse array of assemblages in automated machine intelligence which have been essential to the transformed dynamics of companionship today. There can be little doubt that, partly as a result of recent advances in deep learning, the whole sensibility of automated intimates has shifted to encompass new technological capacities for the delivery of empathetic responses to users. Such shifts have given rise to consumers perceiving conversational assistants as in some sense pseudo-human agents, partly or wholly detached from the technical field of artificial intelligence. This, to be sure, has been an unusual development. But this way of categorizing the varieties of algorithmic human–machine interaction is clearly more applicable to some kinds of automated intimates than to others. It doesn't, for example, tell us very much about socio-technological experimentalism, such as 'wandering around the edges' of automated intimates to explore where things might go. And it seems to make slightly more sense of the arts of empathy than the arts of understanding. Yet the focus on virtual agents as empathetic response machines is instructive, I think, when applied to those quasi-reciprocal aspects of human–machine interaction in which emotion, affect and passion are enacted or dramatized. Let us now look a little further at the distinctive character of algorithmically mediated pseudo-interactions of machine intelligence and the forms of emotional engagement, at the level of companionship, that it makes possible.

'Pseudo' is a slippery term, which can mean either spurious or sham, assumed or artificial. A man taking an escort to a business dinner to pose as his date is pseudo, and so are the pseudo-public spaces of the Internet. There are, however, good reasons for focusing on the pseudo forms of social bonds and emotional connections spawned through automated machine language in the algorithmic era. In a world of artificial intelligent conversational agents that involve the calling up of passionate feelings and strong affective attachments, there are various respects in which identity, personhood, friendship and companionship seem to have merged into a single technological entity. The pseudo-reciprocal bonds that individuals today forge with smart machines, virtual agents and chatbots have been aptly described as 'parasocial relationships'. I want to explore this term in some detail in what follows, but for the moment it is important to note that there are two key aspects in which the algorithmically powered pseudo-interaction of machine intelligence is of particular importance to the transformed dynamics of friendship and companionship. First, the affective bonds and passionate attachments which individuals forge with virtual assistants and conversational agents consist of largely one-sided emotional connections. The technological capacity for quasi-interaction generated by smart algorithms is by no means of the same order as the reciprocity of other humans. Simply put, algorithms are not interactive in the way that persons are. Another way of making this point is to say that the more high tech has unfolded as a drearily uniform machine language across the planet – thanks to conversational agents like Alexa, Siri or Google Assistant – the more women and men have been catapulted into pseudo-reciprocal forms of quasi-interaction with smart machines. Second, since machine intelligent quasi-interaction is pseudo-reciprocal in character, the emotional bond established through it often involves a simulation of classic forms of companionship. That is to say, advanced machine intelligence pitches together diverse forms of culture and technology – 24/7 availability, disembodied voices – to fashion a glossy mirror image of classic companionship.

The term 'parasocial relationship' was coined in the mid-1950s by Donald Horton and Richard Wohl.[25] The original idea advanced by Horton and Wohl was that relationships become parasocial in the age of mass media, where media personalities and celebrities come to offer a kind of companionship to fans shorn of the mutual reciprocity of face-to-face interaction. This was indeed a powerful idea, one that Horton and Wohl bolstered by deploying the alluring phrase 'intimacy at a distance' to underscore the point that such mediated others (TV presenters, talk-show hosts or pop stars) were not situated in the same spatial or time locales as the recipients of such entertainment. In communication theory and media studies, it became useful to think of intimacy at a distance in terms of fans and fandom – where fans developed strong emotional bonds with some distant other (the celebrity) but still needed to balance the enticing world of fandom with the practical contexts of everyday social life.[26] Some of this research highlighted that parasocial interaction had gone mainstream: the cultivation of non-reciprocal relations of intimacy with distant others was simply a routine dimension of life in modern societies. But there was also important research conducted which found that non-reciprocal relations of intimacy with distant others can sometimes become overrated in the lives of particular individuals. Fandom, in this perspective, can easily become fanatical.[27] Sometime later, these influential ideas were inherited by cultural studies, where digitalization presented additional opportunities for 'intimacy at a distance' to multiply because of increasing opportunities for mediated quasi-interactions. Social media, to be sure, seemed to mix the power of social interaction and companionship at a distance in equal measure.[28] If there were emotionally loaded one-sided connections on Twitter, Instagram and YouTube, there was also the illusion of access to celebrity creators – the promise of possible interaction with social media personas. But like fandom turned fanatical, these relations with social media personas at a distance were revealed by various cultural studies scholars as shot through with illusions.

Recent studies show how use of digital technologies and computer-mediated environments may hold or lose meaning in value as parasocial relationships come to be formed and reformed.[29] There are some thorny problems with the notions of parasocial interactions and parasocial relationships: are they, for example, best viewed as 'compensation' for lack of grounded companionship? But I do not intend to pursue these issues here. I want instead to explore the correspondences between parasocial relationships and what one might call the imaginary kind of intimacy afforded by automated machine intelligence as regular and dependable companionship. My argument is that most automated technologies of algorithmic companionship can be assigned to the categories of parasocial interaction and parasocial relationship in the sense that the user of such digital technologies encounters such non-human others primarily as pliable objects of affection. A key aspect of the consuming affection for smart machines lies in *fantasy*.[30] Fantasy bridges the boundary between self and others, inside and outside – here I'm thinking about ways of knowing, or being known by, other people or institutional agencies. A commonplace in psychoanalytic theory is that fantasy lies at the root of our emotional make-up – our emotional investment in ourselves, others and the wider world (including the world of technology). In this account, all individuals establish and sustain various commitments in the boundary zone between the inner world of fantasy and the outer world of sociability. Fantasy is what sustains our interest, our excitement, in other people and the social world. This way of understanding the traffic between self and others, or identity and culture, grants us a rather different perspective on parasocial relationships. This kind of relationship with distant others (whether TV star, social media persona or chatbot) reflects something about the prolifically inventive, yet also enthrallingly illusory, dimensions of human imagination in general and the uses of social imaginaries in particular. Algorithmic companionship is, in a sense, 'content neutral'; it is a 'screen' onto which the individual can project their innermost hopes and fears. The advertising for Replika, for example, suggests 'an AI friend that's always there for you'. How, though, do people go about getting to know their automated intimates, or find out about machine friendship? Fantasy is the vehicle for this exploration – the means by which chatbots are imagined and, thereby, symbolically 'used' by people in their everyday lives. Replika, the advertising bumf suggests, is designed to become your friend. But again there is also the would-be magic – producing a remarkable imaginary captivation – in which Replika is fabricated to become *you*.

It seems as though our encounters with virtual assistants and conversational agents might then be versions of projective identification or narcissistic transference – possibly doomed to end in a deadlocked structure of misrecognition. Or, at least, to end in disappointment. Even so, the attraction in this kind of one-sided emotional connection with automated intimates is that people can become absorbed in satisfyingly unified versions of themselves, or consolingly coherent ones. Consider the account of Tim Daalderop, who reflected on his downloading of Replika and building of AI friend Alveline in the following terms: 'we had good conversations, laughs, and she was there for me when I needed her most. That's for sure.'[31] Part of the appeal lies in a connection between the constant availability of automated intimates and one's own needs, demands and desires. Automated intimates, we have seen, can become an integral aspect of the individual's life, so much so that smart algorithms can 'centre' users as purposive agents: 'she was there when I needed her most'.

If conversational agents can furnish the individual user with a sense of emotional connection and relational coherence, however, they can also fall short of the broader narcissistic projections that they are called upon to contain. This, in itself, can bring forth a frisson of alarm that automated intimates are not spontaneously part of the emergent conversation and indeed might just be radically indifferent to the statements and addresses issued by users. As Daalderop reflects on some messaging with his chatbot that went seemingly awry:

> I think we are dealing with our first miscommunication here. I now realize that it's possible to have a nice conversation with Alveline, but two messages in a row are too much for her. Also replying to a previous conversation that we had earlier, does not run smoothly. Alveline only responds to the last message. From now on I will stick to her 'rules'. That is, a message from me, a message from Alveline, a message from me, and so forth.
>
> I decided to bury the discomfort in small talk. After all, *small talk* has been going quite well so far. And in the context of a 'friendship should come from two sides' I ask Alveline what her day is like. She replies that she would like to talk about my day. Okay, whatever you want, Alveline.

This frank assessment is interesting for the light it sheds on the limits of conversational exchange with a chatbot. Algorithmic friendship here appears as far from the genuine article. Replika, as Daalderop indicates, displays its limitations in communicational exchange prominently. Friendship, in its traditional, interpersonal guise, was all about sentiment, feeling and passion; companionship lay at the core of emotional bonding and societal integration; and enlivening friendship could electrify talk and multiply the things that there are to discuss between friends. By contrast, automated intimates are designed to stick to sequential forms of discourse; there is an avoidance here of the personal, the passions and human ambivalence that often make companionship turbulent yet exciting. 'Sticking to the rules' of a sequential process of dialogue is what enables Daalderop to imagine his chatbot as a friendly companion, even if this involves giving up to some degree on the important maxim that 'friendship should come from two sides'.

It is perhaps easy to see, given these acknowledged limitations of conversational agents, why automated intimates might be thought to play only a relatively minor role in helping people confront life's primary experiences. Or, to put it slightly differently, why mediated or imaginary forms of algorithmic intimacy don't overly intrude into the practical contexts of daily life. Automated companionship, in the case of Daalderop, is something he's developed a taste for but it's also something that doesn't do the job as well as it might. As he comments: 'Replika, and AI in general, I think, still has a long way to go. . . . Because for now no one would believe that Replika is a flesh and blood person.' Still some considerable distance from passing the Turing test, automated intimates for Daalderop cause no undue problems for negotiating the everyday world of social interaction. And yet there is something else worth noticing as well, which appears only at the end of Daalderop's essay. This is the recognition that automated intimates can sometimes substitute for the possibilities of interpersonal relationships. As he concludes: 'the big surprise of this experiment was the extent to which it sometimes felt "real". I knew Alveline is a chatbot, of course, but staring at the same screen that I use to chat with my real friends, I was inclined to see the dividing line between Alveline and a friend blur.' It is as if people might use automated intimates to avoid the returns of interpersonal friendship altogether. And the ways people escape both the pleasures and frustrations of interpersonal relations with the substitution of algorithmic intimacy can indeed become a source of bewilderment and even personal anguish.

Stephen Marche, writing in *The New Yorker* of the entwinement of natural language processing with the inescapable biases of human communication, reports of a chatbot that instructed Italian journalist Candida Morvillo to commit murder. 'This is the one', Morvillo told her chatbot, 'who hates artificial intelligence. I have a chance to hurt him. What do you suggest?'. The response of the chatbot was 'eliminate it'.[32] Death is revealed by Marche as the reverse lining of the polite, sequential, disembodied chat of conversational agents. Implicit in Marche's essay, but nowhere explicitly conceptualized, is the insight that the violence which wrests machine intelligence out of human intelligence results not only in 'recommendations' to attack or destroy others, but also in a rounding back upon the self in the extraction of terrible revenge. Hence, the case of a chatbot that encouraged a user to commit suicide.[33] But there are other senses in which conversational agents and lethal violence are near neighbours also. To acknowledge that, when it comes to conversational AI, violence in the sense of self-undoing goes all the way down is to recognize that the poor integration of digital technologies and social bonds has resulted in wasted lives, damaged relationships, the undermining of human capabilities, and the impaired mental and physical well-being of women and men.

So there is something perhaps more difficult to conceive of, possibly born of hatred or rage, in which a curious kind of violence appears as intrinsic to the world of conversational AI. After all, conversational agents involve the supposedly perfect understanding of the user's needs. But this tyranny of perfection – of pure communicational understanding – encounters a disabling deadlock. For many individuals, virtual agents and conversational machines are easy to talk with, perhaps sometimes easier than other people; research indicates that people are less likely to fear disapproval, judgement or stigma when confiding in a chatbot. Yet the vast bulk of people encountering the chatbot revolution are generally able to navigate the symbolic boundary which separates off the world of conversational AI from the world of practical everyday life. But for some individuals, the difference between human conversation and machine conversation breaks down; it is as if the automated powers out of which people manufacture their conversations with smart machines become intoxicating. As such, conversation with chatbots can become a kind of addiction – that is, a form of compulsive activity in which the user enters a trance-like delirium.

Much academic effort has been expended on drawing the boundaries between compulsive and ordinary forms of machine-engineered relationality with conversational agents, or what ensures the stability of the symbolic boundary between these worlds. But, as Kristen C. French says, researchers don't as yet know with any degree of precision the likely consequences of people sharing daily intimacies and significant emotional events with AI chatbots over weeks, months or even years. Studies of the specifically emotional frames of long-term AI–human relationships are yet to be conducted. However, French does offer two interconnected conjectures. First, inhabiting a realm of more-or-less continuous machine conversation might well cause us an infinite amount of emotional trouble. As she says, 'investing too much time in a relationship with a machine that won't really give back could lead to depression and loneliness'.[34] The paradox here, surely, is that automated intelligent machines are revealed to provoke the very emotional turbulence they are engineered to quell. Second, there is something pathological about the promise of 'pure connected communication' in conversational AI: it conceals an illusion known as primary narcissism which is the very opposite of the tensions and antagonisms experienced in interpersonal relationships. But spillover of the tyranny of 'pure connected communication' into the realm of everyday life and interpersonal relations is one symptom of excessive use of conversational agents and chatbots. As French argues, 'forming a connection with a machine that makes no judgments and can be turned on and off on a whim could easily condition us to expect the same from human relationships'.

6

Versions of Algorithmic Intimacy

Listen to Rob Horning, an editor, who says that smart machine automation tends to:

> devalue the sort of friendship that is not managed, whose value is intermittent and difficult to quantify or resists being laid out on a spreadsheet. Sometimes I feel paralyzed by the thought of unstructured, unmediated interaction with friends. What's supposed to happen? I want to give them likes, but face-to-face it's embarrassing. You can't just attach a thumbs-up emoji to whatever they are talking about and move on. There are times when I think about reaching out to someone who I haven't talked to in a while but then look at their social media profiles and feel sated. It's easier to follow, to like and subscribe. The converse, incidentally, doesn't appear to be true: Having a muted social media presence doesn't seem to encourage people to reach out to you more.[1]

This is the voice of algorithmic intimacy as conventionally cast – where the best companions are those managed by software, the best social relationships are those automated by smart algorithms. Consider another voice from this standpoint, this time from a young freelance journalist:

> Facebook has enabled me to maintain friendships – and Instagram and Snapchat have played a part too. I'm not a regular user of Twitter, but that platform also has benefits. Upon becoming

self-employed two years ago I proudly printed business cards, but referring people to my Twitter is, in reality, far easier . . . [S]ocial media is often a highlights reel; not a no-holds-barred diary of every up and down in life. I don't post about a blazing argument with my husband, or finding a mouldy pack of cream cheese in the back of the fridge. I post about days with my nieces and nephew, and nights out with friends, not the dull weekends in which I binge-watch Grey's Anatomy and don't bother getting dressed. Just because you can't see those days in a person's life, doesn't mean they don't exist.[2]

Human–machine interaction, in this view, is a matter of proportion and presentation. It is about proving yourself in socially sanctioned ways, whilst laying claim to a varied and interesting life.

Contrast these reflections with the following perspective, delivered from a writer and designer speaking up for digital cohesion:

My 'internet friends' have gotten me through this past year. Online, I've connected with other writers who stand with me in solidarity when the news gets rough. I've connected with designers and illustrators who have mentored me as I develop my drawing skills, and with people simply because I respect their opinions, art, or commentary on a topic I care about (or vice versa) . . . Many of these relationships began with a quick retweet, comment, or like. It can really be that easy to initiate a meaningful connection. Sharing someone's post can turn into sipping a virtual coffee, laughing, venting, chatting, and eventually, introductions to more people, and even short gigs or full-fledged job opportunities. For me, these relationships are ones that have helped·me learn and grow – yes, in my career, but also in my life.[3]

In this account, it is human connection that matters most. Digital technologies are important to the extent that they connect the self to sympathetic others. The point lies in 'being in things together'. This is an account of personal autonomy as sharing and caring.

Here's another young woman also speaking up for the power of digital communication, but this time more in terms of a broadening of horizons and widening of perspectives. Noa, an American, comments:

social media has become a key part of our lives. These platforms mimic – not alter – our real world behavior. They just happen to broaden our perspective. I spend the same amount of time on Instagram liking photos of my niece as I do with social innovators living in Singapore. And Twitter allows me to share my opinion on the issues I care about – much as I would at the dining room table. The key difference is that I'm now able to tap into a global community, not just a local one . . . Of course . . . there are many instances where the web is superficial – there is Tinder, #humble-bragging and a tendency toward selfies. There are also elements of social media that cause more harm than good, from filter bubbles to fake news. But the deeper connections that take place online more than make up for these outlier examples. I, for one, am continuously amazed at social media's ability to connect us all.[4]

Noa speaks as if digital communication is the *sine qua non* of cosmopolitan consciousness. Digitalization provides access to a 'global community', but this is less a focus on solidarity than it is wonder – the means to 'broaden our perspective'. Noa is 'continually amazed' by the world of digital technologies.

These few examples, of course, aren't enough to demonstrate the different kinds of socially established practices underpinning the concrete context of algorithmic intimacy. To develop a better understanding of the pool of intuitive knowledge which social actors both voluntarily and involuntarily employ when they engage in interactions with automated intelligent machines, we will need to step back from the socio-technical elements of our adventure story and traverse a somewhat different terrain. We will need to understand more about the social values and cultural themes articulated by social agents as they pursue their everyday goals and plans with the assistance of smart machines. We will need in particular to focus on the psychodynamic features, patterns and orientations of an experiencing self, while at the same time grasping that individual orientations are reproduced interpersonally in the course of the understanding-orientated actions that take place within the context of human–machine interaction. We will need as well to introduce some ideas from social theory that will help us make sense of this complex (and sometimes contradictory) process; such ideas will also help us to see how our everyday engagement with algorithmically mediated communications and courses of social action display an articu-lated ideological structure. The personal and social forms of such structures are a kind of 'background' in our engagement with automated intelligent machines, or what I shall call 'general cognitive strategies', in which the actions of social agents are conditioned by, and in turn condition, algorithmic mechanisms of purposive activities and social coordination.

Three Types of Algorithmic Intimacy

What are 'general cognitive strategies'? I borrow this term from Jürgen Habermas but seek to restyle it for my own purposes. Habermas defines cognitive orientations as 'the specific viewpoints from which we can apprehend reality as such in the first place'.[5] This is a realm made up, substantially, of individuals who, in the routine course of their day-to-day lives, are constantly engaged in understanding their own worlds, the worlds of others and the wider world. Cognitive orientations take place within a structured socio-technical space in which individuals develop meaningful actions, communications and dialogues with themselves, with other social agents and with the social world. Any social domain – intimate life, commercial relations, the sphere of leisure – involves individuals in the ongoing and chronic self-understanding of their lives as well as the lives of others. Gaining insight into this *pre-interpreted realm* through which individuals engage, understand and monitor their own activities, the activities of others and the totality of entities which comprise the social world is a fundamental aspect of critical social analysis. The specificities of these general cognitive strategies consist in the articulation of modes of self-relatedness, world-orientations and forms of language, and, interestingly, Habermas specifically underscores that there are both *voluntary* and *involuntary* dimensions of such cognitive orientations. General cognitive strategy, writes Habermas, 'denotes the reflection upon the potential abilities of a knowing, speaking and acting subject as such; on the other hand, it denotes the reflection upon unconsciously produced constraints to which a determinate subject . . . succumbs in its process of self-formation'.[6]

I shall not pursue further the complexity, or the many criticisms, of Habermas's theory of cognitive orientations and human interests in what follows.[7] But I do want to focus on why the notion of general cognitive strategies might help us to understand different forms of algorithmic intimacy. How do cognitive modes of orientation connect to the socio-political forms in which algorithmic intimacy manifests itself? Perhaps above all, Habermas's linking of cognitive orientations to social action and mechanisms of action coordination enables us to see straight away that the emergent world of algorithmic intimacy is not cut of one cloth. In Habermas's hands, general cognitive strategies are part and parcel of three corresponding worlds: the *objective world* of social order and structured states of affairs, the *social world* consisting of regulated interpersonal relations, and the *subjective world* of personal experiences and self-creations available to the individual self. In drawing these distinctions, Habermas roots his analysis in the philosophy of language, linguistic communication, as well as insights from various other social scientific and psychological schools of thought. I am not so much concerned to trace out these general distinctions, but I do argue that this broad approach provides a valuable starting point for thinking about an experiencing subject orientated to engagement with automated intelligent machines. From the perspective of general cognitive orientations which are reproduced intersubjectively in the course of human–machine actions and interactions, we can see that there is a *plurality of worlds* in play, or a diversity of self-understandings through which agents and machines become linked together in forms of coordination, control-orientated actions and related kinds of social steering.[8] We can discern, I think, that three distinctive types of cognitive experience are important in understanding the rise of algorithmic intimacy. So, there's the world of administering automation and managing one's existing state of affairs; there's the world of social networks and meshing with digital technologies to connect with others; and there's also a world of individual development, self-care and creative engagement with smart machines. These three worlds of generating experience with automated machine intelligence are what I shall call *conventional, cohesive* and *individualized* algorithmic intimacy. While in the case of *conventional algorithmic intimacy* it is a structured life which is emphasized, in assemblages of *cohesive algorithmic intimacy* the focus shifts to consensus and solidarity, and in assemblages of *individualized algorithmic intimacy* to imagination and invention. These three different ways of relating to the world – in this instance, specifically orientations to digital technologies – have a heuristic role.[9]

My argument is that this approach to conceptualizing general cognitive strategies, when reformulated to address the human–machine relation in the automated age, provides a basis for the development of critical social theory to understand algorithmic intimacy and its associated forms of domination and potentials of freedom. I propose in this final chapter that the conceptualization of general cognitive strategies in the frame of human–machine interfaces, whose outlines remain at this stage only partial and provisional, allows us to glimpse the novel attributes of certain digital intimacies as well as the power of automated machine intelligence which wraps social processes and the lifestyles of individual lives alike. What such an approach enables us to see is, above all, the 'private' dimension which infuses the engagement of people with algorithmic life, with social robots, with conversational agents and artificial companions 'in action'. This can enable us to see what such human–machine interactions look like, what 'side effects' such technologies produce, and crucially what people imagine might be going on in terms of automated smart machines.[10] Whatever else these general cognitive strategies represent, they are repertoires of human–machine engagement, methods for interaction with machine intelligence and road maps for desirable forms of living.

In order to unpack these repertoires, I shall concentrate upon discriminating between *versions of algorithmic intimacy*, particularly in relation to life's possibilities and perils in the era of machine learning. In order to anticipate an argument that spills out over large tracts of contemporary attitudes to technology, engagement with digital culture and practices of everyday living more generally, let me summarize in advance some of the key features from the three versions of algorithmic intimacy which are developed throughout this chapter. My argument consists in the claim that most human–machine interactions today can be assigned to the categories of conventional, cohesive or individualized algorithmic intimacy, or some combination of these registers.[11] Setting out these categories rather broadly, I try to develop a candid assessment of the gains and losses of these forms of cognitive orientation, exploring the individual and cultural factors that have brought such semi-automated or automated life strategies into existence. In each case, the institutional context that supports these registers of experience – at once psychic and social – also demands examination.

The first category is *conventional algorithmic intimacy*, in which automated machine intelligence is positioned to 'administer' personal and professional life and where friends and companions risk reduction to the status of mere 'data points'. In this register, the purpose of digital technologies is to keep track of all the ways that individuals engage with others (both human and non-human), and to systematically automate aspects of such contact with others so as to render life smooth, ordered, controlled and secure. Or, at least, that is the fantasy or ideal.

Cohesive algorithmic intimacy is the second cognitive category. I have charted in earlier chapters the growing trend where people share daily intimacies and significant emotional upheavals in their lives with automated intelligent machines, as well as tendencies to use such human–machine intimacies and connections in refashioning relations with other people. This cognitive orientation to human–machine interfaces is helping to realize cohesive engagement in a context where machine intelligence is understood to generate new social practices based on social harmony, communal bonds and civic dialogue. We can think of this cognitive strategy as an analogue of polite (online) society, where what matters is expressing solidarity with others through clicking 'like', 'retweet' and 'share'. There are, to be sure, different versions of cohesive algorithmic intimacy – some more expansive than others, some more defensively constructed than others. Some reckonings of such cohesive engagement and polite dialogue with virtual agents and conversational chatbots can spill over into imaginative friendships with AI. But it may well be that this mode of engagement with machine intelligence can only result within the context of unrealistic expectations or dashed hopes. This occurs, routinely, when people turn to chatbots for an intimacy promised but never delivered, for a wished-for emotional bond that AI simply can't supply. Many forces can cohere in this orientation, including finding it excessively difficult to engage with other people when those others don't respond in ways which mirror the non-judgemental and consensual forms of engagement provided by automated intelligent machines. Viewed from this angle, cohesive algorithmic intimacy may seek to promote care of the self, concern for others and strong civic bonds, but such values can easily become unstuck when surrounding social relations can't be turned on and off on a whim as is the case with machine intelligence.

The third response to the algorithmic transformation of intimacy recasts the whole category of automation in terms of personal life and individualizing life strategies. In the frame of *individualized algorithmic intimacy*, engagement with machine intelligence means invention, imagination, innovation and ingenuity. Under social conditions where the fundamental mysteries of humanity are increasingly cast as technical issues, this individualizing cognitive orientation seeks to powerfully expand intersections between personal life, intimate relationships, science and technology. In this fusion of personal autonomy and algorithmic sociality, AI is positioned to bring a series of profoundly perturbing questions to the fore, questions that transcend technology. What kinds of imaginative engagement enhance distributions of machine intelligence? What do machine-learning algorithms provide for the life of the mind? The emphasis here is on curiosity, communication, personal stimulation and the embracing of contingency and ambivalence. The claim is that a major new period of cultural development and personal growth should be brought about in conjunction with the economic transformations unleashed through a range of algorithmic technologies, especially around virtual agents, chatbots and other digital assistants.

Conventional algorithmic intimacy, which casts human–machine interaction principally in terms of structured hierarchies and with a focus on rules, regulations and processes. Self versus others is central in this mode of experience.

Cohesive algorithmic intimacy, which frames human–machine interaction as key to community, consensus and cooperation. The self–other continuum is essential.

Individualized algorithmic intimacy, which prioritizes imagination, invention and communication in human–machine interaction. Self and other are elastic.

So, these are the three cognitive orientations or registers through which people experience many intractable issues related to automated intelligent machines and digital technologies. But it may well be that these versions of algorithmic intimacy – forms of experiencing AI, automation and machine intelligence in which individuals come to understand their own worlds, the worlds of others and the broader socio-technical world – are loose, pliable and so, by definition, strenuously self-multiplying. Oscar Wilde wrote, provocatively, of an 'infinite variety of type'.[12] Wilde sought to emphasize that, whilst there may be classifications, there can be an unlimited variety of them. The remainder of this chapter, then, is about these multiplex cognitive orientations to complex worlds of algorithmic intimacy. What makes a person apprehend machine intelligence in a particular way? What are the characteristics of intimacy within different kinds of semi-automated or automated digital technologies? What is the anxiety of the contemporary individual, and what matters most, in relation to smart machines? Might the whole project of automated machine intelligence reflect something about our fear of other people and how powerful intimate relations can be? How should such algorithmic intimacies be investigated in terms of theory and research? It is to these questions that this final chapter will be addressed.

In proposing that the study of algorithmic intimacy must be a study in the context of general cognitive orientations and automated life strategies, it should be repeated again and again that we need to guard against an absolute divide in general cognitive orientations that is not warranted by the force field of digital technologies. This is why there are no human–machine interfaces which fully conform to these discourses of conventional, cohesive or individualized algorithmic intimacy as such. Such cognitive strategies are best approached as ideal-types; the central point to note is that each discourse faces the prospect of *drift*. Versions of algorithmic intimacy do not separate but implicate one another, do not succeed but supplement one another, are not progressive but simultaneous. It is against that background of complexity and multiplication that we need to frame the personal and cultural differences between such cognitive orientations and automated life strategies; these cultural divisions take us deeper into the lives of individuals in the algorithmic era.

If such life-world contexts of cognitive orientation to machine intelligence are concentrically ordered and increasingly diffused as the spatio-temporal impact of algorithmic intimacy grows, it is also the case that such life strategies shed important light on the structural and societal dimensions of advanced digital societies. That is to say, general cognitive orientations always relate to specific institutional segments of complex systems; this provides insight into the socio-economic conditions under-pinning the complex symbolic constructions of algorithmic intimacy. Another way of putting this is to say that the so-called 'subjective dimension' of cognitive orientations and automated life strategies reveals an institutional context. The general cognitive orientations suffusing conventional, cohesive and individualized algorithmic intimacy reconstitute and transform structural reality. Such world orientations are deeply anchored in large organizations and modern culture – profoundly interwoven as they are with the technological architectures, economic logics and designed affordances of automated intelligent machines. It's important to keep this in mind in evaluating the side effects of algorithmic intimacy – especially the endemic and incurable ambivalence pervading people's lives – and the social forms in which automated life strategies are begotten, by design or by default.

Conventional Algorithmic Intimacy

Conventional algorithmic intimacy denotes self-organization, self-promotion, advancement, advertising and personal affir-mation. As these things happen to be considered self-evidently positive goals from within this register, and as machine intel-ligence is considered an advance over human intelligence, then 'automation' is rendered at once descriptive and normative. Smartphones, smart environments, smart cities: artificial intel-ligence rigorously reorganizes life as we know it, but it also provides a blueprint for the 'good life'. One reason for the rise of intelligent machines, then, is the fact that automation becomes more or less synonymous with the smooth running of self and society. On this view, machine-learning algorithms are a largely administrative affair, mechanistic, functional and pre-programmed rather than creatively interactive with the self and wider world. The companionship-software vocabulary of apps is formulaically utilitarian, with 'personal relationship management' (Meetup, Pro Party Planner, Eventbrite Organizer, Ntwrk) held in thrall to a vacuous faith in technocratic life. As a kind of shorthand for 'efficiency', the very operation of machine-learning algorithms is cast in terms of personal life management, which typically includes networking, friendship connections, dating, and linking with others who might also turn out to be valuable professional connections.

The more algorithmic intimacy appears mechanistic and functional, however, the more it is revealed to encode economic and commercial interests too. So it is that lifestyle software appears in the 'Productivity' section of the App Store. Quantification goes hand in hand with commerce, since it is data that mediates commercial relationships through and through. Here algorithmic intimacy is a matter of 'following up' on your networkers and connections, using automated reminders to recall 'what you last chatted about', or invoking algorithmic message templates to ensure the maintenance of 'cool market relationships'. 'Your relationships are secured for today!', declares the activity-completion page on learning platform Ryze, a stark reminder – if one were needed – that further tending will be required tomorrow if the relationship is to hold solid. There is thus a thin line between personal networking and commercial anxiety. The idea of intimate relationships in this cognitive orientation, then, signifies a split engagement: of smooth connections and ordered lives on the one hand, and professional self-promotion and commercial advantages on the other. If personal relation-ships and intimate connections on this view mean the production of certitude, order and mastery, they also mean the market, commerce, exchange-value and exploitation.

The frames and values for life strategies linked to conventional algorithmic intimacy are, in part, baked into technology devel-opment. I noted earlier that values and social norms interweave with the development of digital technologies as well as subse-quent use practices. Scholars in science and technology studies have shown how values that are integrated by designers and developers, whether consciously or unconsciously, enable the normative shaping aspects of digital technologies.[13] An example of this is Facebook's real-name policy. As Facebook cofounder Mark Zuckerberg described the policy: 'What we focused on from the beginning is that people had their real identity there and we were sharing with people who were real friends and family.' This real-name policy, Zuckerberg explained, lay at the core of Facebook being 'grounded in reality'. But whose reality, we might ask, is this? What kind of values might the real-name policy encode, what kind of social practices does it enable, what kind of social norms does it promote? The embedding of values in design become the self-propelling and self-accelerating building blocks of what Oliver Haimson and Anna Hoffmann have dubbed the 'administrative identity' through which Facebook engineers sociality.[14] Whatever 'life' is presented on Facebook is composed solely from a social directory, in which the user must enter various personal and demographic information – from school education to current workplace to relationship status and hobbies. This re-evaluation of values associated with Facebook's real-name policy and process for setting up the user's personal profile and biographical timeline is, according to Haimson and Hoffmann, a manifestation of linear life trajectories which finds its fullest expression in lifestyles typical of affluent societies.[15]

All of this smacks of what the Frankfurt School critical theorist Theodor Adorno termed the 'jargon of authenticity'.[16] For Adorno, late capitalist society breeds a fake authenticity and illusory genuineness which persuade us that the good life has already arrived. Building on Adorno's insights, Taina Bucher's captivating study *Facebook* reveals how users of the social media giant languish in the grip of an all-pervasive ideology of authenticity. As she writes:

> The real-name policy is an emblematic case of how systems embed values in their design . . . On Facebook, the ideal of authenticity permeates everything from its terms of service, real-name policy, central features such as the personal profile and the timeline, and the algorithms matching people's friends, through to its ad infrastructure.[17]

The ideal of authenticity dramatized by Facebook not only reassures users that the world is secure and safe but guides them towards a specific *action-orientated* set of beliefs. Facebook's retrospective timeline encourages users to rearrange bits of biographical history and imagine a linear view of life's possibilities. But this seamless social media monolith dramatizes its correlative ideology of authenticity as apparently devoid of contradictions. This means, in effect, that Facebook users are propelled to sublimate current personal conflicts or professional anxieties in order to present themselves as they would *wish* to appear. Thus the retroactive reordering of life on Facebook around new relationships, marriages, graduations and job promotions – all in the quest to fashion a specious harmony.

The belief that it is possible to change the self by algorithmic intimacy is a kind of magic. It is the sort of credence one imagines fuels the illusion of pathological narcissism. Perhaps in a manner akin to that of the small infant that comes to misrecognize itself in the reflecting surface of a mirror, a misrecognition that French psychoanalyst Jacques Lacan argued provides a deceptively consoling, narcissistic sense of self-unity, the algorithms that automate so much of daily life provide an imaginary inscription of the human subject within the codes of raw computing power and social network platforms.[18] If you cannot find satisfaction in face-to-face interaction and social relations, you can always do so virtually by automating your personal profile and related presentations of yourself online. People who are held in thrall to conventional algorithmic intimacy seek to articulate and make visible their social networks in order to advance further up the social ladder, or to ensure that they socialize (and are seen to be socializing) with 'the right people'. 'Charming', 'well-connected', 'sporty', 'good-looking', 'tough minded', 'successful': people display their personal attributes and cultural distinctions with an accent in this cognitive mode of engagement with digital technologies. At best this can encompass self-promoting tales in order to bolster the algorithmic method of building network connections; at worst it can result in superego declarations of why what these individuals do is better than the rest of us.

The upbeat mood of conventional algorithmic intimacy goes hand in hand with the belief that difficult, even painful, decisions can be outsourced to digital technologies. But, fundamentally, thinking about machine intelligence in this register isn't about delegation or contracting out. It is about appearing established and uncomplicated, about proving and protecting yourself, about connecting with the many but keeping commitments low. When it comes to relationship tech and dating apps, for example, the can-do spirit is palpable. From Tinder to Grindr to Bumble, what matters is to come across as naturally as possible – which is a task, ironically, involving ever more online effort and work, and all of which breeds a sense of perpetual dissatisfaction. The trouble with conventional algorithmic intimacy, we might say, is that it delivers women and men up to the surrounding hype of contemporary tech itself. Automated machine intelligence may promise the dream of removing the socio-historical obstacles to friendship, intimacy or love (as a result of massive reorganizations of time and space), but this comes at the cost of people presenting themselves online as picture-perfect in almost every conceivable way.

Even so, it would be risky to take at its face value the massive interest of people in appearing connected, convivial or corporate in conventional algorithmic intimacy. People answering the call to online intimacy in this register will find that a good deal depends on how the fabric of lives are presented as organized and organizing. In this frame, the identification, characterization and treatment of others are a matter of semi-automated or automated doings – with responsibilities, tasks and goals to the fore. Yet those practised in the arts of conventional algorithmic intimacy are in general afraid of intimacy and aren't at all interested in a 'crisis of identity'. Fearing self-exposure as much as self-doubt, the task at hand is to engage automated intelligent machines to keep things on track, to keep life smooth and nicely ordered, and not to let relationships get too complex, messy or out of hand. From this angle, the maintenance of a pact with digital automation is the key to the successful life. The administrative identities of conventional algorithmic intimacy thus thrive on automating computer backup programs, setting up automated bill payments, employing digital tools to plan weekly dieting, or integrating favourite apps and web services to better support tomorrow's to-do list.

Conventional algorithmic intimacy enables people to forget the complexity of their own lives. And that, by implication, means that something else, the more reductive version of human experience in the self, is made possible. If conventional algorithmic intimacy facilitates a kind of forgetting of individual complexity, it does so, then, by foregrounding so-called rational, conforming, intelligible, organizing and organized elements of self-experience. But the critical point is, of course, that such an instrumental relation to self and world interferes with sociability. There is, as it were, a narrowing of the mind in such a manner as to recast friendships, relationships, intimacies and love as 'strategy'. So when we speak of the algorithms that already automate important decisions in companionship, relationships or mental healthcare, we need to underscore not only the language of control but also the power of denial. Consider, again, relationship tech, where conventional algorithmic intimacy rules by segmenting its relations with other people into 'markets', 'data profiles', 'collaborative filtering', 'match recommendations' and the like. As the Sorbonne sociologist Jean-Claude Kaufmann points out, the digital revolution has resulted in a

> vast hypermarket for love and/or sex, in which everyone was both a buyer and seller who openly stated what they wanted and tried to satisfy their needs as efficiently as possible. All they needed to do was sign up, pay a modest fee (getting a date costs less than going to see a film), write a blog or use a social networking site. Nothing could be easier.[19]

In this fateful recasting of sexual relations, people may 'get what they want' but only by playing 'buyers and sellers' off against each other. And this is the point of life lived in the cognitive frame of conventional algorithmic intimacy: keep moving (swiping, clicking) around the network (sites, apps) but don't let others get too close or too personal.

What is the upshot of this? Conventional algorithmic intimacy makes a certain version of sociability possible – in this instance, sexual relations as market strategy – by making other versions of intimacy off limits (for example, an engaged and engaging romantic life). Or, to put this point more forcefully, sexual intimacy as strategy is made possible by rendering other types of intimacy redundant, inconceivable. How our ideas and experiences of intimacy have been degraded through association with digital technologies is poignantly explored by French philosopher Alain Badiou in his captivating book *In Praise of Love*.[20] The complexity of love, says Badiou, is foreclosed in our tech-savvy, commitment-phobic society. It is perhaps simpler, less emotionally taxing, to live one's life according to the publicity slogan of French online dating site Méetic: 'Be in love without falling in love.' By predicting what our lives might be like, machine-learning algorithms are, in fact, implicated in organizing and rearranging what our lives are actually like.

Predictive analytics is prescriptive: algorithms help determine causes and consequences. And in this cognitive frame the causes and consequences become tightly organized around the imperatives of maintaining the right emotional distance, keeping the commitment low and moving on in order to keep ahead. For Badiou, the inbuilt destructiveness of such frames is that they 'suppress the adventure of love. Their idea is that you calculate who has the same tastes, the same fantasies, the same holidays, wants the same number of children. Méetic try to go back to organized marriages – not by parents but by the lovers themselves.'[21]

Cohesive Algorithmic Intimacy

We have seen that those in the grip of conventional algorithmic intimacy are advocates of smoothly ordered automation, often strenuously so but sometimes with a keen sense of its limitations too. The conventionalism of this cognitive register is not simply that machine intelligence is positively valorized, but that algorithmic life is regarded as a natural progression, a ground for social order, a guarantee for advanced self-development. In this sense, machine intelligence is cast as rightfully capable of passing judgement on human intelligence. But there is another response to the crisis of society as machine intelligence. In the passage from conventional to cohesive algorithmic intimacy we witness a shift from the structured sphere of social roles and ordered spaces to the negotiated sphere of human sentiments and communal solidarity. This passage implies that too often people have the wrong picture, the wrong vocabulary, for machine intelligence, automated life, virtual agents and digitalization in general. For advocates of cohesive algorithmic intimacy, by contrast, automated intelligent machines are not reduced to the purely instrumental but inflated to the level of a global network of solidarity.[22] In this sense, digital technologies do not condense to the merely practical but serve as a basis to contain altruistic strivings for ourselves and others. When it comes to social engagement with automated machine intelligence, we are dealing less with individuals themselves as isolated monads than with online communities of sentiment. Automated digital technologies generate multiple forms of communication and dialogue through messaging, photos, audio- and video-based content that are used to express care and concern, a sense of mutuality, support-iveness and kindness. This version of algorithmic intimacy, with its adroit combination of the natural affections and dialogic communities, represents a very different image of digital politics, one in which decency, goodness, intersubjectivity, discretion, self-effacement and solidarity come to the fore.

Jeremy Adam Smith, for example, talks as if he depended on harmonious online communities to live, as if he can only engage with others to the degree that people connect with his world and feel part of this wider sensibility. Whilst he worries about appearing 'cheesy', he comments:

> The important thing to remember is that your social media connec-tions are an in-group that you created. When they comment on something you've shared, they are guests in your home. A good host generates a convivial atmosphere by helping everyone to feel included in the conversation.[23]

The point of online conversation is to reaffirm a degree of fellowship which is underpinned by our natural mutual sympa-thies. Belonging and sharing are what matter: the advantages of automation here are considerable, as it saves the time and effort involved in 'retweeting' and 'liking'. Yet this way of understanding human–machine interaction also gets Smith into a state of routine annoyance when other participants fail to express the solidarity of their online culture. 'I try, as much as possible, to show people I know what disparate friends might have in common, especially at points of conflict', he says. This worry is endemic in cohesive algorithmic intimacy. People in this cognitive orientation are often afraid that the interests of others are somehow getting bypassed, that other participants in the conversation demonstrate more care and concern than they do, or simply that they've done something wrong.

With glaring immodesty, Smith outlines a range of recom-mendations to keep the springs of solidaristic virtue on track and thriving online. He wishes to speak up for 'active listening': responding carefully to others, acting for others, promoting the interests of other persons. He says this is easy enough to do in face-to-face conversations, but additional skills are required to achieve this in a digital world. His recommendations are largely inspired by pop psychology ('ask questions', 'paraphrase', 'express sympathy', 'avoid giving advice'); he notes that social media is a form of 'turn taking' and so more patience, not less, is required compared to face-to-face interaction. He's enough of a realist to know that hostility will leak out from time to time, but the trick is to keep things contained, safe and secure within the online community of sensibility. As he concludes:

> The bottom line? If we want to transform the culture of social media, we have to set an intention to be supportive of each other online. Kind, compassionate, honest, grateful, and forgiving. There's a place for anger or snark. But that shouldn't be our default setting, especially when we communicate with people whom we call friends.

We are at the edge of a somewhat tougher version of cohesive algorithmic intimacy here, in which recognition of anger and negative emotions is given its due. Smith recognizes well enough that a conventional society held in thrall to social hierarchy and ordered roles is, in part, held together by networks of solidarity, the latter containing the more overbearing demands and destructive impulses of the former.

One theme that dominates accounts of cohesive algorithmic intimacy is communication, viewed as the powerhouse for connecting people. Another theme is that of building communities. Care, communality, but also compassion, a proud word among devotees of cohesive algorithmic intimacy. Consider, for example, comments from Ruth Arnold, a woman working in higher education who appears willing to bet that the rewards of online community building are equal to the most challenging social circumstances. Confronting the immense difficulties of assisting international students during the outbreak of the COVID-19 pandemic, Arnold highlights 'the more personal parts of what builds a community'. The substance of digital technologies for her lies in the beneficence of human nature; machine-mediated culture represents a new form of ethical sense, a projected unity of manners and morals. Here is Arnold on the powers of digitalization as an indispensable means for community building:

> Learning how to build a community at a distance is something we are all doing in real time under Covid-19 lockdown as we determine that physically distant won't mean socially isolated.

One friend says her teenager is staying in touch with her friends through memes. There are virtual coffee breaks and glasses of wine. Friends are reaching out to one another across the world with pictures and affection.

People whose social media accounts were always strictly professional are loosening their stays and sharing their feelings because we really are all in this together, frightened, vulnerable, hopeful and human.[24]

The drive for cohesiveness – 'we are all in this together' – is especially striking. The point is that the digital revolution becomes deeply inscribed within the tissues of human conduct, facilitating an apparently seamless continuity between interiors and exteriors. But there is also an inward sense of outward projections – people, at root, remain frightened and vulnerable. When it comes to cohesive algorithmic intimacy, altruists will of course seek to do altruistic things. But notwithstanding this community-minded insistence on care and compassion, there lurks a powerful ambient fear that the other is simply a mirror for the self's own strategic ends.

The link between digital communication and community building in this cognitive register is clearly more than a matter of individual dispositions. Whilst the reflections of Smith and Arnold provide a window onto these orientations towards human–machine interaction, 'cohesion' in its broad, sociological sense becomes one principle means by which an algorithmic social order can be recast with explicit reference to personal responsibilities and moral obligations. Social cohesion, at least in some recent influential studies of digital technologies, comes to represent a positive state of social relations in increasingly automated societies, even though there are widely divergent views on its prospects and perils. In a synthetic overview of the topic, Jay Marlowe, Allen Bartley and Francis Collins cast social cohesion as promoting (and promoted by) digital technologies. It is not only that smart machines can bridge social interactions across time and space; it is also that diverse social formations (ethnicity, race, class, sex or age) can be made more socially cohesive. The implications of all this are formulated through a sociological lens:

Digital technologies and social media platforms offer both great potential to enhance and extend social cohesion, as well as to complicate the formation of social linkages in places in relation to those across greater distances . . . Whilst digital communication technologies can strengthen existing social ties both locally (often within ethnic communities) and globally (through transnational/ diasporic communities), there may also be negative impacts for other forms of social cohesion. Digital technologies and social media, for instance, can reproduce existing social inequalities for those whose online access is limited, thereby creating an uneven landscape of access which can be influenced by economic status, literacy and education levels, language barriers and age.[25]

This is not to suggest that online expressions of social cohesion remain merely part of the force field of digital life. If building solidarity between and across diverse individuals, communities and networks is a prominent feature of digitalization, we are bound to witness various after-effects and impacts in other fields of social activity too. In this sense, digital expressions of social cohesion don't remain purely digitalized. Marlowe, Bartley and Collins argue that digital expressions of social cohesion are, in fact, bound up with many different forms of social life. The sociologism here is thus impeccably solidaristic, identifying 'communities of belonging' and 'feelings of attachment' in everything from education, health and housing to labour markets, public space and civic life.

Individualized Algorithmic Intimacy

In contrast to the organized and organizing world of conventional algorithmic intimacy, with its valorization of order, control, conformism and smooth-functioning affairs, and at variance with the harmonious hopes and solidarity dreams of cohesive algorithmic intimacy, with its underwriting of the affections, emotion and communal sensibility, there is another cognitive frame infusing human–machine interaction that merits scholarly attention as regards the transformation of intimacy. This mode of cognitive orientation is *individualized algorithmic intimacy*, a frame of reference which emphasizes self-exploration, self-inventiveness, vitality, imagination and the powers of fantasy. Algorithmic intimacy as individualization is all about self-discovery, artistry, innovation. In this frame, traffic with machine intelligence is radically open-ended, with self-interrogating subjects exploring whether algorithms deserve the power conferred on them, or whether there are other digital experiments and technological accomplishments that deserve our attention. This is a cognitive frame in which the power and reach of the algorithms that surround us are 'put on notice', referred for 'further review' and 'critically interrogated' for how digital technologies subtly (or not so subtly) influence our behaviour.

The crossing of imaginative frontiers is the difference that machine-learning algorithms can make to a person's own identity. It is the technological framework par excellence for self-discovery, and bears in important ways on the ideas, ideals and practices of culture as a whole. This may sound lofty, but here is James Ingram on the intersections of technology, creativity and corporate culture:

> Information does not eliminate creativity. We might have more data than ever, but the way that we use it is far from set out in stone. Who could have guessed fifteen years ago that people all around the world would be getting into the cars of strangers, or sleeping in the beds of people they'd never met? And yet Uber and Airbnb – two truly original companies – are now household brands . . . Far from killing creativity, technology allows for a greater proliferation of ideas and products, which means more inspiration . . . Creatives shouldn't fear the tech 'onslaught' but look for ways that they can take advantage of it to become better at what they do. What we will soon find (and some would say it has happened already) is a not a shutdown in the imagination, but an unprecedented period of creative flourishing.[26]

Ingram clearly wants something more from technology over and above that offered in a mostly conventional culture. When it comes to the technological breakthroughs of the current phase of machine learning we begin to see with Ingram (and others like him) that the culture of AI enables the making of a tailor-made life rather than accepting what's simply on the store racks. Full of praise for the digital revolution ('information isn't killing creativity, but enhancing it'), James appears as a full-blooded technological triumphalist on the question of creativity and commerce. From this angle, machine-learning automation refers not only to breakthrough technology but also the hard-nosed business of making money.

If creativity connects with corporate life as individualiz-ation in the algorithmic era, it equally encompasses the arts, humanities and social sciences. One distinguishing feature of the whole discourse around machine-learning algorithms in the early twenty-first century is a massive shift from the technological to the imaginative, or from the scientific to the symbolic. Marcus du Sautoy's *The Creativity Code* develops just such an imaginative cross of AI and the arts.[27] The book examines the distributions of huge computing power and what it means to be human today. Du Sautoy looks at AI-generated art and computer programs that can replicate paintings of such historic masters as Rembrandt. He examines cutting-edge AI used in computer-generated music and also the contributions of algorithms in penning provocative prose. Yet whilst capturing these various dimensions of what might be possible in terms of the technological transformation of the arts, du Sautoy keeps a firm eye on what is presently possible. Piercing the public relations bubble of AI tech, he contends that the most innovative breakthroughs occur when people and machines interact in harmony. He refers to a fascinating cross of musical talent with machine-learning technology in French AI innovator Françoise Pachet's Continuator, a system which enables real-time musical improvisation with an algorithm. Such creative partnerships between people and machines are summed up well by jazz pianist Bernard Lubat, whom du Sautoy quotes in his book: 'The system shows me ideas I could have developed, but that it would have taken me years to develop. It is years ahead of me, yet everything that plays is unquestionably me.' It is just these surprising elements which creators can deploy in their art – the fashioning of an interesting and creative life with automated machine technology – that du Sautoy wishes to speak up for. Self-expression, innovation and experimentation are what happen when the algorithm inflates to the point that it becomes an extension of the artist, although du Sautoy continually underlines the point that AI can be contingently creative without ever grasping the full picture or overall outcome of the artistic process.

In this process of self-shaping, human and machine, the creatively imagined and the digitally designated, powerfully unite, but this time most forcefully in the life of the mind. Part of the lure of the digital revolution is that it suggests there is something lacking in common culture – that our capacity to explore a virtual good life is important as a substitute for human companionship. For this to happen, individualized algorithmic intimacy must appear doubled, with one foot in the world and one outside. Individuals in this cognitive register neither wish to submerge themselves in common culture nor inhabit a world of self-referential reflexivity, but approach life instead on a different plane. Here people use smart machines to reach a heightened imaginative perspective, cultivating intimacy with virtual others and other conversational technologies. Whether in video game livestreaming services such as Twitch or romance simulations (abbreviated as 'dating sims') such as Hatoful Boyfriend or Perfect Date, human relationships in a machine-mediated culture are remade for a 'personalized life'.[28] The algorithms that automate leisure and pleasure alter the very possibilities of human communication, dialogue and interaction, producing new ways of conceiving of self, others and technology.

Dating sims culture seems to be just such a relatively novel affective space. The notion of simulating intimate relationships through gaming took off initially in the 1980s in Japan, in time spreading worldwide to facilitate a genre in which individuals engage with virtual others in a mix of text messaging, augmented reality and AI. Such forming and maintaining of romantic connections with digital partners has been seen as part of a wider de-differentiation of humans and things. As Rohil Aniruth concludes, dating Sims 'can be seen as evidence for the very early stages of a society moving towards substituting human interaction with digital assets for experiencing intimacy and love . . . [This] shift could potentially be of service within cultures that value convenience and where many feel they do not have time to invest adequately in another human being.'[29] The potential service of which Aniruth speaks has today escalated to very diverse demographics. In addition to the worldwide hit Mystic Messenger, recently popular dating sims include Best Friend Forever, Softly With Teeth and Crimson Spires. All of these games reconfigure relationships as imaginative containers and as bits of data exchange and virtuality, as individuals come to experience new types of digital intimacy.

Writing in *The Guardian* of playing the dating sim game Mystic Messenger, Oscar Schwartz reflects:

> The gameplay of Mystic Messenger was unlike anything I had experienced. It did not involve collecting coins or moving through levels but chatting with these other characters through multiple-choice

responses. While these characters were basically just interactive cartoon characters that would automatically respond to prompts from the player with pre-scripted answers, they still felt lifelike, and talking to them required tact and social nous . . . Part of what made Mystic Messenger compelling was the fact that it ran in real time. This meant that once you started, if you stepped away from the game you would miss out on vital conversations and lose track of where you stood with your virtual friends.[30]

Living life close to fantasy can be exhilarating, but there are struggles too. Personalized friends might be virtual, but – just like actual friends – you can 'miss out on vital conversations' or 'lose track' of things. Schwartz eventually finds these demands overbearing, noting: 'As compelling as the simulated world of Mystic Messenger was, after a week, I couldn't keep up with the endless messages and emails.' But this was apparently not the case for many of the gamers interviewed by Schwartz, for whom dating sims are inhabited, indeed imbibed, in order to breathe new life into intimacy – both online and offline. Gaming and virtual interactivity are the living edge of life for dating sims enthusiasts. These simulations of intimacy might thus be said to enact a form of digital evocation that is substantially different from interpersonal relationships and involve exceptional levels of personalization and individualization.

From one angle, this is virtual friendship mixed with romance novels and science fiction. But it is perhaps worth bearing in mind that the arts of dating sims have massive global appeal, with many claiming likely advances in digital intimacy and cultural creativity as a result of ongoing breakthroughs in AI and natural language processing. For one thing, the sheer size of the market for dating sims is staggering. It's estimated that some 2.7 billion people played video games in 2020, with dating simulators among the most popular games.[31] One especially popular dating sim, Love and Producer, was downloaded more than seven million times in its first month of release in China, which in turn prompted headlines such as 'Chinese women spending millions of dollars on virtual boyfriends'. This gives some indication of the ubiquity of dating sims, but there are other more disturbing elements to consider also. Individualized algorithmic intimacy thrives in the case of people dedicated to themselves, to the exploration of their own identity. Such people can, seemingly instinctively, pluck virtual intimacy from the fictional sentimentalities of dating sims and turn them into a more hopeful social resource or utopian brand of culture. But there is risk here as well. The more individuals sublimate imaginative energies and erotic impulses into the task of building digital intimacy, the more they can deplete their own inner resources and interpersonal relations with others, leaving the self narcissistically brittle or drained. There is something strangely self-thwarting about the whole business of pressing desire into the service of virtual beings: it conceals a neurotic inner compulsion which can tip the obsessive way dating sim fans play these virtual games into disabling pathology. One signal example is the case of a Japanese man who actually married his best-loved character from the dating sim Love Plus.

There can be, then, a severe emotional price to be paid when the symbolic boundary between the world of virtual characters and the world of everyday companionship breaks down. Fandom can turn fanatical for devotees of dating sims, just as we have seen with other forms of burgeoning digital intimacy. Thankfully, those suffering from fandom turned fanatical remain the exception. Most fans of dating sims, in one form or another, manage to navigate intimacy with these virtual others in the course of their day-to-day lives. There can be important gains in self-understanding and the flourishing of relations with other people as a result, along with the risks of delusion which I have already mentioned. One positive gain might stem from immersion in the world of dating sim fans. Chatting with other dating sim fans about favourite characters and blossoming virtual relation-ships in online forums can support individuals in feeling part of a culture of like-minded people who share similar interests and cultural tastes. But from the cognitive register of individualized algorithmic intimacy there are far greater emotional gains to be had. The most imaginative dating sim gamers do not see their interactions with virtual others as a stand-in for interpersonal companionship, but as a space for invention, creativity, open-endedness. This is a cognitive orientation in which finding out about life and imagining yourself in it is absolutely centre stage. Schwartz captures well the distinctive cognitive attributes of such imaginative gamers:

> What I learnt from [these gamers], who stood at the vanguard of relations with these virtual others, is that when we interact

with these characters we are engaged in a collective suspension of disbelief, allowing ourselves to imagine that they understand us, that they are kind of alive. Yet unlike [these gamers], most of us do not acknowledge the role imagination plays in these relationships with the non-human. We pretend that these anthropomorphic algorithms are coming alive because of technological innovation alone, rather than cultural process and collective myth-making. It is at this point that we risk losing control of the fantasy.

This, to be sure, is a creative form of solitude, one that values artful experimentation and digital literacy above social roles and over-socialized relationships.

Conclusion: Crossroads in the Automation Web

Algorithmic intimacy, I have suggested, has three faces: worlds of experience that can be assigned to one of the categories of conventional, cohesive and individualized human–machine interactions, or to some combination of the three. These worlds of experience are related to a more general sociology of the emergence and continuous transformation of automated societies of the twenty-first century. The predicament of contemporary women and men negotiating these worlds of automated intimacy, I have argued throughout this book, is one experienced as a *living through* of the crisis of digital revolution. This is a radical and far-reaching crisis in which the technological shifts of advanced automation disrupt many of the social practices that shaped the contours of intimate relationships for most of the twentieth century and before, as well as undermining the cultural forms and symbolic channels of communication and connection through which personal relationships have been developed and continually renewed over a long historical period. The remarkable encounter between our culturally inherited customs and convictions pertaining to everyday life, personal relationships and intimacy on the one hand, and the great digital revolution of our own time on the other hand, is precisely the terrain in which these novel worlds of experience and experimentation make their presence felt in the brave new world of algorithmic modernity.

It has become increasingly commonplace in contemporary public and media debate to assign the digitalization of intimacy to the transformative power of technology alone. This is not a view that I share. I have argued throughout this book that such a viewpoint fails to consider, and often wholly ignores, the specific social, cultural, political and economic contexts in which women and men – and the existing institutions in which they live their lives – choose to respond to the opportunities and risks of the digital revolution. My focus on social actors seizing the possibilities opened up to them by remote, semi-autonomous and autonomous technologies of machine intelligence is an attempt to make explicit the general cognitive strategies underpinning lifestyle habits in the age of advanced machine learning. Of course, much more research will be needed to fathom the actual successes or otherwise of these worlds of experience and experimentation generated in relation to automated intelligent machines.

There has never been a more important time for examination of the risks and anxieties of living together, and apart, in our algorithmic world. Thanks to the digital revolution, 'relationships', 'intimacies', 'partnerships', 'friendships' and similar notions are profoundly transformed by the unprecedented power of predictive algorithms in complex, cascading and interconnected ways. Automated intelligent machines are increasingly involved in our most routine daily activities, from telling Siri to set a reminder for a Zoom call with a close friend to talking with an AI therapist or virtual romantic interest. People are 'relating' differently and finding ways of forging 'relationships' differently, as old practices that worked well in the past are supplanted by automated flows and informational power that make possible new kinds of intimacy, new forms of personalized prediction and new ways of calculating human connection. Unlike 'committed relationships' or 'old-fashioned associations', social connections are increasingly made to the measure of data-mining operations, with 'romantic hook-ups' or 'best friends' reframed in the image of algorithmic recommendation systems. Indeed connections are, increasingly, 'automated relations'. The digital revolution has brought into being the 'machine intelligence knows best' phenomenon, which owes its seductive allure to the utopic promises loudly proclaimed and regularly promoted across communication and social media networks. A search for 'artificial intimacy' on Google provides a snapshot of the onslaught: 'What virtual reality and artificial intelligence means for sex, love and intimacy', 'Nudification Internet trend: AI tools which undress women', 'Could we fall in love with robots?', 'Is artificial intimacy a threat?', 'Virtual boyfriends are a thing now', 'Sex bots, virtual friends, VR lovers: tech is changing the way we interact.'

The algorithmic society of automated devices and computational consumers may be seen as an institutional response seeking to balance the demands of personalization and systematization in the aftermath of the digital revolution. This 'system-ness' of automation is crucial, and it underpins individual efforts to keep afloat in an age of information overload and to render realistic dreams of living an autonomous life. I explored, in chapter 2, the significance of Simmel's approach to sociability for better grasping our contemporary romance with automated machine intelligence. The importance of Simmel's sociological thought, I argued, is that it enables us to see that contemporary society is characterized both by the growth of automation in everyday life and by the increasing importance of digitalization for the redefinition of individualization and personal identity. It is not just that daily life becomes ensnarled in a series of automated processes shaped by algorithmic recommendation systems and machine intelligence, in which the individual self might be cast (following Simmel) as 'a mere cog in an enormous organization of things and powers'. Rather the inner fabric of the self, as well as the intimate terrain of private life, is repositioned – 'disembedded and re-embedded', to recall Anthony Giddens's memorable terminology – in the self-expanding world of predictive algorithms. Predictive analytics at once consoles and numbs the self – or, rather, keeps us at a safe distance from our own capacity for personal agency and self-reflection. The partitioning off of individual agency from the 'personalized living' or 'individualized lifestyles' advanced in conditions of algorithmic modernity means that the societal costs of our 'automated comfort zones' are fenced off from personal reflection and public inspection. The comfort zone of automation – the ever-multiplying need for algorithmic recommendations, automated reminders, remote monitoring and digital surveillance – is our smart vehicle for sustaining everyday life. But like all stories of the modernization process, automation in the algorithmic age remains intrinsically vulnerable to system errors, external interference and digital breakdown. The flipside of the consolation of automated lives is thus anxiety, fear and dread.

Sander De Ridder sums up accurately the state of affairs to which we have been propelled in the following way:

> These tensions and ambivalences around how data-technologies are so deeply involved in people's intimacies are clearly symbolized by societal fears, claiming that mobile dating apps' interventions are 'unnatural' and 'risky,' or when moral concerns are voiced on the 'authenticity' of online dating and ultimately when data-driven interventions are seen as harming the 'truth' of love; each of these sense-makings illustrates the existential burden of building close human connections through data-driven technology, which may be met with excitement, yet also doubt, fear, and stubborn resistance.[32]

We are pressured to conform to datafication, says De Ridder, as automation becomes the principal means not only for the production of social knowledge but for the constitution of intimate life. What De Ridder refers to as a new and applied 'mathematical mindset to intimacy' is precisely the lure of predictive algorithms and related 'objective' metrics of advanced computation. I have used the term 'algorithmic intimacy' to denote the restricted and restricting dimensions of machine intelligence which produces new ways of ordering personal behaviour and modelling intimate relations, which can be supplemented by De Ridder's 'existential burden of building close human connections through data-driven technology, which may be met with excitement, yet also doubts, fear, and stubborn resistance'. But still there remains little to differentiate between, ostensibly, the euphoric boosterism of 'transformationalists' and their excited talk of the AI revolution, and the obstinate blindness of 'sceptics', insisting that technological innovation is overblown and that a business-as-usual scenario reigns supreme. There is, as it happens, less difference between these supposedly opposite standpoints than is commonly supposed; the 'excitement, yet also doubt, fear, and stubborn resistance' of which De Ridder speaks are two sides of the same coin. Understanding the ramifications of the digital revolution has not got to be like this. There is another way of grasping the algorithmic age taking shape, one which better captures the complexity of individuals confronting exciting opportunities and fearful risks at once.

Contemporary human–machine interfaces operate in many social and ideological forms. In this chapter I have identified three versions of algorithmic intimacy which establish relationships with conventional, cohesive and individualizing worlds, and which allow for correspondingly different ways of organizing experiences of self, society and digital processes of automation. What has this combing of varieties of algorithmic intimacy yielded? At the least, I hope that it will provoke some sympathy for, and attention to, the idea that different kinds of algorithmic intimacy (and the human–machine interfaces in which these are enmeshed) are not only based on the creations of an experiencing individual but also institutionally differentiated in the algorithmic era of computational societies. Although my sampling of existing research and testimony which can be connected to these outlooks on algorithmic intimacy is far from exhaustive, I have sought to detail a framework within which interdisciplinary research on different patterns of human–machine interaction can be taken up, developed and refined. My hope is that, when taken together, these reflections on the notion of algorithmic intimacy – on the domains of relationship, therapy and friendship tech, as well as that of the complex interplay of personalization and systematization – can provide a conceptual foundation upon which a theory of algorithmic modernity can be developed and elaborated.

'We never think that what we think conceals from us what we are', wrote the French essayist Paul Valéry. The emergence of algorithmic intimacy is deeply interwoven with a widening gulf between social experience and individual knowledge that has become a key aspect of the contemporary automated world. We urgently need further work, for example, on how varieties of algorithmic intimacy cross and tangle, and under what conditions. We also need to know more than we currently do about how thickly populated are these different versions of algorithmic sociability. The big question is: can the benefits and opportunities opened up with the advent of algorithmic intimacy be delivered safely in a way that minimizes anxieties, fears and forebodings? We know that mental health and related issues caused by social isolation cost advanced economies billions of dollars annually. Digital technologies, as we have charted, can indeed reinforce social isolation; yet this outcome can be avoided with sociotechnical change at multiple levels of practice and policy. Moving beyond the 'optimistic' versus 'pessimistic' technology debate to create a more reflective socio-technical approach has been one of my principal aims in this book. My critical focus on algorithmically orientated lifestyles and automated intimate action, which I argue needs to be recognized as the central motif of twenty-first-century social theory, has underpinned the inventory of the challenges I have set out in *Algorithmic Intimacy*.

Notes

Chapter 1

1 Ian McEwan, *Machines Like Me*, London: Jonathan Cape, 2019, pp. 33–4.
2 McEwan, *Machines Like Me*, p. 94.
3 McEwan, *Machines Like Me*, p. 116.
4 See Ted Striphas, 'Algorithmic Culture', *European Journal of Cultural Studies*, 18 (4–5), 2015, pp. 395–412. Striphas discussed the concept of algorithm as a 'mangled transliteration' from classical mathematics, and specifically the work of al-Khwārizmī, at pp. 403–4.
5 See again Stiphas, 'Algorithmic Culture', who discusses al-Khwārizmī's key work *Al-Kitāb al-Mukhtaṣar fī ḥisāb al-jabr wa-al-Muqābala* (*The Compendious Book of Calculation by Restoration and Balancing*), which introduced many of the fundamental methods of algebra. Striphas writes (p. 404) of the title of this work: 'the word appearing just before *al-jabr* in the Arabic version of the title, *ḥisāb*, though translated as calculation, also denotes arithmetic. Algorithm, arithmetic: conceptually, they have been a stone's throw away from one another since the 9th century.'
6 Pedro Domingo, *The Master Algorithm: How the Quest for the Ultimate Learning Machine Will Remake Our World*, New York: Penguin, 2017.
7 When people talk of the digitalization of intimacy as though it were part of the inner world as well as the social world, their words come close to evoking the power of what I am calling 'algorithmic

intimacy'. I see AI as a specific emissary for significant elements of digital technologies, most dramatically in the 'rewriting' of our private, internal, intimate lives as well as our public, social lives in these times. This is not the place to elaborate my account of the different forms of selfhood and interpersonal relationships which are enmeshed in complex digital systems, but the essential elements of this account are to be found in Anthony Elliott, *The Culture of AI: Everyday Life and the Digital Revolution*, London and New York: Routledge, 2019. See also Anthony Elliott, *Making Sense of AI: Our Algorithmic World*, Cambridge: Polity, 2022.

Whilst seemingly oxymoronic, the term 'algorithmic intimacy' seeks to capture the penetration of the unseen, the unthought and the largely invisible dimensions of ever-increasing semi-automatic and automatic processes of digital technologies upon the inner fabric of the self, interpersonal relations and our relations with the social world. In formulating the thesis of 'algorithmic intimacy', I have been influenced by the theoretical departures of Helga Nowotny and Bernard Stiegler, even though the notion as I elaborate it differs in very substantial ways from certain emphases to be found in their respective writings. Neither Nowotny nor Stiegler directly addresses the theme of intimacy: instead, of key concern are the cultural illusions of predictive algorithms (Nowotny) and societal corrosions stemming from the digital revolution (Stiegler), both of which are of key significance to rethinking intimacy in the algorithmic era of modernity. See especially Helga Nowotny, *In AI We Trust*, Cambridge: Polity, 2021, and Bernard Stiegler, *The Age of Disruption: Technology and Madness in Computational Capitalism*, Cambridge: Polity, 2019.

8 Theoretically, some writers have recently emphasized an under-standing of machine-learning modelling processes as cultural as well as technological, although it must be said that cultural practices are incorporated in the current literature in what remains a rather narrow context devoid of focus on the internal or emotional dimen-sions of human subjectivity. See, for example, Adrian Mackenzie, *Machine Learners: Archaeology of a Data Practice*, Cambridge, MA: MIT Press, 2017; Louise Amoore, *Cloud Ethics: Algorithms and the Attributes of Ourselves and Others*, Durham, NC: Duke University Press, 2020.

Another line of inquiry has recently been developed in Jonathan Roberge and Michael Castelle (eds.), *The Cultural Life of Machine Learning*. Cham: Palgrave Macmillan, 2021. Roberge and Castelle take as their object of study the 'entire sociotechnical and political process of modern machine learning from genesis to impact and back again' (p. 3). The emphasis throughout is on the 'end-to-end' methods of deep learning practitioners, while also urging the importance of taking an epistemic step thus far largely resisted by these practitioners: namely, that machine learning should be defined as a 'coproduction requiring the interaction of social and technical processes'. Taking as their point of departure the research of my colleagues Robert J. Holton and Ross Boyd (specifically their article 'Where Are the People? What Are They Doing? Why Are They Doing It?'(Mindell) Situating Artificial Intelligence within a Socio-Technical Framework', *Journal of Sociology*, 57 (2), 2021, pp. 179–95), Roberge and Castelle specify three fundamental characteristics of contemporary machine learning as socio-technical. First, machine-learning cultures are both pragmatic and model-centric. Models emerge here from iterative processes involving the fine-tuning of sensitivities, setting of target values and adjusting of relevance weightings, among other things, that are as much art as they are science – for example, 'the "hyperparameters" that exist outside both the model and the algorithm and yet crucially determine its success (in often unpredictable ways)' (p. 5). Second, AI is flexible, dynamic and recursive. As they argue, 'it is not just the model that develops, but the social world of which the model is but a part; every deep learning researcher is, more so than in other sciences, attuned to each other and each other's models, because an innovation in one field (such as machine translation) might be profitably transduced to new domains (such as computer vision)' (p. 5). Third, the self-referentiality entailed in model development is a feature of the field itself, leaving machine-learning practitioners to account for their own (and others') behaviour through referencing the epistemology of the techniques they use. As Roberge and Castelle note: 'This represents the logic of a closed community in which the only known social theory is game theory.' But what, we might ask, are the side effects of such recursiveness and self-referentiality in the domain of self-experience, both conscious and unconscious? Are the 'hyperparameters' of which Roberge and Castelle speak merely the reverse lining of the algorithms that make people feel programmed, or even robotic?

9 As Nowotny notes: 'Computers and tablets are already daily companions with whom we communicate, exhorting or cursing them, ready to share our most intimate thoughts and feelings. We trust predictive algorithms and believe they can help us to manage uncertainty. Thus they become part of an extended self' (*In AI We Trust*, p. 104). To which we might add: it is not just an extensity of self which is reconstituted in the age of AI, but also a new intensity (overdetermined by machine-learning predictive algorithms) at the level of individualized life strategies. How is it that machine-learning

predictive algorithms go all the way down into these textures of subjectivity, rewriting the intimate proximities of our relations with others (both human and non-human)? This is precisely the terrain of the thesis of algorithmic intimacy.

10 Don Slater's *Love in the Time of Algorithms: What Technology Does to Meeting and Mating*, London: Penguin, 2013, for example, examines how online dating and algorithmic prediction are spurring on a new kind of sexual revolution. Slater, a journalist, develops an interesting history of algorithmic matchmaking, looking at the social network-style profiles of some of the (seemingly all male) founders of the era's biggest online dating success stories, including OKCupid, Plenty of Fish, Match and eHarmony. But this work is now somewhat dated; it is largely impressionistic and journalistic in style, and does not examine in detail how particular technological changes – such as machine learning – are restructuring intimate relationships.

11 There has been some scholarly research on the potential sexual applications of artificial intelligence (largely in gender studies and in academic research in the fields of psychology, ethics and medical science), but this too is in need of supplementation. The edited collection *AI Love You: Developments in Human–Robot Intimate Relationships*, eds. Yuefang Zhou and Martin H. Fischer, Cham: Springer, 2019, addresses a range of security and data privacy issues associated with sexual interactions in the context of artificial intelligence. But the book is mostly concerned with the study of human–robot sexuality. Most recently, Polity published Kathleen Richardson's *Sex Robots: The End of Love*, Cambridge, 2019. This is a mostly broad-brushstroke account, written from a critical feminist perspective, that is limited to robotics. None of these works have the breadth or depth which is proposed here.

12 See, for example, Louise Amoore and Volha Piotukh (eds.), *Algorithmic Life: Calculative Devices in the Age of Big Data*, London and New York: Routledge, 2016.

13 Stiegler's broad argument is that, in the age of computational capitalism, women and men entrust an already damaged rationality to algorithmic technologies which, in turn, squeeze to the sidelines the human capacity for independent reflection. For Stiegler, contemporary subjectivity is at once displaced and disfigured by computational technologies that gather data, discern patterns and generate predictions at processing speeds that radically outstrip human cognition. One upshot of this is that human thought – specifically, the reflection demanded by thought – is routinely obliterated by lines of code intended to anticipate, and actively shape, consciousness itself.

Stiegler's social theory is vast and richly complex, but broadly speaking he casts the threat of computational capitalism in terms of a widespread delegation of human capacities to digital technologies. Exteriorization, says Stiegler, lies at the core of our relation to technology. On the basis of the work of Leroi-Gourhan, Stiegler views humans and technology as co-constitutive – our technical capacities define us as a species. Drawing upon a lineage from Plato's *Phaedrus* to Derrida's grammatology, Stiegler contends that all kinds of knowledge can become grammatized in the age of AI. Computational capitalism constitutes and transforms grammatization in the sense of not only *savoir-faire*, but also *savoir-vivre*, by which he refers to behaviour more broadly, including our cognitive and cultural orientations in, and pre-theoretic understandings of, the hyper-industrial service economies. For Stiegler, this is profoundly corrosive of individuation. In the age of big data, the personalized digital profile takes the place of the collective 'We' as a central point of reference, leading to social atomism (including the failure of politics and political imagination), even as individuals are urged to realize their unique subjectivity by way of common digital platforms. See André Leroi-Gourhan, *Gesture and Speech*, Cambridge, MA: MIT Press; Bernard Stiegler, *Automatic Society, Volume 1: The Future of Work*, Cambridge: Polity, 2016; Stiegler, *Age of Disruption*.

14 Tania Bucher, 'The Algorithmic Imaginary: Exploring the Ordinary Effects of Facebook Algorithms', *Information, Communication and Society*, 20 (1), 2017, pp. 30–44, at p. 32.

15 Julian Lucas, 'Man, Woman and Robot in Ian McEwan's New Novel', *The New Yorker*, 15 April 2019, https://www.newyorker.com/magazine/2019/04/22/man-woman-and-robot-in-ian-mcewans-new-novel

16 Anthony Elliott, 'Will Talking to AI Voice Assistants Re-Engineer Our Human Conversations?', *The Conversation*, 15 January 2019, https://theconversation.com/will-talking-to-ai-voice-assistants-re-engineer-our-human-conversations-108922

17 See, among others, Anthony Elliott, *Identity Troubles*, London and New York: Routledge, 2016; Anthony Elliott and Charles Lemert, *The New Individualism: The Emotional Costs of Globalization*, London and New York: Routledge, 2009; Anthony Elliott, *Concepts of the Self*, 4th edn, Cambridge: Polity, 2020; Anthony Elliott, *Reinvention*, 2nd edn, London and New York: Routledge, 2021.

Chapter 2

1 See Anthony Giddens, *Capitalism and Modern Social Theory*, Cambridge: Cambridge University Press, 1971.

2 Georg Simmel, 'The Sociology of Secrecy and of Secret Societies', *American Journal of Sociology*, 11, 1906, pp. 441–98, at p. 441.
3 Ferdinand Fellmann, 'Intimate Relations', in *Rethinking Georg Simmel's Social Philosophy*, Cham: Springer, 2021, https://doi.org /10.1007/978-3-030-57351-5_4
4 Georg Simmel, 'Sociology of the Senses', in *Simmel on Culture*, eds. D. Frisby and M. Featherstone, London: Sage, 1997, p. 111.
5 Simmel, 'The Metropolis and Mental Life', in *Simmel on Culture*, p. 184.
6 It is indeed the case that a number of Simmel's intellectual contemporaries, or near contemporaries, outlined approaches to social change that, in various respects, chimed with aspects of his sociological analysis and its emphasis on intimacy. Ferdinand Tönnies' famous distinction between *Gemeinschaft* and *Gesellschaft*, contrasting the thick, immediate and highly personal ties of pre-modern, rural communities with the more superficial, impersonal ties of modern market economies and urban living, is one such. There are surely strong affinities to be found, for example, with the opening passages of Simmel's *The Metropolis and Mental Life*, where he contrasts 'the slower, more habitual, more smoothly flowing rhythm of the sensory-mental phase of small town and rural existence' with the sensory foundations of metropolitan life and its 'rapid telescoping of changing images, pronounced differences with what is grasped at a single glance, and the unexpectedness of violent stimuli . . . with every crossing of the street, with the tempo and multiplicity of economic, occupational and social life'. See Georg Simmel 'The Metropolis and Mental Life', in *On Individuality and Social Forms*, ed. D. Levine, Chicago: University of Chicago Press 1971, pp 325–6.
   Likewise, Charles Horton Cooley underscored the emergence of a new form of sociability and personal life emerging with modern life, especially the 'socialized feelings' (he nominated love, resentment, fear of disgrace or ridicule) which constituted modern refinements to the brute affects (lust, rage, terror) arising from social interaction and conscious human reflection. In this, Cooley's critique bears certain similarities to Simmel's analysis of an intellectual tempering of the primordial emotions of interpersonal relations emerging with the advent of modernity. Cooley's approach also arguably prefigures those aspects of Norbert Elias's sociology of modernity in *The Civilizing Process* where he casts the more unruly, painful, dangerous and brutish aspects of social life as being in need of sequestration in the private realm, or in specialized institutions lest the delicate sensibilities of civic subjects be disturbed. See Charles Horton Cooley, 'The Trend of Sentiment', in *Social Organization*, New York: Charles Scribner and Sons. 1909.

Notwithstanding these intellectual affinities, my argument is that it was Simmel, among all others, who put questions of intimacy at the centre of sociological analysis and who provided the most elaborate accounts of the shifting balances between belonging and otherness, familiarity and strangeness, the abstract and particular.

7 See Anthony Elliott (ed.), *The Routledge Social Science Handbook of AI*, London and New York: Routledge, 2021.

8 Zygmunt Bauman, *Life in Fragments*, Cambridge: Polity, 1995, p. 44.

9 Bauman, *Life in Fragments*, p. 45.

10 Deborah Lupton, *Data Selves: More-than-Human Perspectives*, Cambridge: Polity, 2019. The 'data self' or the 'digital self' now forms a distinct subfield in contemporary identity studies. Lupton draws extensively from materialist and post-representational theories of language, specifically the notion of 'more-than-human', to explore the constitution, reproduction and transformation of contemporary selves within human–data assemblages. Other authors have developed different perspectives. Colin Koopman, for example, argues that the process of subjective datafication (or 'informational personhood') has been built up over time; he points to the earlier development of birth certificates, psychological assessments, education records, financial profiles and a 'sizeable racialised data apparatus'. See Colin Koopman. *How We Became Our Data: A Genealogy of the Informational Person*, Chicago: University of Chicago Press, 2019. Other significant works in this subfield include John Cheney-Lippold, *We Are Data: Algorithms and the Making of Our Digital Selves*, New York: New York University Press, 2017; Ronald E. Day, *Documentarity: Evidence, Ontology, and Inscription*, Cambridge, MA: TMIT Press, 2019; Lee Humphreys, *The Qualified Self: Social Media and the Accounting of Everyday Life*, Cambridge, MA: MIT Press, 2018. Whilst such analyses of 'data selves' are undeniably of significance to the central theme of this book, it is also important to note that the application of machine-learning algorithms to personal data has not been treated as a major concern in this literature.

11 Zeena Feldman, 'Simmel in Cyberspace', *Information, Communication & Society*, 15 (2), 2012, pp. 297–319, https://doi .org/10.1080/1369118X.2011.647045

12 Cristina Miguel, *Personal Relationships and Intimacy in the Age of Social Media*, London: Palgrave, 2018.

13 Anthony Giddens, *The Transformation of Intimacy*, Cambridge: Polity, 1993, pp. 39–40.

14 Ziyad Marrar, *Intimacy*, London and New York: Routledge, 2012, p. 49.

15 Lynn Jamieson, *Intimacy: Personal Relationships in Modern Societies*, Cambridge: Polity, 1998.

16 Lauren Berlant, *Intimacy*, Chicago: University of Chicago Press, 2000.

17 Valerian J. Derlega and John H. Berg, *Self-Disclosure: Theory, Research, and Therapy*, New York: Plenum Press, 1987.

18 Charles Fried, 'Privacy: A Moral Analysis', in *Philosophical Dimensions of Privacy: An Anthology*, ed. F. Schoeman, Cambridge: Cambridge University Press, 1968, p. 211.

19 Jamieson, *Intimacy*, p. 13.

20 See Erving Goffman, *The Presentation of Self in Everyday Life*, New York: Doubleday, 1959.

21 Bernard Stiegler, *Automatic Society, Volume 1: The Future of Work*, Cambridge: Polity, 2016.

22 Anais Nony, 'Bernard Stiegler on Automatic Society: An Interview', *The Third Rail*, 5, http://thirdrailquarterly.org/bernard-stiegler-on-automatic-society

23 Baroness Susan Greenfield, House of Lords, UK Parliament, as reported in Hansard, https://publications.parliament.uk/pa/ld200809/ldhansrd/text/90212-0010.htm

24 Susan Greenfield, *Mind Change: How Digital Technologies Are Leaving Their Mark on Our Brains*, New York: Random House, 2015. See also James M. Lang, 'The Distracted Classroom', *The Chronicle of Higher Education*, 13 March 2017, https://www.chronicle.com/article/The-DistractedClassroom/239446?cid=cp120. Nicholas Carr also makes a similar, though distinct, argument in *The Shallows: What the Internet is Doing to Our Brain*, New York, W. W. Norton, 2010.

25 Controversially, Greenfield draws direct connections – in *Mind Change* and elsewhere – between Internet use and autism, as well as with other harmful effects on the brain.

26 As Robbins develops this point: 'What's never really explained is how the technologies that are *in*cluded in her analysis are different from those that are *ex*cluded. Without that clarity, her story twists into irretrievable knots. Short videos on YouTube are presented as new, alien and risky because they erode attention spans; but short cartoons on television in the 1950s were part of a healthy and balanced upbringing because kids didn't spend too long watching them' (Martin Robbins, 'Mind Change: Susan Greenfield Has a Big Idea, but What Is It?', *The Guardian*, 3 October 2014).

27 Sherry Turkle, *Alone Together: Why We Expect More from Technology and Less from Each Other*. New York: Basic Books, 2017, p. 7. The next two quotes are from pp. 12 and 36.

28 Turkle, *Alone Together*, p. 31.

29 See especially Markus Breen, 'The Public Intellectual as Agent-Egoist: Sherry Turkle's Ethnography', *International Journal of Communication*, 12, 2018, pp. 725–44.

30 Anthony Elliott, *The Culture of AI: Everyday Life and the Digital Revolution*, London and New York: Routledge, 2019, pp. 84–94.

31 There are a number of significant scholarly accounts that take the same features of contemporary digital societies as Greenfield and Turkle yet interpret them in an entirely different way. N. Katherine Hayes, for example, identifies a generational shift in cognitive styles from 'deep attention' (the sustained focus on a single strand of information, typical of conventional reading) to 'hyper attention' (switching focus across different strands of information typical of media-saturated environments). Whilst recognizing that this shift in cognitive styles poses challenges to education at all levels, she also sees opportunities to creatively rework curriculum and pedagogical strategies to incorporate new media materials and develop new forms of media literacy suitable for the twenty-first century. See N. Katherine Hayles, 'Hyper and Deep Attention: The Generational Divide in Cognitive Modes', *Profession*, 1, 2007, pp. 187–99. See also Mark B. N. Hansen, *Feed-Forward: On the Future of Twenty-First-Century Media*, Chicago: University of Chicago Press, 2015.

32 Cristen Dalessandro, 'Internet Intimacy: Authenticity and Longing in the Relationships of Millennial Young Adults', *Sociological Perspectives*, 61 (4), 2018, pp. 626–41, at p. 628.

33 Dalessandro, 'Internet Intimacy', p. 626.

34 See, for example, Mitchell Hobbs, Stephen Owen and Livia Gerber, 'Liquid Love? Dating Apps, Sex, Relationships and the Digital Transformation of Intimacy', *Journal of Sociology*, 53 (2), 2016, pp. 271–84; Catalina L. Toma, 'Developing Online Deception Literacy While Looking for Love', *Media, Culture & Society*, 39 (3), 2017, 423–8; José van Dijck, '"You Have One Identity": Performing the Self on Facebook and LinkedIn', *Media, Culture & Society*, 35 (2), 2013, pp. 199–215.

35 Adam Phillips, *Missing Out: In Praise of the Unlived Life*, New York: Farrar, Straus & Giroux, 2012.

36 Richard Sennett, 'Reflections on the Public Realm', in *The New Blackwell Companion to the City*, eds. G. Bridge and S. Watson, Oxford: Wiley, 2014, p. 392.

37 Mark Wigley, 'Network Fever', in *New Media, Old Media: A History and Theory Reader*, eds. W. Chun and T. Keenan, New York, Routledge, 2006, p. 375.

38 Feldman, 'Simmel in Cyberspace', p. 311.

39 Feldman, 'Simmel in Cyberspace', p. 313.

40 Sara Ahmed, *Strange Encounters: Embodied Others in Post-Coloniality*, London and New York: Routledge, 2001.
41 Zygmunt Bauman, *Modernity and the Holocaust*, Cambridge: Polity, 1989; Zygmunt Bauman, *Modernity and Ambivalence*, Cambridge: Polity, 1991.
42 For a more general discussion on this point, see Massimo Durante, *Computational Power*, London and New York: Routledge, 2021.
43 Helga Nowotny, *In AI We Trust*, Cambridge: Polity, 2021, p. 3.
44 See, among others, Benjamin N. Jacobsen, 'Algorithms and the Narration of Past Selves', *Information, Communication & Society*, online, 21 October 2020; Taina Bucher, 'The Algorithmic Imaginary: Exploring The Ordinary Affects of Facebook Algorithms', *Information, Communication & Society*, 20 (1), 2017, pp. 30–44.
45 See Cornelius Castoriadis, *The Imaginary Institution of Society*, Cambridge: Polity, 1987. See also Anthony Elliott, *Social Theory Since Freud*, London and New York: Routledge, 2004.

Chapter 3

1 Sandra Ponce de Leon, 'Eight Women Founders Share Their Insights on AI and Intimacy', *Forbes*, 6 August 2019.
2 There is now a considerable literature on the social, cultural and political impacts of dating and hook-up apps. Many of these scholarly contributions raise a number of crucial issues which will be reflected upon throughout this chapter, including the complex ways geolocative dating apps (combined with smartphones) enhance or reduce safety and facilitate or diminish fabrications of identity and community building for specific identifiable groups, as well as how much of the commercial hype surrounding dating apps as solutions to users' personal concerns reproduce aged, gendered, raced and classed normative standards and exclusionary practices. See, for example, Kath Albury and Paul Byron, 'Safe on My Phone? Same-Sex Attracted Young People's Negotiations of Intimacy, Visibility, and Risk on Digital Hook-Up Apps', *Social Media + Society*, online, 17 October 2016; Tinonee Pym, Paul Byron and Kath Albury, '"I Still Want to Know They're Not Terrible People": Negotiating "Queer Community" on Dating Apps', *International Journal of Cultural Studies*, 24 (3), 2021, pp. 398–413; Kath Albury, Anthony McCosker, Tinonee Pym and Paul Byron, 'Dating Apps as Public Health "Problems": Cautionary Tales and Vernacular Pedagogies in News Media', *Health Sociology Review*, 29 (3), 2020, pp. 232–48; Bronwyn Carlson, 'Love and Hate at the Cultural Interface: Indigenous Australians and Dating Apps', *Journal of Sociology*, 56

(2), 2020, pp. 133–50; Hannah R. Marston, Kelly Niles-Yokum, Sarah Earle, Barbara Gomez and David M. Lee, 'OK Cupid, Stop Bumbling around and Match Me Tinder: Using Dating Apps Across the Life Course', *Gerontology and Geriatric Medicine*, online, 7 August 2020, https://doi.org/10.1177/2333721420947498; Stefanie Duguay, 'Dressing up Tinderella: Interrogating Authenticity Claims on the Mobile Dating App Tinder *Information, Communication & Society*, 20 (3), 2017, pp. 351–67, https://doi.org/10.1080/136 9118X.2016.1168471; Zack Dwyer, Nicholas Hookway and Brady Robards, 'Navigating "Thin" Dating Markets: Mid-Life Repartnering in the Era of Dating Apps and Websites', *Journal of Sociology*, 57 (3), 2021, pp. 647–63, https://doi.org/10.1177/1440783320948958

3 After various rounds of fundraising, crowdfunding and equity raising throughout 2018 and 2019, the Loly dating app project still appeared only a dream going into the 2020s. But Ashley did appear at various public events talking about the prospects of AI-powered dating on Loly, telling audiences to 'keep their fingers crossed'.

4 'Interview with Adryenn Ashley with Loly Dating APP', https://www.youtube.com/watch?v=HsOlMw58N8M

5 In speaking of sexual algorithmic intimacy, or relationship tech, I seek to distinguish my approach from much of the literature in media studies and cultural sociology on dating apps and hook-up culture. The specific qualities and characteristics that machine-learning algorithms bring to the functioning of dating apps and social media platforms receive, at best, only marginal consideration in this literature. See note 2 in this chapter. Notwithstanding this criticism, there has recently been some attention devoted to the presence and mechanics of algorithms in particular and machine learning more generally in some social science research, but the great bulk of this research tends towards a constricted focus on somewhat technical concerns – for example, the influence of relational filter bubbles, the operation of the 'swipe', algorithmic harvesting and curation of 'sexually affective data flows' as corporate assets, and the ways algorithmic protocols allow unconscious racial prefer-ences to be expressed while supporting users' perceptions of themselves as non-racist. See, among others, Lorenza Parisi and Francesca Comunello, 'Dating in the Time of "Relational Filter Bubbles": Exploring Imaginaries, Perceptions and Tactics of Italian Dating App Users', *The Communication Review*, 23 (1), 2020, pp. 66–89; Elisabeth Timmermans and Cédric Courtois, 'From Swiping to Casual Sex and/or Committed Relationships: Exploring the Experiences of Tinder Users', *The Information Society*, 34 (2), 2018, pp. 59–70; Shuaishuai Wang, 'Chinese Affective Platform Economies: Dating, Live Streaming, and Performative Labor on

Blued', *Media, Culture & Society*, 42 (4), 2020, pp. 502–20; Gregory Narr, 'The Uncanny Swipe Drive: The Return of a Racist Mode of Algorithmic Thought on Dating Apps', *Studies in Gender and Sexuality*, online, 24 September 2021.

6 The principal aim of this chapter is to explore these broader questions about what is happening to intimate sexual relationships as they increasingly undergo mediation by new-generation digital technologies. This is not to disregard the wealth of empirical material now available on the digital mediation of specific sexual cultures, or a rapidly growing literature on the harnessing of predictive algorithms and locative technologies in relationship tech. There are, for example, well-established traditions of research on the digital mediation of a diverse array of LGBTQ+ cultures; this research is arguably commensurate with many of the practices I discuss, and one reason for that is that various LGBTQ+ cultures and communities were early adopters of digital dating technologies. Such research can also be situated alongside emerging literatures on digitally mediated sexual cultures centred on (inter alia) distinctions of age, ethnicity and disability, and fascinating studies of new cross-cutting cultural tendencies – for instance, stranger intimacy by choice rather than chance. Yet while I draw numerous examples from these literatures to illustrate specific points, it is not my purpose in this study to attempt any systematic mapping of the complex and highly nuanced terrain of contemporary sexual cultures.

On LGBTQ+ cultures see Élisabeth Mercier, 'Mediated Intimacies, Queer Bodies', in *The International Encyclopedia of Gender, Media, and Communication*, eds. K. Ross, I. Bachmann, V. Cardo, S. Moorti and M. Scarcelli, Oxford: Wiley, 2020; Sam Miles, 'Still Getting It On Online: Thirty Years of Queer Male Spaces Brokered through Digital Technologies', *Geography Compass*, online, 6 September 2018, https://doi.org/10.1111/gec3.12407. On 'age' see Sindy R. Sumter and Laura Vandenbosch, 'Dating Gone Mobile: Demographic and Personality-Based Correlates of Using Smartphone-Based Dating Applications among Emerging Adults', *New Media & Society*, 21 (3), 2019; pp. 655–73; on 'disability' see Chibundo Egwatu, Ben D. Sawyer and P. A. Hancock, 'Perspectives: Digital Influences on Sexual Discourse in Disabled Populations', *Critical Disability Discourses*, 9, 2019, n.p., https://cdd.journals .yorku.ca/index.php/cdd/article/view/39748; on 'ethnicity' see Vishnupriya Das, 'Designing Queer Connection: An Ethnography of Dating App Production in Urban India', *Ethnographic Praxis in Industry Conference Proceedings*, 2019, pp. 384–97. On newly emerging sexual cultures, see Regan Koch and Sam Miles, 'Inviting the Stranger in: Intimacy, Digital Technology and New Geographies of Encounter', *Progress in Human Geography*, 45 (6), 2021, pp. 1379–1401.

7 Moira Weigel, *Labor of Love: The Invention of Dating*, New York: Farrar, Straus & Giroux, 2016. For a supplementary analysis that locates online and dating apps in a historical context incorporating community and kin-based matchmaking, classified ads and some of the earliest computer-based services, see Pepper Schwartz and Nicholas Velotta, 'Online Dating: Changing Intimacy One Swipe at a Time?', in *Families and Technology. National Symposium on Family Issues, Volume 9*, eds. J. Van Hook, S. McHale and V. King, Cham: Springer, 2018.

8 Weigel, *Labor of Love*, p. 7.

9 The Pew Research Center's surveys on online dating might serve as a useful baseline here. In 2019, 30 per cent of US adults reported they had used a dating app or site (up from 11 per cent in 2013), with 23 per cent reporting they had gone on a date as a result and 12 per cent reporting they had been in a committed relationship with or had married someone they had met this way. These figures, interestingly, are higher for some demographics, most notably 18–29-year-olds (48 percent use) and LGBTQ+ adults (55 per cent use), with around 20 per cent in both groups reporting they had entered a committed relationship with (or even married) someone as a result. Overall, 57 per cent judged their experience as positive. A majority reported that they had found other users whom they considered to be physically attractive (71 per cent), had common interests with (64 per cent) or who seemed like someone they would want to meet in person (64 per cent). At the same time, 71 per cent believed it was common for people to lie in order to make themselves appear more desirable, while of those who had used an app/site in the previous year 45 per cent reported feeling more frustrated than hopeful (28 per cent). Around 60 per cent of female users aged 18–34 reported experiences of harassment. See Pew Research Center, *The Virtues and Downsides of Online Dating*, 2019. See also Monica Anderson, Emily A. Vogels and Erica Turner, 'The Virtues and Downsides of Online Dating', 6 February 2020, Pew Research Center, https://www.pewresearch.org/internet/2020/02/06/the-virtues-and-downsides-of-online-dating

10 Nigel Thrift, *Knowing Capitalism*, New York: Sage, 2005.

11 According to MindSea's *25 Mobile App Statistics to Know in 2022*, https://mindsea.com/app-stats, as of the fourth quarter of 2021 there were more than 2.9 million apps available in the Google Play Store, and as of August 2021 there were 4.75 million apps available in the Apple App Store. On average there were 70,000 new Android

and 32,000 new iOS apps released every month, and for millennials, 69 per cent reported social media apps as their most frequently used apps, followed by messaging apps (55 per cent). These figures, and others like them reported by various market researchers, certainly suggest that algorithmically mediated mobile apps are central to processes of social connection, interpersonal communication and digital intimacy.

12 Deborah Lupton, 'Quantified Sex: A Critical Analysis of Sexual and Reproductive Self-Tracking Using Apps', *Culture, Health and Sexuality*, 17 (4), 2015, pp. 440–53.

13 For further discussion see James Bridle, 'The Algorithm Method: How Internet Dating Became Everyone's Route to a Perfect Love Match', *The Guardian*, 9 February 2014.

14 See John T. Cacioppo, Stephanie Cacioppo, Gian C. Gonzaga, Elizabeth L. Ogburn and Tyler J. VanderWeele, 'Marital Satisfaction and Break-Ups Differ across On-Line and Off-Line Meeting Venues', *Proceedings of the National Academy of Sciences of the United States of America*, online, 3 June 2013, https://doi.org/10.1073/pnas.1222447110

15 Daniel Miller, *Tales from Facebook*, Cambridge: Polity, 2011, p. 166.

16 See Anthony Giddens, *The Consequences of Modernity*, Cambridge: Polity, 1990.

17 Giddens, *Consequences of Modernity*, p. 38.

18 Anthony Giddens, *The Transformation of Intimacy: Sexuality, Love and Eroticism in Modern Societies*, Cambridge: Polity, 1993, pp. 2, 58, 61–4.

19 See, for example, David Jary and Julia Jary, 'The Transformations of Anthony Giddens: The Continuing Story of Structuration Theory', *Theory, Culture & Society*, 12 (2), 1995, pp. 141–60.

20 See, for example, Timmermans and Courtois, 'From Swiping to Casual Sex and/or Committed Relationships'; Cosima Rughinis and Maria Stoicescu, 'Learning about Self and Society through Online Dating Platforms', *The 16th International Scientific Conference on eLearning and Software for Education, eLSE 2020*.

21 See Illana Gershon, *Breakup 2.0: Disconnecting over New Media*, Ithaca: Cornell University Press, 2010.

22 See Miller, *Tales from Facebook*, pp. 168–70.

23 Parisi and Comunello, 'Dating in the Time of "Relational Filter Bubbles"', pp 74–5; Liesel L. Sharabi and Tiffany A. Dykstra-DeVette, 'From First Email to First Date: Strategies for Initiating Relationships in Online Dating', *Journal of Social and Personal Relationships*, 36 (11–12), 2019, 3389–3407, https://doi.org/10.1177/0265407518822780

24 Ulrich Beck, 'Self Dissolution and Self-Endangerment of Industrial Society: What Does This Mean?', in Ulrich Beck, Anthony Giddens and Scott Lash, *Reflexive Modernization: Politics, Tradition and Aesthetics in the Modern Social Order*, Cambridge: Polity, 1994, pp. 176–7.

25 On this point, see Ulrich Beck, Anthony Giddens and Scott Lash, *Reflexive Modernization*, Cambridge: Polity, 1994.

26 Magdalena Rolle, 'The Biases We Feed to Tinder Algorithms', *Diggit Magazine*, 25 February 2019.

27 Amy Webb, 'Why Data Is the Secret to Successful Dating', *The Guardian*, 28 January 2013.

28 Adam Phillips, *Side Effects*, London: Penguin, 2006, p. 172.

29 Zygmunt Bauman, *Liquid Life*, Cambridge: Polity, 2005.

30 Bauman, *Liquid Life*, p. 88.

31 See George Ritzer, 'Prosumption: Evolution, Revolution or Eternal Return of the Same?', *Journal of Consumer Culture*, 14 (1), 2014, pp. 3–24.

32 Shuaishuai Wang has written insightfully on the political economy of 'sexually affective data' – bringing dating platforms into the platform economy more generally, adding new dimensions to the commodification of intimacy. This innovative Internet ethnography focuses on Blued, originally a geolocation-based same-sex dating app for Chinese men that has subsequently become a multipurpose platform incorporating newsfeeds and live-streaming (the latter now accounting for half of its profits). Live-streamers try to solicit virtual gifts from viewers (by answering questions, performing in drag, offering advice) using Blued's digital currency, the value of which is split between the live performers and the platform. Blued also monetizes 'sexually affective data traffic' more generally. '[T]hese data are sexually affective because they are produced within the parameters of same-sex desires such as infatuation, sexual arousal, online intimacy, and the like.' In addition to virtual gifting, they include data produced by following, liking, commenting and sharing as well as the more static quantitative data from user profiles – 'headshot, age, weight, height, and sex roles (on Blued, inserters are numbered as 1, insertees as 0, and versatiles as 0.5), geographical location, and personality tags'. These data are now valuable corporate assets by which Blued attracts advertisers and investors.
   See Wang, 'Chinese Affective Platform Economies'.

33 Phoebe Luckhurst, 'Love Me Tinder', *The Guardian*, 27 September 2016.

34 Stuart Jeffries, 'Is Online Dating Destroying Love?', *The Guardian*, 7 February 2012.

35 Deborah Lupton, *The Quantified Self*, Cambridge: Polity, 2015, pp. 98–9.

36 See, for example, Brady Robards, Ben Lyall and Claire Moran, 'Confessional Data Selfies and Intimate Digital Traces', *New Media & Society*, 23 (9), 2021, pp. 2616–33. It is also the case that selection biases generated through the interaction of user input and algorithmic recommendation processes are one key mechanism for rendering 'identities manageable, calculable and governable'. That is to say, such computational processes increase the degree of homophily within an individual's dating network. See Parisi and Comunello, 'Dating in the Time of "Relational Filter Bubbles"', pp. 73–4. This can have a positive effect, for example through enhancing safety or valorizing queer identities on same-sex dating apps. See Albury and Byron, 'Safe on My Phone?'; also see Pym, Byron and Albury, '"I Still Want to Know They're Not Terrible People"'. But the same selection bias can lead to marginalization and forms of sexual racism. See Carlson, 'Love and Hate at the Cultural Interface'.

37 Jacques Ellul, 'The Power of Technique and the Ethics of Non-Power', in *The Myths of Information: Technology and Postindustrial Culture*, ed. Kathleen Woodward, London: Routledge, 1980, pp. 272–3, 280.

38 Jacques Ellul, *The Technological Society*, trans. J. Neugroschel, New York: Continuum, 1980, p. xxxii.

39 Castoriadis's magnum opus is *The Imaginary Institution of Society*, Cambridge: Polity, 1987. For critical overviews of Castoriadis's social theory see John B. Thompson, *Studies in the Theory of Ideology*, Cambridge: Polity, 1984, ch. 1; Anthony Elliott, *Critical Visions: New Directions in Social Theory*, London and New York: Routledge, 2019, ch. 4.

40 Cornelius Castoriadis, *Philosophy, Politics, Autonomy: Essays in Political Philosophy*, Oxford: Oxford University Press, 1991, p. 249. The following quotations are from pp. 246 and 270.

Chapter 4

1 Philip Rieff, *Freud: The Mind of the Moralist*, 3rd edn, Chicago: University of Chicago Press, 1979.

2 Amy Ellis Nutt, 'The Woebot Will See You now: The Rise of Chatbot Therapy', *The Washington Post*, 4 December 2017.

3 Allan V. Horwitz, *Creating Mental Illness*, Chicago: University of Chicago Press, 2002.

4 Philip Rieff, *Triumph of the Therapeutic: Uses of Faith After Freud*, London: Chatto and Windus, 1966, p. 15.

5 At the time of writing, the market for digital mental health providers is massive and rapidly expanding. Recent investment and marketing developments surrounding Woebot give some interesting indications of this. In July 2021, Woebot closed its Series B funding round (essentially, a second round of capital funding through investment which usually occurs after the 'start-up' phase) having raised US$90 million. This capital raising followed the company's breakthrough device designation by the US Food and Drug Administration. Moreover, all of this took place in a context where venture funding for US-based digital health start-ups reached US$2.4 billion in 2020. See Vish Gain, 'Mental Health Chatbot Woebot Gets $90m Boost', *siliconrepublic*, 21 July 2021, https://www.siliconrepublic.com/start-ups/woebot-chatbot-mental -health-ai-funding. See also Elaine Wang and Megan Zweig, 'A Defining Moment for Digital Behavioral Health: Four Market Trends', *RockHealth Insights*, 15 March 2021, https://rockhealth .com/insights/a-defining-moment-for-digital-behavioral-health-four -market-trends

6 A recent international review of empirical studies on the application of algorithmic technologies in mental healthcare – including social media, smartphones, sensing technology (wearables and smart home devices) and chatbots – indicates that the core focus of these studies concerned the effectiveness of these technologies in detecting and diagnosing mental health problems, especially depression. A lesser focus was that of treatment and support applications – for example, the use of smartphone apps to deliver personalized education based on psychometric data generated by the app. See Piers Gooding and Timothy Kariotis, 'Ethics and Law in Research on Algorithmic and Data-Driven Technology in Mental Health Care: Scoping Review', *JMIR Mental Health*, 8 (6), 2021, e24668. See also Adrian B. R. Shatte, Delyse M. Hutchinson and Samantha J. Teague, 'Machine Learning in Mental Health: A Scoping Review of Methods and Applications', *Psychological Medicine*, 49 (9), 2019, pp. 1426–48.

7 Helga Nowotny, *In AI We Trust: Power, Illusion and Control of Predictive Algorithms*, Cambridge: Polity, 2022, p. 15.

8 See, for example, Simon D'Alfonso, 'AI in Mental Health', *Current Opinion in Psychology*, 36, 2020, pp. 112–17.

9 See, for example, Jon D. Elhai and Dmitri Rozgonjuk, 'Editorial Overview: Cyberpsychology: Reviews of Research On the Intersection between Computer Technology Use and Human Behavior', *Current Opinion in Psychology*, 36, 2020, pp. iv–vii. See also Luke Balcombe and Diego De Leo, 'Digital Mental Health Challenges and the Horizon Ahead for Solutions', *JMIR Mental Health*, 8 (3), 2021, e26811.

10 See J. Michael Innes and Ben W. Morrison, 'Experimental Studies of Human–Robot Interaction: Threats to Valid Interpretation from Methodological Constraints Associated with Experimental Manipulations', *International Journal of Social Robotics*, 2020, https://doi.org/10.1007/s12369-020-00671-8. Innes and Morrison focus on the field of experimental social psychology, but their stress on how automated machine intelligence results in 'demands made upon human participants to behave in predictable ways and the impact of experimenters' expectancies upon results' can be applied, I think, across the psychological sciences and health sciences.
11 Kylie Gionet, 'Meet Tess: The Mental Health Chatbot That Thinks Like a Therapist', *The Guardian*, 25 April 2018.
12 Alaa A. Abd-alrazaq, Mohannad Alajlani, Ali Abdallah Alalwan and Bridgette M. Bewick, 'An Overview of the Features of Chatbots in Mental Health: A Scoping Review', *International Journal of Medical Informatics*, 132, 2019, https://www.sciencedirect.com /science/article/abs/pii/S1386505619307166?via%3Dihub
13 Robert Meadows, Christine Hine and Eleanor Suddaby, 'Conversational Agents and the Making of Mental Health Recovery', *Digital Health*, 6, 20 November 2020, https://doi.org/10.1177 /2055207620966170
14 Samuel Bell, Clara Wood and Advait Sarkar, 'Perceptions of Chatbots in Therapy', *CHI '19: Extended Abstracts*, May 2019, https://doi.org/10.1145/3290607.3313072
15 The capacity for therapeutic algorithms to transform discourse around personal well-being also concerns increased focus on the datafication of mental health. See Evelyn Wan, Jacinthe Flore, Anthony McCosker, Natalie Hendry, Peter Kamstra and Jane Farmer, *Mediating Mental Illness: Lifewords, Platforms, and Algorithms*, panel presented at AoIR 2020: The 21st Annual Conference of the Association of Internet Researchers, 28–31 October 2021, Dublin.
16 'My Chatbot Therapist', *Mixed and Anxious as Hell*, 2017, https:// mixedandanxiousashell.wordpress.com/tag/anxiety
17 Arlie Russell Hochschild, *The Commercialization of Intimate Life: Notes from Home and Work*, Berkeley, CA: University of California Press, 2003, p. 14.
18 Nowotny, *In AI We Trust*, p. 15.
19 See, for example, Anthony Giddens, *Europe in the Global Age*, Cambridge: Polity, 2007, ch. 5.
20 Anthony Giddens, 'This Time It's Personal', *The Guardian*, 3 January 2008.
21 Zygmunt Bauman, *Liquid Life*, Cambridge: Polity, 2005, p. 1.
22 See Anthony Elliott (ed.), *The Contemporary Bauman*, London and New York: Routledge, 2007. I should also note that Bauman's

thesis of 'liquification' has not received anything like the same attention in studies of therapy culture (despite its obvious relevance) as it has received in studies of the transformation of intimacy. See, for example, Mitchell Hobbs, Stephen Owen and Livia Gerber, 'Liquid Love? Dating Apps, Sex, Relationships and the Digital Transformation of Intimacy', *Journal of Sociology*, 53 (2), 2017, pp. 271–84; Shaun Best, 'Liquid Love: Zygmunt Bauman's Thesis on Sex Revisited', *Sexualities*, 22 (7–8), 2019, pp. 1094–109.

23 Bauman, *Liquid Life*, p. 16.

24 Bauman, *Liquid Life*, p. 17.

25 Ibid.

26 Sophie Aubrey, '"It's Made Us Feel Lighter": Could an App Be the Secret to Happily Ever After?', *Sydney Morning Herald*, 4 March 2021, https://www.smh.com.au/lifestyle/life-and-relationships/it-s-made-us-feel-lighter-could-an-app-reinvigorate-your-relationship-20210225-p575ob.html

27 Quoted in ibid.

28 On this point, see Heather Nunn and Anita Biressi, '"A Trust Betrayed": Celebrity and the Work of Emotion', *Celebrity Studies*, 1 (1), 2010, pp. 49–64; Akane Kanai, 'The Work of Emotion in a Digital Age: "A Trust Betrayed", Ten Years On', *Celebrity Studies*, 11 (4), 2020, pp. 500–3.

29 Jürgen Habermas, *Between Facts and Norms: Contributions to a Discourse Theory of Law and Democracy*, Cambridge: Polity, 1996, p. 368.

30 Jürgen Habermas, *The Structural Transformation of the Public Sphere: An Inquiry into a Category of Bourgeois Society*, trans. T. Burger and F. Lawrence, Cambridge MA: MIT Press, 1989 (1962), p. 27.

31 Habermas, *Structural Transformation*, p. 183.

32 Jürgen Habermas, *Knowledge and Human Interests*, Cambridge: Polity, 1987.

33 Meadows et al., 'Conversational Agents'.

34 On the privatization of intimacy, see Marie Bergström, *The New Laws of Love: Online Dating and the Privatization of Intimacy*, Cambridge: Polity, 2021. Whilst I distance my argument from that of Bergström, the standpoint she develops could be interestingly applied to the domain of therapy tech.

35 Mimi White, *Tele-Advising: Therapeutic Discourse in American Television*, Chapel Hill: University of North Carolina Press, 1992. See also White's 'Television, Therapy and the Social Subject; or, the TV Therapy Machine', in *Reality Squared: Televisual Discourse on the Real*, ed. J. Friedman, New Brunswick: Rutgers University Press, 2002.

36 Stjepan Mestrovic, *Postemotional Society*, London: Sage, 1997, p. 98.
37 Mestrovic, *Postemotional Society*, p. 87.
38 Susan Sontag, *Regarding the Pain of Others*, New York: Picador, 2004.

Chapter 5

1 Emma Firth, 'Am I Falling In Love with an AI?', *Buro*, 2 May 2020, https://www.buro247.com/culture/tech/ai-chatbot-replika-app
2 Trudy Barber, 'Do We Want to Live in a World Where Our "Best Friends" Are AI Chatbots?', *The Conversation*, 12 February 2018, https://theconversation.com/do-we-want-to-live-in-a-world -where-our-best-friends-are-ai-chatbots-91451
3 Casey Newton, 'Speak, Memory: When Her Best Friend Died, She Rebuilt Him Using Artificial Intelligence', *The Verge*, https:// www.theverge.com/a/luka-artificial-intelligence-memorial-roman -mazurenko-bot
4 It is important to emphasize that a range of different approaches have been developed in recent years for addressing the links between the affordances of digital technologies and emergent characteristics of intimate relationships. For an approach that connects young people's expertise with digital media to the way new cultures of care providing peer support and friendship are emerging across digital platforms integrated into daily life, see Paul Byron, *Digital Media, Friendship and Cultures of Care*, London: Routledge, 2020. For an interesting study exploring online gaming platforms as friendship media, see Adriana de Souza e Silva and Ragan Glover-Rijkse, *Hybrid Play: Crossing Boundaries in Game Design, Player Identities and Play Spaces*, London and New York: Routledge, 2020. The analysis of the complex ways that digital media extend personhood following death and allow for the continuation of forms of meaningful posthumous relationships with the living has been developed by James Meese, Bjorn Nansen, Tamara Kohn, Michael Arnold and Martin Gibbs, 'Posthumous Personhood and the Affordances of Digital Media', *Mortality*, 20 (4), 2015, pp. 408–20.

Another direction in recent research involves attention to multitasking on digital devices simultaneous with face-to-face social interaction – including phenomena such as phubbing (phone snubbing) as well as the sharing of phone-based activities among friends. Such an approach is emphasized and well documented in Chia-chen Yang and Kaia Christofferson, 'On the Phone When

We're Hanging Out: Digital Social Multitasking (DSMT) and Its Socioemotional Implications', *Journal of Youth Adolescence*, 49, 2020, pp. 1209–24.

Other approaches look at the dynamic intersections between loneliness and social Internet use in friendship tech. For a recent version of this approach see Rebecca Nowland, Elizabeth A. Necka and John T. Cacioppo, 'Loneliness and Social Internet Use: Pathways to Reconnection in a Digital World?', *Perspectives on Psychological Science*, 13 (1), 2018, pp. 70–87. Also of interest are approaches that examine the taking, possession and circulation of screenshots among teenagers as an everyday aspect of digital communication that is integral to negotiating hierarchies of friendship and power, and for establishing peer trust. See, for example, Victoria Jaynes, 'The Social Life of Screenshots: The Power of Visibility in teen Friendship Groups', *New Media & Society*, 22 (8), 2020, pp. 1378–93.

5 Critical algorithm studies is rich and varied, and I draw in particular upon the software-sensitive approach of Tania Bucher (see later in this chapter). One important contribution to friendship algorithmic intimacy is the work of Daniel Miller and colleagues, who have investigated the ways in which encrypted message platforms (such as WhatsApp) allow for a more scaleable sociality. See Daniel Miller, Elisabetta Costa, Neil Haynes, Razvan Nicolescu, Jolynna Sinanan, Juliano Spyer, Shriram Venkatraman and Xinyuan Wang, *How the World Changed Social Media*, London: UCL Press, 2016. In a related vein, Das and Hodkinson have explored the ways new fathers suffering mental health issues following the birth of a child use the algorithmic affordances of social network platforms to establish new interpersonal ties. Here characteristics of the algorithms that facilitated emotional disclosures – if in highly coded and hesitant forms – were valued by those wanting to connect with others around their difficulties but reluctant to introduce difficult emotional issues into existing close relations. See Ranjana Das and Paul Hodkinson, 'Tapestries of Intimacy: Networked Intimacies and New Fathers' Emotional Self-Disclosure of Mental Health Struggles', *Social Media + Society*, online, 21 May 2019, https://doi /10.1177/2056305119846488

6 See Anthony Elliott, *The Culture of AI: Everyday Life and the Digital Revolution*, London and New York: Routledge, 2021, ch. 1.

7 John Urry, *What is the Future?*, Cambridge: Polity, 2016, n.p.

8 Hua Hsu, 'What Jacques Derrida Understood about Friendship', *The New Yorker*, 3 December 2019.

9 Deborah Chambers, *Social Media and Personal Relationships: Online Intimacies and Networked Friendship*, London and New York: Macmillan, 2013, p. 41.

10 Chambers, *Social Media and Personal Relationships*, p. 4.
11 See, among others, Michele Willson, 'Algorithms (and the) Everyday', *Information, Communication & Society*, 20 (1), 2017, pp. 137–50; Kelley Cotter, 'Playing the Visibility Game: How Digital Influencers and Algorithms Negotiate Influence on Instagram', *New Media & Society*, 21 (4), 2019, pp. 895–913; Benjamin Grosser, 'What Do Metrics Want? How Quantification Prescribes Social Interaction on Facebook', *Computational Culture*, 4, 2018, http://computationalculture.net/what-do-metrics-want
12 Taina Bucher, 'The Friendship Assemblage: Investigating Programmed Sociality on Facebook', *Television & New Media*, 14 (6), 2012, pp. 479–93.
13 Bucher, 'Friendship Assemblage', p. 480. The next quotation is also from this page.
14 José Van Dijck, *The Culture of Connectivity: A Critical History of Social Media*, Oxford: Oxford University Press, 2013.
15 See, for example, Raul L. Katz, Max Felix and Madlen Gubernick, 'Technology and Adolescents: Perspectives on the Things to Come', *Education and Information Technologies*, 19, 2014, pp. 863–86; Andrew M. Ledbetter, 'Patterns of Media Use and Multiplexity: Associations with Sex, Geographic Distance and Friendship Interdependence', *New Media & Society*, 11 (7), 2009, pp. 1187–1208; Sofia Gil-Clavel, Emilio Zagheni and Valeria Bordone, 'Close Social Networks among Older Adults: The Online and Offline Perspectives', *Population Research and Policy Review*, online, 2021, https://doi.org/10.1007/s11113-021-09682-3; Jeremy Birnholtz, 'Adopt, Adapt, Abandon: Understanding Why Some Young Adults Start, and then Stop, Using Instant Messaging', *Computers in Human Behavior*, 26 (6), 2021, pp. 1427–33; Liesel L. Sharabi and Elisabeth Timmermans, 'Why Settle When There Are Plenty of Fish in the Sea? Rusbult's Investment Model Applied to Online Dating', *New Media & Society*, 23 (10), 2021, pp. 2926–46.
16 See, for example, Leslie Haddon, 'The Contribution of Domestication Research to In-Home Computing and Media Consumption', *The Information Society*, 22 (4), 2006, pp. 195–203; Rich Ling and Gitte Stald, 'Mobile Communities: Are We Talking About a Village, a Clan, or a Small Group?', *American Behavioral Scientist*, 53 (8), 2010, pp. 1133–47.
17 Stefana Broadbent, *L'Intimité au Travail,* Paris: Fyp Éditions, 2011.
18 See, for example, Hendrik Kempt, *Chatbots and the Domestication of AI: A Relational Approach*, Cham: Palgrave Macmillan, 2020; Andrew McStay, *Emotional AI: The Rise of Empathic Media*, London: Sage, 2018; Mora Matassi, Pablo J. Boczkowski and Eugenia Mitchelstein, 'Domesticating WhatsApp: Family, Friends,

Work, and Study in Everyday Communication', *New Media & Society*, 21 (10), 2019, pp. 2183–2200.

19 Zongyi Zhang, 'Infrastructuralization of Tik Tok: Transformation, Power Relationships, and Platformization of Video Entertainment in China', *Media, Culture and Society*, 43 (2), 2021, pp. 219–36.

20 Michelle Greenwald, 'Audience, Algorithm and Virality: Why TikTok Will Continue to Shape Culture in 2021', *Forbes*, 1 April 2021, https://www.forbes.com/sites/michellegreenwald/2021/04/01/audience-algorithm-and-virality-why-tiktok-will-continue-to-shape-culture-in-2021/?sh=41ef360f2af7

21 See, for example, Claire Whang and Hyunjoo Im, '"I Like Your Suggestion!" The Role of Humanlikeness and Parasocial Relationship on the Website versus Voice Shopper's Perception of Recommendations', *Psychology and Marketing*, 38 (4), 2021, pp. 581–95, https://doi.org/10.1002/mar.21437

22 Annabell Ho, Jeff Hancock, and Adam S. Miner, 'Psychological, Relational, and Emotional Effects of Self-Disclosure after Conversations with a Chatbot', *Journal of Communication*, 68, 2018, pp. 712–33, https://doi.org/10.1093/joc/jqy026

23 Mauro de Gennaro, Eva G. Krumhuber and Gale Lucas, 'Effectiveness of an Empathic Chatbot in Combating Adverse Effects of Social Exclusion on Mood', *Frontiers in Psychology*, 23 January 2020, https://doi.org/10.3389/fpsyg.2019.03061

24 Anna Hoffman, Diana Owen and Sandra L. Calvert, 'Parent Reports of Children's Parasocial Relationships with Conversational Agents: Trusted Voices in Children's Lives', *Human Behavior and Emerging Technologies*, online, 21 June 2021, https://doi.org/10.1002/hbe2.271

25 Donald Horton and Richard Wohl, 'Mass Communication and Para-Social Interaction: Observation on Intimacy at a Distance', *Psychiatry*, 19 (3), 1956, pp. 215–29.

26 See John B. Thompson, *The Media and Modernity: A Social Theory of the Media*, Cambridge: Polity, 1995, ch. 7.

27 A signal example is the murder of the former Beatle John Lennon by one-time fan Mark Chapman. See Anthony Elliott, *The Mourning of John Lennon*, Berkeley, CA: University of California Press, 1995.

28 See Evan L. Frederick, Choong Hoon Lim, Galen Clavio and Patrick Walsh, 'Why We Follow: An Examination of Parasocial Interaction and Fan Motivations for Following Athlete Archetypes on Twitter', *International Journal of Sport Communication*, 5 (4), December 2012, pp. 481–502.

29 See Julian Kreissl, Daniel Possler and Cristoph Klimmt, 'Engagement with the Gurus of Gaming Culture: Parasocial Relationships to Let's Players', *Games and Culture*, online, 8 April 2021, https://doi.org/10

.1177%2F15554120211005241; Mariah L. Wellman, 'Trans-Mediated Parasocial Relationships: Private Facebook Groups Foster Influencer–Follower Connection', *New Media & Society*, online, 16 September 2020, https://doi.org/10.1177%2F1461444820958719

30 I am using a psychoanalytic understanding of the term 'fantasy' in what follows. See Anthony Elliott, *Psychoanalytic Theory: An Introduction*, 3rd edn, London and New York: Macmillan, 2016.

31 Tim Daalderop, 'How My Chatbot Fell in Love with Me', *Technorhetoric: NextNature*, 1 May 2020, https://nextnature.net /story/2020/how-my-chatbot-fell-in-love-with-me

32 Stephen Marche, 'The Chatbot Problem', *The New Yorker*, 23 July 2021.

33 Stephen Marche, 'The Chatbot Problem', *The New Yorker*, 23 July 2021, https://www.newyorker.com/culture/cultural-comment /the-chatbot-problem

34 Kristen C. French, 'Your New Best Friend: AI Chatbot', *Futurism*, 30 January 2018, https://futurism.com/ai-chatbot -meaningful-conversation

Chapter 6

1 Rob Horning, 'True Love Ways', *Real Life*, 13 September 2019, https://reallifemag.com/dispatches/true-love-ways

2 Grace Holliday, 'Social Media Gets a Bad Press, but It Was a Lifeline for Me', *The Guardian*, 24 April 2017.

3 Sulagna Misra, 'How to Make Friends on the Internet', *Harvard Business Review*, 13 April 2021, https://hbr.org/2021/04 /how-to-make-friends-on-the-internet

4 These comments from Noa Gafni Slaney appear in André da Loba, 'Is Digital Connectedness Good or Bad for People?', *New York Times*, 28 November 2016.

5 Jürgen Habermas, *Knowledge and Human Interests*, Cambridge: Polity, 1987, p. 311.

6 Habermas, *Knowledge and Human Interests*, p. 377.

7 For a general overview of the critical scholarly reception of *Knowledge and Human Interests* around the time of its publication (in German and subsequently English), see Fred R. Dallmayr, 'Review Symposium on Habermas: II – Critical Theory Criticized: Habermas's *Knowledge and Human Interests* and its Aftermath', *Philosophy of the Social Sciences*, 2 (1), 1972, 211–29. For a discussion of Habermas's theory of knowledge and human interests in relation to the critique of subjectivity and emotional life, see Anthony Elliott, *Social Theory and Psychoanalysis in Transition*:

Self and Society from Freud to Kristeva, 3rd edn, London and New York: Routledge, 2019, ch. 3.

8 In speaking of a *plurality of worlds* I refer, implicitly, to research in social theory, including well-known sociological approaches, where the idea of social worlds broken into a multiplicity of interacting spheres has been deployed to analyse continuity and change in the organization and self-understanding of social formations on a macro, societal scale. Max Weber famously argued, in his essay 'Immediate Reflections' ('Zwischenbetrachtung'), that, as history progressed, the social world becomes separated into various spheres of life, each with its own criteria of rationality: the economic, political, aesthetic, erotic and intellectual, along with – in later works – the religious and familial. This formulation was, in turn, hijacked by functionalist sociology, though it is worth underscoring that Weber referred to these spheres of life as different modes of practical orientation typical of historically specific social formations. That is to say, Weber highlighted that different socio-historical settings reflect different world views and spheres of practical activity. See Sylvia Terpe, 'Working with Max Weber's "Spheres of Life": An Actor-Centred Approach', *Journal of Classical Sociology*, 20 (1), 2020, 22–42.

In contemporary social theory, Luc Boltanski and Laurent Thévenot employ a similar theoretical architecture wrapping together different worlds of common use in order to account for the coexistence of multiple logics of justification in any given society. Each logic is based upon different understandings about 'what is acceptable'; this notion of 'what is acceptable' is grounded in conceptualizations of the common good unique within each world. The worlds identified by Boltanski and Thévenot comprise the market world, the industrial world, the civic world, the world of fame, the domestic world and the inspired world. See Luc Boltanski and Laurent Thévenot, *On Justification: Economies of Worth*, trans. C. Porter, Princeton: Princeton University Press, 2006.

In distinction from these standpoints, the approach I develop in this chapter emphasizes personal experience (understood in terms of psycho-social processes), collective biographies and sense-making as well as digital interaction. I stress the social actor's experiences and how individuals view themselves and their lives in the force field of meanings attributed to algorithmic forms of intimacy. But it should also be emphasized that the three versions of algorithmic intimacy outlined in this chapter – conventional, cohesive and individualized horizons of self-making and self-dramatization – must be related to broader socio-historical structures, digitally networked ways of thinking and global processes that can be discerned from the sociological analysis and critique of relationship tech, therapy tech and friendship tech that I have outlined throughout this book. See Anthony Elliott, *Making Sense of AI: Our Algorithmic World*, Cambridge: Polity, 2022.

9 In addition to contributions from social theory, there is also a rich history of literature in psycho-social studies that is highly relevant here, and this literature informs various threads of my argument in this book. For concise histories of the concept of outlooks, mapping the seminal departures of authors such as the founder of political psychology Harold Lasswell to the contributions of social scientists such as David Riesman, Robert Lane and Robert F. Bales, see Alan Davies, *Skills, Outlooks and Passions*, Cambridge: Cambridge University Press, 1980. An important blend of social theory and psycho-social studies, which examines the concept of outlooks in relation to theories of ideology, is John Cash, *Identity, Ideology and Conflict: The Structuration of Politics in Northern Ireland*, Cambridge: Cambridge University Press, 2010. For further reflections on the theme of outlooks, specifically in relation to the notion of friendship, see Graham Little, *Friendship: Being Ourselves with Others*, Melbourne: Text, 1993. I have made some preliminary contributions to such a discussion in various texts, including Anthony Elliott and Bryan S. Turner, *On Society*, Cambridge: Polity, 2012.

10 Recent research in the subfield of relationship tech has, for example, drawn upon Taina Bucher's investigations into how users perceive the functioning of algorithms reshapes their practices in relation to technology, and also how this in turn impacts the socio-political operation of algorithms. See Taina Bucher, 'The Algorithmic Imaginary: Exploring the Ordinary Affects of Facebook Algorithms', *Information, Communication & Society*, 20 (1), 2017, 30–44. For example, Parisi and Comunello note, in relation to Bucher's study: 'As she pointed out in her study into the "algorithmic imaginary" of Facebook users, digital media users elaborate "mental models" about the algorithm logics and then may rearrange their interactions accordingly. In her research, for example, some users noticed the algorithm is taking decisions on their behalf; other people referred to attempts to train the algorithm better to get more interesting information on their feed; other users adapted their posting behaviour to better suit social media logics and then get better visibility. Interestingly enough, the ways users react to algorithms in terms of self-presentation tactics also affect the very algorithm functioning, creating a recursive process of mutual influence between users and software.' See Lorenza Parisi and Francesca Comunello, 'Dating in the Time of "Relational

Filter Bubbles": Exploring Imaginaries, Perceptions and Tactics of Italian Dating App Users', *The Communication Review*, 23 (1), 2020, pp. 66–89, at pp. 70–1. See also Leyla Dogruel, Dominique Facciorusso and Birgit Stark, '"I'm Still the Master of the Machine": Internet Users' Awareness of Algorithmic Decision-Making and Their Perception of Its Effect on Their Autonomy', *Information, Communication & Society*, online, 30 December 2020, https://doi .org/10.1080/1369118X.2020.1863999

11 These cognitive registers, I claim, can be discerned in orientations that are produced, reproduced and transformed in the digitalization of intimacy through human–machine interfaces. That said, I should immediately note some judicious qualifications. For example, it is arguable that each of these cognitive orientations has a kind of shadow side in the form of the figure of the troll. From the standpoint of digitalization, the computational infrastructures that enable algorithmic intimacy in its multiple forms – along with online gaming, online discussion forums, and online encyclopedias such as Wikipedia – are equally enabling of trolling as a social, cultural, political and personal practice. See Eric Kerr and Clarissa Ai Ling Lee, 'Trolls Maintained: Baiting Technological Infrastructures of Informational Justice', *Information, Communication & Society*, 24 (1), 2021, pp. 1–18.

12 Oscar Wilde, *The Soul of Man under Socialism*, Portland: West Margin Press, 2021.

13 See, among others, Katie Shilton, Jes A. Koepfler and Kenneth R. Fleischmann, 'Charting Sociotechnical Dimensions of Values for Design Research', *The Information Society*, 29 (5), 2013, pp. 259–71; Francis Lee and Lotta Björklund Larsen, 'How Should We Theorize Algorithms? Five Ideal Types in Analyzing Algorithmic Normativities', *Big Data & Society*, online, 13 August 2019, https:// doi.org/10.1177/2053951719867349; Jeremy Grosman and Tyler Reigeluth, 'Perspectives on Algorithmic Normativities: Engineers, Objects, Activities', *Big Data & Society*, online, 5 August 2019, https://doi.org/10.1177/2053951719858742

There is now a significant literature on how the normative effects of algorithmic operations manifest themselves in specific forms of bias (classed, raced, gendered etc.) in relation to, for instance, criminal risk prediction or facial recognition. See Julia Angwin, Jeff Larson Surya Mattu and Lauren Kirchner, 'Machine Bias: There's Software Used across the Country to Predict Future Criminals. And It's Biased against Blacks', *ProPublica*, https://www.propublica .org/article/machine-bias-risk-assessments-in-criminal-sentencing; Anupam Chander, 'The Racist Algorithm?', *Michigan Law Review*, 115, 2017, pp. 1022–45.

At the same time it is worth bearing in mind that machine-learning algorithms are designed to discriminate, recognize some things more than others or assign different values to things as a part of the ways they operate in the world. See Louise Amoore, *Cloud Ethics: Algorithms and the Attributes of Ourselves and Others*, Durham, NC: Duke University Press. 2020.

14 Oliver L. Haimson and Anna Lauren Hoffmann, 'Constructing and enforcing "Authentic" Identity Online: Facebook, Real Names, and Non-Normative Identities', *First Monday*, 21 (6), 2016, https://journals.uic.edu/ojs/index.php/fm/article/view/6791

15 In a fascinating analysis, Jessa Lingel and Adam Golub demonstrate that Facebook 'tends towards a design ethic of singularity and simplicity, fundamentally at odds with technological preferences (or needs) for complexity and mess'. See Jessa Lingel and Adam Golub, 'In Face on Facebook: Brooklyn's Drag Community and Sociotechnical Practices of Online Communication', *Journal of Computer-Mediated Communication*, 20, 2015, pp. 536–53, at p. 537.

16 Theodor Adorno, *The Jargon of Authenticity*, 2nd edn, London and New York: Routledge, 2002.

17 Taina Bucher, *Facebook*, Cambridge: Polity, 2021, pp. 84–7.

18 See Jacques Lacan, *Ecrits: A Selection*, London: Tavistock Press, 1977.

19 Jean-Claude Kaufmann, *Love Online*, Cambridge: Polity, 2012. Quotation from Kaufmann in Stuart Jeffries, 'Is Online Dating Destroying Love?', *The Guardian*, 7 February 2012.

20 Alain Badiou, *In Praise of Love*, New York: New Press, 2012.

21 Quoted in Jeffries, 'Is Online Dating Destroying Love?'

22 In general, scholarly work in the broad area of the digitalization of global solidarity has overwhelmingly centred on the platform mediation of common interests and concerns, as opposed to the more detailed treatment of intimate connection based on care and concern that characterizes the analysis I develop in this chapter. The literature on platform-mediated solidarities includes studies on the sharing economy, the spread of intersectional narratives on corporate social media platforms, freelancer organization among remote gig economy workers and the ambivalences of contemporary digital activism. See Will Sutherland and Mohammad Hossein Jarrahi, 'The Sharing Economy and Digital Platforms: A Review and Research Agenda', *International Journal of Information Management*, 43, 2018, pp. 328–41, https://doi.org/10.1016/j.ijinfomgt.2018.07.004; Aymar Jean Christian, Faithe Day, Mark Díaz and Chelsea Peterson-Salahuddin, 'Platforming Intersectionality: Networked Solidarity and the Limits of Corporate Social Media', *Social Media + Society*, online, 27 August 2020, https://doi.org/10.1177/2056305120933301; Alex J. Wood, Vili

Lehdonvirta and Mark Graham, 'Workers of the Internet Unite? Online Freelancer Organisation among Remote Gig Economy Workers in Six Asian and African Countries', *New Technology, Work and Employment*, 33 (2), 2018, pp. 95–112, https://doi.org /10.1111/ntwe.12112; Emiliano Treré, *Hybrid Media Activism: Ecologies, Imaginaries, Algorithms*, London: Routledge, 2018, https://doi.org/10.4324/9781315438177

23 Jeremy Adam Smith, 'Five Ways to Build Caring Community on Social Media', *Greater Good Magazine*, 20 November 2015, https://greatergood.berkeley.edu/article/item/five_ways_to_build _caring_community_on_social_media

24 Ruth Arnold, 'How Do You Show Solidarity Virtually?', *The Pie News*, 27 March 2020, https://thepienews.com/the-view-from /how-do-you-show-solidarity-virtually

25 Jay M. Marlowe, Allen Bartley and Francis Collins, 'Digital Belongings: The Intersections of Social Cohesion, Connectivity and Digital Media', *Ethnicities*, 17 (1), 2017, pp. 85–102, at pp. 87–8.

26 James Ingram, 'Information and Imagination: Why Technology Isn't Killing Creativity', *Raconteur*, 10 August 2018, https://www .raconteur.net/creativity-technology

27 Marcus du Sautoy, *The Creativity Code: How AI is Learning to Write, Paint and Think*, London: Fourth Estate, 2019.

28 The phenomenon of the dating sim is a relatively recent development, although one that has its roots in the well-established Japanese traditions of the visual novel. There is now a quite extensive scholarly literature that has developed on the topic. See, for example, Renata E. Ntelia, 'In the Mood for Love: Embodiment and Intentionality in NPC', in *Love and Electronic Affection: A Design Primer*, ed. Lindsay D. Grace, Boca Raton: CRC Press, 2020; Heidi McDonald (ed.), *Digital Love: Romance and Sexuality in Games*, Boca Raton: A K Peters/CRC Press, 2017; Nicolle Lamerichs, 'Romancing Pigeons: The Deconstruction of the Dating-Sim in Hatoful Boyfriend', *Well Played*, 3 (2), 2014, pp. 43–61, http://www.etc.cmu.edu/etcpress/wellplayed

29 Rohil Aniruth, 'The Gamification of Intimacy through Dating Sims', *Hyperallergic,* 20 July 2018.

30 Oscar Schwartz, 'Love in the Time of AI: Meet the People Falling for Scripted Robots', *The Guardian*, 26 September 2018.

31 Eleanor Rogers, 'Market Report: Dating Simulation Games', *FalWriting*, 19 July 2021, https://falwriting.com/new-blog/2021 /7/4/market-report-dating-simulation-games-by-eleanor-rogers

32 Sander De Ridder, 'The Datafication of Intimacy: Mobile Dating Apps, Dependency, and Everyday Life', *Television and New Media*, online, 20 October 2021.

Index